Her Honor

HER HONOR

Rosalie Wahl *and the* Minnesota Women's Movement

LORI STURDEVANT

With a foreword by Senator Amy Klobuchar

Best wishes!
Lori Sturdevant

Minnesota Historical Society Press

The publication of this book was supported by the Eugenie M. Anderson Women in Public Affairs Fund, Kathleen C. Ridder, and gifts from friends of Rosalie Wahl.

©2014 by the Minnesota Historical Society. All rights reserved. No part of this book may be used or reproduced in any manner whatsoever without written permission except in the case of brief quotations embodied in critical articles and reviews. For information, write to the Minnesota Historical Society Press, 345 Kellogg Blvd. W., St. Paul, MN 55102-1906.

www.mhspress.org
The Minnesota Historical Society Press is a member of the Association of American University Presses.
Manufactured in the United States of America

10 9 8 7 6 5 4 3 2 1

♾ The paper used in this publication meets the minimum requirements of the American National Standard for Information Sciences—Permanence for Printed Library Materials, ANSI Z39.48-1984.

International Standard Book Number
ISBN: 978-0-87351-806-2 (paper)
ISBN: 978-0-87351-934-2 (e-book)

Library of Congress Cataloging-in-Publication Data

Sturdevant, Lori, 1953– author.
    Her honor : Rosalie Wahl and the Minnesota women's movement / Lori Sturdevant, With a foreword by Amy Klobuchar.
        p.   cm.
    Includes bibliographical references and index.
    ISBN 978-0-87351-806-2 (pbk. : alk. paper) — ISBN 978-0-87351-934-2 (ebook)
        1. Wahl, Rosalie E. (Rosalie Erwin), 1924–2013. 2. Judges—United States—Biography. 3. Lawyers—United States—Biography. 4. Feminism—Minnesota—History. I. Title.
KF373.W26S78   2014
347.776'03534—dc23
[B]
                                                        2013045119

Contents

Foreword

U.S. Senator Amy Klobuchar

"I never saw a woman judge," Rosalie Wahl once said. "I never had a chance to practice in front of one."

These are remarkable words to come from the first woman to serve on the Minnesota Supreme Court. But what's truly remarkable is that this reality never fazed Rosalie Wahl. For Rosalie, the lack of any women role models, like all the challenges she overcame, was not an obstacle in her path, it was the path—a path she marched down with an uncanny combination of grit and grace.

Rosalie truly paved her own way, laying each flagstone of her distinguished legal career on her own. In doing so, she built a foundation, not just for women in the law, not just for working mothers, but for all women.

Like so many women in law and politics in our state, I stand on Rosalie's sturdy, sensible shoulders. In fact, the very year that Rosalie was appointed to serve on the Minnesota Supreme Court, my own political career began—albeit modestly—leading a Life Saver lollipop drive to salvage our high school's prom. But as Rosalie's life has shown us, you have to start somewhere.

In Rosalie's case, she grew up in Kansas during the Depression. Her mom died when she was three. She and her brother went to live with their grandmother on the Kansas family farm. At age seven Rosalie lost her brother and grandfather in a train accident, and her family couldn't sue the train company because the lawyer required $100 in advance. The farm was sold. A fiancé died in the Army Air Corps during World War II. She went to college in Kansas and didn't enroll in law school until 1962, when she was thirty-eight years old, the mother of four, only one of two women in her class.

Ask anyone who crossed Rosalie's path and they will tell you that she was tough as nails. She learned to "lean in" decades before the phrase became cool. She decided to enroll in law school because she was "tired of sitting outside doors waiting for the men inside to make the decisions." After defeating three men in her reelection to the state's highest court, she heard countless cases, argued persuasively in judicial conference, and tackled gender discrimination and racial bias in our judicial system—and she did all of this with uncommon humility and an unerring commitment to justice.

As I walk that path forged by Rosalie, I think of what life was like for her, both as the first woman elected to the state's supreme court and as a mother who put herself through law school, taking just one week off after giving birth to her fifth child. As the first woman elected to serve as Hennepin County attorney and the first woman elected to the U.S. Senate from Minnesota, I find solace in knowing that whatever trials I face in balancing my family and my job and in navigating a male-dominated political world, Rosalie faced them first and against even greater odds.

It's no surprise that the legal tradition lives on in Rosalie's family. I was fortunate to have her daughter, Sara Wahl, working with me as an accomplished civil litigator and manager in the Hennepin County attorney's office. And Rosalie's legacy extends beyond her family.

When Rosalie was the first woman to don the judicial robes on Minnesota's highest court, did she ever imagine that one day there would be a majority of women on the Minnesota Supreme Court? Did she envision that three women would sit on the U.S. Supreme Court? Despite the fact that there were no women in the Senate when she was sworn in as a judge, did she foresee a Senate with a record twenty women senators serving as we have today?

The answer to these questions is simply yes, she did. She understood. She had the vision and faith to see far into the future, imagining that one day women would fill boardrooms, classrooms, locker rooms, and labs. One day they would orbit the earth, scale our highest peaks, and explore our deepest seas. She knew that other women, like herself, would never take no for an answer.

In this book, Lori Sturdevant captures the trials and triumphs of one of our state's most endearing icons. And Rosalie's story is but one of Sturdevant's many narratives thoughtfully recounting Minnesota's unique history. From the Pillsbury family, to prominent civil rights leader W. Harry Davis, to feminist diplomat Arvonne Fraser, Sturdevant writes the stories about Minnesota that need to be told. This book, like her other works, reflects both the spirit of its subject and the essence of our state. It reminds us once again of the debt of gratitude we owe to those who came before us. It inspires us to make our life's work worthy of Rosalie Wahl's legacy.

Introduction and Acknowledgments

Rosalie Wahl's story is inseparably intertwined with that of Minnesota's mid-twentieth-century women's movement. The same might be said of any number of her contemporaries. These women were born when votes for women were new in America, and the feminist spirit that engineered the ratification of the Nineteenth Amendment to the U.S. Constitution was rapidly receding. As they came of age, they experienced both the trauma and the opportunity caused by war. They chafed against gender-based norms that became more rigid in war's wake. Then, at midlife—seeking fulfillment, financial security, or both—they decided *en masse* that the strictures were too tight. Finding each other, supporting each other, showing each other the way, they broke free of these strictures and broke new ground. With ample justification, Rosalie often said that she could not have been the state's first female supreme court justice had there been no Minnesota women's movement.

Yet within that movement, Rosalie Erwin Wahl stood out. She was someone around whom feminists could reliably rally. Midwestern values "sprouted by the hearth," as she described them, ran deep in her. She was a hard worker, self reliant, faith grounded, family focused, and community involved. Tragedy and trauma had tested and toughened her without wilting her compassion. A Methodist-cum-Quaker, she saw godly potential in all people. A poet, she employed language as justice's sword. A singer, she raised her voice in chorus with others to reveal the beauty and strength in numbers.

If she had been merely a gender pioneer in Minnesota's judiciary, Associate Justice Rosalie Wahl would be noteworthy. But she also believed that with personal achievement comes responsibility. She seized the opportunity to be an agent of change for all Minnesota women whose lives are touched by the state's courts, and would later do as much for racial minorities. She was also in the vanguard of a reform movement within legal education that still unfolds today, with great potential to improve the legal profession's service to society.

This book sets Rosalie's story in its essential context, the movement for women's equality in Minnesota. This movement made her public service possible; she made it exceptional. It's fitting that in the reading area of the Minnesota State Law Library, a bust is displayed of only one of the ninety-nine justices to have served through the first 155 years of Minnesota statehood. Rosalie Wahl's kindly face, preserved in stone, offers enduring inspiration to justice seekers.

While this book emphasizes Rosalie's connection to the women's movement, a larger connection should not go unstated. Rosalie and other feminists were motivated by a shared belief that if a greater measure of liberty and justice were available for women, all of society would benefit. The lives of men and children would also improve. Rosalie held the converse also to be true. As she said in a recorded conversation in 1990 with her law clerk Laura Kadwell and her ally in court reform Norma Wikler, "The thing I think about justice is that if there's injustice out there anywhere, then justice for everybody is in danger."

The quest to make society more humane, inclusive, and just is always unfinished. Throughout history, advances toward that goal have come in waves of sudden and impressive progress. It behooves us to reflect on the conditions, the ideas, the values, and, most of all, the character of the people who made the last wave happen, as a foundation for considering what can be done now to start the next wave rolling.

While this book owes its origin to many people, it has one godmother: Kathleen Ridder. A stalwart among Minnesota feminists, Ridder called me in 2009 with a plan for a book about Rosalie Wahl and a plea: If you are willing to write it, please drop what you are doing and meet with Rosalie now. The former justice's health was deteriorating. Interviews at a later date may not be possible, Ridder advised.

I was willing and eager. Although my career as a *Minneapolis Star Tribune* journalist has focused on the other two branches of Minnesota state government, I knew and much admired Rosalie Wahl. Probing her story and presenting it to readers in its rightful context struck me as a worthy sideline to my newspaper "day job."

With the support of my *Star Tribune* editor, Scott Gillespie, and an editorial board of talented colleagues, and by the leave of the good man with whom I was already working on a project—the late George Pillsbury, a feminist in his own right—I was soon on my way to Jenny Wahl Blaine's house in St. Paul to interview her mother. Rosalie was frail, but her voice was strong and rich with emotion as she patiently related tales of her life. I'm honored and thankful for that opportunity, and grateful to sisters Sara Wahl and Jenny Blaine for joining those sessions and spurring their mother's memory when it lagged. I later met son Tim Wahl and son-in-law Michael Davis, and was again impressed by the generous spirit that characterizes the Wahl family.

My next stops were the Minnesota State Law Library, where I sat under Rosalie's stone visage, and the Minnesota History Center library to dig through seventeen boxes of painstakingly organized papers preserved from Rosalie's long public career. These facilities and their staffs are Minnesota treasures. So are the not-yet-digitized archives at the *Star Tribune*. I'm grateful to have had access to all three—and I worry about the fate of the deteriorating newspaper clippings at the *Star Tribune*. A history-minded angel is needed soon to finance their digital preservation.

Several of Rosalie's oldest and dearest friends kindly provided help. A happy coincidence brought Fronzena Jackson Sizer, Rosalie's University of Kansas (KU) contemporary, to Minnesota at about the same time the Wahls arrived. Mary Alice Harvey, the widow of Elmer Harvey, shared memories of the "intentional community" they sought to create in Circle Pines, Minnesota. The Society of Friends congregations that spiritually nurtured Rosalie in her new home included Frank and Raquel Wood, Wayne Kassera, and, later, her 1990s tenant, Gail Lewellan, and her law clerk Paul Landskroener. They deepened my understanding of Rosalie's early years in Minnesota and the inspiration she drew from her faith.

I also returned to trusted sources and friends—the leaders of the Minnesota women's movement that I had covered as a young reporter in the 1970s and 1980s. It was a joy to renew acquaintances and reminisce about what Rosalie would call "a yeasty time." My gratitude to Kathleen Ridder redoubled as I became aware that delay would have denied me a chance for some of those conversations. Indeed, only a few months after my April 2011 interview with the founding leader of the Minnesota Women's Consortium, Gloria Griffin died. Sadly, Jeri Rasmussen is now the resident of a care facility. I regret that I missed chances to meet and interview the late C. Paul Jones and Nancy Dreher. But I am grateful that I could speak with Carol Connolly, Don and Arvonne Fraser, Koryne Horbal, Emily Anne Tuttle, Marilyn Bryant, Aviva Breen, Nina Rothchild, Bonnie Peace Watkins, Joan Growe, Gretchen Fogo, Judy Schuck, Sally Pillsbury, Mary Pattock, Linda Berglin, Rahm Westby, Grace Harkness, Dottie Rietow, Phyllis Kahn, Ernee McArthur, Nancy Brataas, Ember Reichgott Junge, and Josie Johnson. I was pleased to reconnect with Ellen Dresselhuis, Rosalie's only female law school classmate, whose work I had covered decades earlier. Kathleen Ridder was a steady source of information and encouragement as my research progressed.

I also count among the sources for this book people now deceased whom I knew well and whose stories linger in my memory. They include Governors Rudy Perpich and Elmer Andersen, chief justice Douglas Amdahl, former state senator George Pillsbury, former senate majority leader Nicholas Coleman, and feminist leaders Mary Peek, Sue Rockne, Peggy Specktor, and Ann O'Loughlin.

It was a joy to relive the Perpich administration with my esteemed former *Star Tribune* colleague Betty Wilson, Rosalie's friend and the author of the fine biography *Rudy! The People's Governor* (Nodin Press, 2005). Also generous with their memories of the Perpich years were Rudy Perpich Jr.; Connie Perpich, the governor's sister-in-law; former lieutenant governor Marlene Johnson; former aide Ray Bohn; University of Minnesota historian Hy Berman; and the former cabinet member who is now Minnesota's governor, Mark Dayton. Chuck Slocum, a dear friend who was the nation's youngest state Republican Party chairman in the 1970s, offered helpful memories about that era. I caught up with former governor Al Quie at age eighty-nine, shortly after one of his still-frequent horseback rides, to hear his account of the appointment of Associate Justice M. Jeanne Coyne.

A number of Minnesota judges and law professors enhanced my understanding of the profession Rosalie chose and developed. Judge Harriet Lansing, Rosalie's invaluable partner in crafting the 1989 Gender Fairness Task Force report, was a great friend of this project. I'm also grateful to judges Mary Lou Klas, Kathleen Blatz, Esther Tomljanovich, A. M. "Sandy" Keith, Leslie Metzen, and Paul Anderson; and law professors Ann Juergens, Douglas Heidenreich, and Roger Haydock at William Mitchell College of Law. Juergens's insights about Rosalie, research help, and editing comments were important guides. Barbara Burwell, the daughter of Rosalie's late colleague Associate Justice C. Donald Peterson, was generous with material about the joint Peterson-Wahl campaign of 1978. Several of Rosalie's former law students, now distinguished attorneys—Sandra Nevens, Tom Miller, Ross Kramer, Eric Magnuson—also shared memories.

This project benefited from the work of scholars, authors, and journalists who wrote previously about portions of this story. The notes for each chapter provide a particular account, but more generally I must acknowledge a large debt to the important work done by Sally Kenney, formerly of the Humphrey School of Public Affairs' Center on Women and Public Policy, now of Tulane University and author of the 2013 book *Gender and Justice: Why Women in the Judiciary Really Matter* (Routledge). I'm grateful for her kind review and helpful comments about this book's manuscript. I was also glad to have access to the insights of Gail Collins, whose 2009 book *When Everything Changed: The Amazing Journey of American Women from 1960 to the Present* (Little, Brown & Co.) is the best, most readable history to date of the social revolution of the past fifty years. The written words and, more specifically, the transcribed interviews of Rosalie Wahl by two law professors, Ann Juergens of William Mitchell College of Law in 2002 and Laura Cooper of the University of Minnesota in 1994, were of great help.

I'm grateful to Minnesota Historical Society Press and its editor in chief, Ann Regan, for taking on this project and guiding it well, and for tolerating my tardiness in completing it. It would have taken even longer, but for the *Star Tribune*'s grant of two leaves of absence of several weeks' duration. One of those absences was made possible financially by a 2012 Mondale Research Fellowship. A new program of the Humphrey School's Center for the Study of Politics and Government, this fellowship promises to help Minnesota historians, amateur and otherwise, tell the stories that have given this state a distinctive political character and a rich shared life. I'm honored to have been among the first in what is already, in its second year, a distinguished roster of awardees.

Above all, I owe thanks to my family for their tolerance of my avocation as an amateur Minnesota historian. My indulgent husband Martin Vos is an electrical engineer who is also a willing and very able copy editor. My three grown children, Ted, John, and Emelia Carroll, cheer me on. Son Ted is a staff member at the American Bar Association (ABA) in Washington, DC, providing me with a personal link to Rosalie's ABA work on legal education reform. It felt good to hear from a leading Minnesota jurist, Cara Lee Neville, "I work with your son at the ABA." Daughter Emelia's recently declared intention to pursue a career in the law gave this project fresh purpose. Idealistic young women like Emelia can see the law today as a path not only to a satisfying career, but also to a more just society, because of the way cleared by Her Honor Rosalie Wahl and the Minnesota women's movement. It is to the next generation of women lawyers that this book is dedicated.

Her Honor

Chapter One

Among Sturdy Women

Rural living in America's broad midsection in the 1920s and 1930s tempered the women who survived it. The time and place required that women of the Dust Bowl combine intelligence, adaptability, and grit to keep homes and farms functional and families intact through bad weather and worse markets, poorly understood disease, and heartbreaking loss. Rosalie Wahl spoke to all of that when she described herself as a "farm girl" who had been "raised by sturdy women."

Sara Rosalie Erwin wasn't originally a farm girl. The third daughter of oil pipeline maintenance engineer Claude Erwin and his wife, Gertrude Patterson Erwin, of Gordon, Kansas, she was born August 27, 1924—four years and one day after American women achieved suffrage. Sisters Mary and Jeanette were, respectively, six and four years older. Little brother Claude William, called Billy, was born two years and three months later. Their father's work took him away often, sometimes as far away as Minnesota, and the family moved several times. The Erwin relatives were either dead or scattered by the 1920s.[1]

Those circumstances drew the young family close to Gertrude's family, the Pattersons. Harry and Effie Ellis Patterson farmed 160 acres and raised six children near Birch Creek, Kansas, not far from the Oklahoma border. Gertrude was their eldest child. Effie's family, the Ellises, were originally from Ohio, then Iowa. Staunch Yankees in the Civil War, they migrated to Kansas to establish a farm alongside Birch Creek in the mid-1870s. By the 1920s, Great-grandma Ellis was an elderly widow and had moved "out west" to Montana with some of her children. But the Ellis matriarch still held the title to the place where Harry and Effie raised their family. The Pattersons paid rent each year. Harry's family had come to Kansas from West Virginia, a state that seceded from the rest of Virginia in order to remain with the Union during the Civil War. They became neighbors of the Ellises. Though West Virginia came into being to be distinct from the Confederacy, Great-grandma Ellis never quite forgave her eldest daughter for marrying "a Southerner."

The little girl called Rosalie—to distinguish her from her namesake, Gertrude's younger sister, Sara—became a farm girl at nearly age four under sad circumstances. The Erwins were living in Augusta, near Wichita, in 1928 when Gertrude Erwin died at the age of thirty-two. Rosalie carried through life the mental picture of her bedridden mother and her two-year-old brother sitting at the sick woman's side, trying to comfort her. A doctor was summoned, but Gertrude died before medical help arrived. The psychological scar that early loss left on young Rosalie was lasting. A 1975 poem Rosalie titled simply "Gertrude Patterson Erwin, 1896–1928," gives haunting voice to the lingering void it caused:

> Let me find you
> So that I can say
> Goodbye.
> Hold me tight.
> Fill the phantom form
> With laughter,
> Flesh it out with living tissue,
> Break the solemn stillness
> Of the photographic face.
> Let your little girl come running.
> Be the child I never knew.
> Weep again behind the woodstove
> When Beth died in Little Women.
> I have it still—your copy—
> Your unknown bequest to me.
> And your glasses, in my hand,
> Funny little gold-rimmed glasses,
> Put them on.
> Weigh and measure, once again,
> Through those deep-set eyes,
> Blue, like mine.

No one told me you were dead—
But I knew.
Is it true?
Is the sad all gone?
Can I come, too?[2]

A family conference soon thereafter determined that the four Erwin kids would separate. Mary and Jeanette would stay with their father and share his itinerant life and eventual remarriage. Rosalie and Billy would live with the Pattersons, joining Grandpa Harry and Grandma Effie and their two youngest children, Bill and Bob, who were teenagers still at home. "I was lucky," Rosalie often said. "I got to stay with Grandma."[3]

Strong, self-reliant Effie Ellis Patterson became the central figure in Rosalie's childhood. Born in 1877, the eldest daughter in a large family, Effie loved learning and reading but had no school to attend until she was

Rosalie Erwin on the Patterson farm, 1930. *Courtesy Wahl family.*

ten years old. She learned well the skills farm women passed on to their daughters—raising poultry, milking cows, butchering meat, selling eggs and butter, growing an abundance of garden produce and preserving it for winter consumption, plus the domestic arts of cooking, cleaning, and sewing. She was also the family healer, and was so skillful that, on their long daily walks to retrieve the mail, Rosalie and Billy agreed that if Grandma had been at their mother's sickbed (she had not been told that her daughter was ill), Gertrude Erwin would not have died. Grandma would have known what to do.

But Grandma's "magic" was not up to the next tragedy that befell

Harry and Effie Patterson. *Courtesy Wahl family.*

the family. On May 19, 1932, seven-year-old Rosalie and five-year-old Billy were riding with their grandfather on a wagon drawn by horses Bill and Old Maud—his usual conveyance for farm chores. Harry Patterson didn't own a tractor. He enjoyed working with horses and had taught Rosalie how to drive a team. She loved to sit between his knees, with his big hands around her small ones on the reins, and call commands to the horses.

They were on a routine late-afternoon errand to fetch timber from the wooded area on Birch Creek's banks. The trip required crossing a railroad track; the road across the track was gated on both sides. A nearby hill made it a blind crossing, but no train was expected at that hour. Rosalie climbed out of the wagon, opened the first gate, and ran to open the opposite one. Just as the big wagon lumbered forward, a fast-moving train appeared from behind the hill. It was running late and running fast, the engineer acknowledged afterward. No horn sounded, contrary to the law's requirement. The horses bolted, but not quickly enough. Grandpa tried to throw Billy clear of the oncoming locomotive, but it was too late.

In mere seconds, the wagon was in pieces in the tall weeds alongside the track, and both Grandpa and Billy were dead. The little boy's body was found on the locomotive's cowcatcher.

Blessedly, the collision and its immediate aftermath left a blank in Rosalie's memory. Some things are too awful for young minds to absorb. Her memory skipped from opening the gate to resting her sad and weary head on Aunt Sara's lap in a car, driving away from the horrible scene. But the Patterson family's struggle in the days and weeks following shaped Rosalie's thinking about government, the law, and the obligations people have toward one another. There was no insurance on Harry Patterson's life. Neither the railroad nor any level of government shouldered any responsibility for the speeding train or the unsafe crossing. No compensation check was written to the Pattersons. No widow's benefit from the government was available to Effie Patterson. The advent of Social Security was still three years away. The family looked into filing a wrongful death lawsuit, but the lawyer they contacted in nearby Coffeyville told them he would need $100 in advance before taking the case. It might as well have been $100,000. Not many Great Plains farm families in 1932 could muster $100 in cash. A sense lodged in Rosalie's mind that the system had done too little to right an injustice and that ordinary people deserved better treatment. The next year, a spark from a train passing on the same track would set one of the family's fields afire and destroy a crop. That time, the railroad sent a check for $25—a token that rekindled the widow's anger. Was a crop worth more than two lives? Witnessing Effie's tears quickened Rosalie's thinking about what justice meant and required.

While legal recompense was denied the widow and her granddaughter, the extended family's support was not. Not long after Harry's death, Rosalie overheard a conversation between her visiting father and grandmother. "You won't take Rosalie away, will you?" Effie pleaded. He would not. Instead, Claude Erwin sent Effie money now and then for his daughter's support. More consistent aid came from the five surviving Patterson siblings. At first, Rosalie's young uncle, Bob, and his new wife, Marie, moved back to the home place, but Bob did not fancy farming. He hoped for a potentially more lucrative career in the oil industry. Gertrude's other two brothers, Bill and Ellis, weren't interested in taking over the enterprise either. The family decided to sell the farm's livestock and implements, bringing Effie precious little return at the nadir of the Depression. The land, still owned by the Ellis family, would be rented to others.

In March 1933, Effie and Rosalie moved from the large house where Effie had raised her children to the old Patterson place, a small, unoccupied house over a hill from the farm. The Pattersons' "Old Stone House" had been Effie's home when she was a bride. It was not in good condition, but the family's efforts made it a cozy haven for a grandmother and granddaughter in need of shelter from life's storms. Aunt Sara borrowed money on an insurance policy to pay for a new kitchen and dining room addition. Effie's poultry enterprise relocated with her, as did a cow named Bossy that Rosalie learned to milk. A plot was plowed for Effie's garden; a battered hen house was restored. The place lacked indoor plumbing, but Aunt Gladys offered Effie and Rosalie the use of her laundry facilities each week. Gertrude's brothers visited often to bring firewood, help with chores, and drive Effie and Rosalie to Niotaze Methodist Church each Sunday and to Caney, a larger town seven miles away, for errands, meetings, or elections, as needed. Grandpa's car had gone to Uncle Ellis on the strength of his promise to get Effie and Rosalie wherever they needed to go. (Effie never learned to drive, but she never missed an election. Her sons told Rosalie how excited she was when they took her to vote for the first time in 1920, the year the Nineteenth Amendment to the U.S. Constitution was ratified. Without ready access to a car as a teenager, Rosalie would not learn to drive until she was a young wife with small children.)[4]

On weekends, Aunt Sara frequently joined Rosalie and Effie at the Old Stone House. The younger of Gertrude's two sisters had not followed the conventional path for farm girls in rural Kansas. She refused to become a farm woman. Aunt Sara lived in Emporia, then Kansas City, and eventually Lawrence, Kansas. She was an unmarried, well-educated nurse—an occupation of her choosing, despite her family's reservations. She became one of the first teachers hired to staff a new nursing school in what would become part of Emporia State University, and eventually earned a master's degree at the University of Chicago. Sara also became the most dependable financial provider for the little household at Birch Creek. Faithfully each month, she sent a stipend—initially $25 for Effie and $3 for Rosalie. A letter arrived from Aunt Sara each week, and Grandma and Rosalie reciprocated. Rosalie discovered later that not long after

Harry's death, Sara "had a young man" who was studying to be a doctor. She had had a chance to marry. But in those years, marriage meant the end of a woman's career and a loss of financial independence. The responsibility she had shouldered for her mother and niece factored into her decision to remain single, Rosalie learned as she grew older. Sara's example taught Rosalie a lesson about the importance of family obligations, and their cost.

Rosalie adored Aunt Sara. Her visits were blasts of energy through the tiny, quiet house Effie and Rosalie shared. Her stories about city life and work were exciting. Her political thinking was more liberal than that of the other Pattersons, something seldom discussed openly with the rest of the staunchly Republican family but that Rosalie came to understand during long, private conversations with her aunt. Sara Patterson instilled in Rosalie a sense of purpose to carry her through the lonely hours. "Aunt Sara said she never worried about Grandma because I was there. I felt

Aunt Sara, Rosalie, and
Grandma Effie, about 1938.
Courtesy Wahl family.

proud . . . I was taking care of Grandma," Rosalie recalled. Sara made simple things fun—going for walks, washing dishes, baking cookies, decorating for Christmas. "She was somebody," Rosalie said. "She had ideas." She gave Rosalie ideas about feminine independence.[5]

Rosalie's grade school teachers, all of them young unmarried women, reinforced those ideas. She attended grade school at the one-room Birch Creek School, a half mile from the Old Stone House. Country schools had their limitations, but for students with quick minds, they offered one advantage over larger, structured grade schools—the opportunity to advance at one's own pace. A second grader could listen to the seventh graders' lessons and absorb as much information as she was capable of acquiring. "There in that one-room country school, education got a hold of me," Rosalie would say much later. "I was a goner from the time I learned to read, in my thirst for knowledge and my quest for learning more." Soon she would be a county spelling and arithmetic champion.[6]

Birch Creek School afforded students ample attention from teachers. Paid too little to afford independent lodging, teachers typically boarded in their students' homes. For Effie, renting a room to a teacher meant extra income and an extra measure of adult companionship; for Rosalie, having her teacher as her housemate meant extra lessons and a closer bond to an influential adult. Late in life, Rosalie could recall with ease the names of teachers who boarded at the Old Stone House.

But teachers didn't stay long, and Aunt Sara always had to return to work. Rosalie was often alone with Grandma in the mid-1930s as nature punished the farmers of the Great Plains for a half century of over-tilling the fragile prairie. Kansas was near the epicenter of the American Dust Bowl. In 1935, Kansas topsoil blew east as far as Washington, DC. The sky wasn't dark every day, however. Rosalie loved being outdoors, doing chores, walking to and from school, or just daydreaming as she admired the view from the hill on which the Old Stone House stood. As a young woman, she penned lines of poetry that invoked her childhood love affair with nature:

> There is some part
> Of me would die
> If kept too long
> From the Earth and sky—

From sweep of field
From rush of cloud
And unreality
Would shroud
That innermost
Vitality
That sense of being—
Even me.[7]

Family, school, church, and the beauty of Birch Creek shaped and sustained Rosalie Erwin. They prepared her for study at Caney High School, from which her mother's generation of Pattersons had graduated. It was seven and one-half miles from the Old Stone House. No school bus or family car was available for Rosalie to use to commute to school, so Grandma arranged for her to board during the week with one of Grandpa Harry's nephews, Jack Cooper, and his family. That lasted for two years, even though Cooper's unemployed young-adult son and pregnant daughter-in-law returned to the parental nest in year two, pushing Rosalie onto the living room couch. Effie understood that times were hard, but she thought that Rosalie deserved better. She prevailed on her family for more help, and found an inexpensive apartment to rent in Caney. It was their home during Rosalie's junior and senior years.

SCHOOL DAYS
1939–40

Rosalie at sixteen. *Courtesy Wahl family.*

In that small-town setting, grandmother and granddaughter thrived. New neighbors became fast friends. Rosalie excelled at her studies. A favorite English teacher, Marie Jones, inspired a love for literature and "taught us grammar like you wouldn't believe," Rosalie said years later. She put her English skills to use as co-editor of the school newspaper. Both Effie

and Rosalie joined the Caney Methodist Church. At Methodist Youth Fellowship, Rosalie found a special friend, Eldon Peck, who lived with his
family south of Caney just across the Kansas-Oklahoma state line.[8]

Through four changeable high school years, Rosalie learned adaptability and self-reliance. Those traits would be required of her entire
generation. During Rosalie's senior year, she and her schoolmates filed
into the auditorium on Monday, December 8, 1941, to listen together to
the radio as President Franklin Roosevelt called on Congress to declare
war on Japan.

As much as she admired Aunt Sara and her nursing career, Rosalie wanted a different course. She loved writing and fancied a career in
journalism, a field that would allow her to "be out there all around and
influence people." She set her cap on the University of Kansas (KU) in
Lawrence. Aunt Sara, by then a member of the KU nursing faculty, not
only paid Rosalie's tuition but put Rosalie's name on her own checking
account so that Rosalie could function financially. Meanwhile, Eldon
Peck followed his older brothers into the Army Air Force in September
1942 and trained in Tonkawa, Oklahoma. He occasionally hitchhiked to
Lawrence to visit Rosalie. Later that school year, as Rosalie visited Eldon
while he was on leave at his parents' house in Tahlequah, Oklahoma, they
came to an understanding. Though they made no formal announcement
outside their immediate families, they were engaged before he headed to
South Carolina to continue flight training. They spoke about a wedding
after the school year ended in 1944.[9]

Her engagement and the steady departure of young men and some
women from the University of Kansas in the spring of 1943 made Rosalie
feel that "school didn't seem so important." She was susceptible to a new
direction when her Uncle George, a member of the Birch Creek school
board, told her, "We need somebody to teach in Birch Creek. It's tough
to find teachers with the war on." Young women suddenly had a chance
to make more money, as jobs opened that had been closed to them when
male labor was in ample supply. Rosalie borrowed money from Grandma
Effie and enrolled in the brief summer school required to obtain a teaching certificate. Aunt Sara disapproved of Rosalie's choice, but she accepted it, telling the young woman that her Grandpa Harry had always
wished that a girl in the Patterson family would teach at Birch Creek
School. Effie Patterson had returned to country living when Rosalie was

Rosalie in college. *Courtesy Wahl family.*

at the University of Kansas. The sociable senior citizen was delighted to have her granddaughter's company again.[10]

Rosalie took charge of eleven children in eight grades at Birch Creek. She was settling into that challenging assignment in November when tragic news arrived. Eldon had been severely injured in a training accident in South Carolina. Rosalie quickly borrowed a hundred dollars from one of her sisters and bought a train ticket to join him. When the train passed through Kansas City, Aunt Sara met her at the station and, noticing that Rosalie lacked a warm coat, gave Rosalie her own. The train was agonizingly slow and, for Rosalie, too late. During one of the train's last stops before reaching her destination, Rosalie felt a sensation of deep chill. She learned later that it was at about that moment that Eldon died.[11]

It was as if the blackboard on which Rosalie had been carefully writing her life's plan was suddenly, violently erased—a shattering experience shared that bloody year by countless young people the world over. "If the Methodist Church had had a religious order, I would have probably stomped off and joined it," she said years later. She had no close-in-age peers at hand with whom to share her grief or pass the time. She did, however, have the benefit of familiar surroundings and a caring family as she mourned and considered what to do next with her life. The place itself nurtured and comforted her, judging from a poem she wrote years later, "Birch Creek":

> Here I have lived
> Here let me die
> By yonder Birch Creek let me lie.
> Birch leaves drifting on the sands

Where I built castles with my hands
In youth, and listened to the call
Of meadowlarks on grasses tall.
Black oaked horizons, skies above,
Bound for me this land I love.
Birch Creek, within your heart I lie.
As long as you live, so shall I.[12]

Despite the solace of home—or perhaps because of its healing effect—
Rosalie grew restless as spring arrived. "I really thought it through. I
decided that whatever I did, I had to go back into society and work with
people," she recalled years later. She concluded that she did not want to
continue teaching. She wanted more education and more possibilities.
The war was putting American women into new roles and changing the
way Americans thought about women's capabilities. Rosalie wanted to
be part of that change. In the summer of 1944, she was back at the University of Kansas with a new major—sociology. She wanted to prepare
for a life spent "doing something that made the world better, and helped
people."[13]

Intent on making a fresh start, Rosalie flung herself into academic
work and university life, and thrived. Initially, she paid her tuition with
the savings she had accumulated while teaching, and earned her room
and board by waiting tables in Corbin Hall, a dormitory populated by
female students who were not part of the Greek sorority system. She
quickly became acquainted with other students. Soon she was involved
in student government and the student newspaper, at which she excelled.
The next year, she was the editor of the *Daily Kansan* and contemplat-
ing a career in social work. A female sociology professor, Esther Trottie,
fueled her ambition. She was drawn to the possibility of going to California to aid the migrant workers there who were economic refugees from
the 1930s Dust Bowl in Oklahoma and Kansas.[14]

An early wave of the twentieth century American civil rights movement reached Rosalie in 1944-45 via the Young Women's Christian Association (YWCA). Founded in New York City and Boston in the mid-
nineteenth century, "the Y" was a well-established national presence by
the 1940s. It also had a history of defying social convention. Even before
the turn of the twentieth century, the YWCA was reaching out to African

American and Native American women and was calling for racial equality under the law.[15]

Rosalie had grown up in an all-white community in which racism was ambient in the culture. She carried into adulthood the memory of grown-ups talking about a woman in her county who discovered after marriage that her husband had an African American grandparent. She immediately divorced him, the gossips reported approvingly. The YWCA opened Rosalie's eyes to the bigotry of such thinking. Unlike most student organizations at KU, the Y welcomed students of all races and religions. In the Y's spacious headquarters, Henley House (donated to the campus chapter by a Mrs. A. Henley in 1922), black and white students became friends. Together they questioned the university's housing policy that offered dormitory rooms for rental to white students but barred black students. The chapter's executive secretary, a professor's wife named Rachel Vanderwerf, pointed out to the chapter's student leaders that Henley House had sleeping rooms on its second floor that were offered to visitors and used occasionally by graduate students. Might those rooms be used "in a way more in keeping with our principles?" she asked. The students' answer to that question gave rise to the first integrated housing on the KU campus—a women's cooperative for up to a dozen students, half white, half black. Rosalie, who would be YWCA chapter president in her senior year, was one of the first two white residents; Fronzena Jackson Sizer was one of the black housing pioneers. "We brought in other people," related Sizer, who, like Rosalie, would later become a Minnesotan. "Rosalie came up with many good ideas."[16]

Some of those ideas involved winning campus and community approval. Rosalie and the other co-op founders needed their parents' permission. (Tellingly, Rosalie opted to get the requisite letter from Aunt Sara, who was then working on a master's degree at the University of Chicago—and not Grandma.) The students took their case personally to the YWCA's local governing board, which included townspeople among its members, and to university chancellor Dean Malott. He was "pretty supportive," Rosalie recalled, and he took some heat for that stance. He told her later that a parent of a student in the sorority house next door called him to complain about Henley House's experiment in integrated living. The chancellor told the irate parent, "Well, then take her to live someplace else." The Henley residents suspected a disapproving owner of another adjacent house removed the device on Henley House's side that automatically kept its coal-burning furnace fed. "We shoveled coal all that winter," Rosalie related with a laugh, as if to say, "and it was worth it!" Henley House residents looked for opportunities to put their commitment to civil rights on display. Rosalie spoke years later about swim-ins at a segregated university pool and staging a sit-in at a local restaurant that refused to serve African Americans. The experience shaped her ideas about racial equality and reinforced her thinking that the law could be a tool for social justice.[17]

Henley House also introduced Rosalie to the Religious Society of Friends, better known as the Quakers. The residents chose as their housemother Mary McCracken, the sister of a female philosophy professor whom the young women admired. Mary was a Quaker who regularly attended a Friends Meeting and who willingly answered Rosalie's questions about the Quakers' commitment to racial equality, women's rights, and pacifism. Rosalie began to accompany her housemother to Friends Meetings. By 1946 she considered herself a member. She was especially drawn to the Quaker "testimony of equality," the notion that every human being is God's creation and everyone can know and respond to the will of God. Quaker worship, values, and congregational life fed two sides of Rosalie's nature. As she described herself years later, she was drawn to solitary, contemplative mysticism as well as to social activity aimed at advancing justice. Sundays with the Society of Friends offered elements of both.[18]

In addition to opening her eyes to racial injustice, the YWCA enlarged Rosalie's world in another way. Her chapter sold sandwiches at fraternity houses to raise three hundred dollars to send her to the YWCA Presidents' School, a leadership training program for college chapter presidents. The school was at Union Theological Seminary in New York City in the eventful summer of 1945. Being in the nation's largest city for two months between the end of the war in Europe and the dramatic bombing of Japan that would end the war in the Pacific was "pretty exciting," Rosalie would say later in Kansan understatement. "We did everything . . . Our horizons just expanded all over the place."

Among the things she did was write poetry. For years she had enjoyed the solitude and mental exercise required to write spare, evocative verse. "Words were lovely things to me," she said. As a student leader, she discovered that retreating in solitude to write poetry revived her energy and recharged her spirit during days that were packed with activity. It helped her process new experiences and prepared her to experience more. Writing poetry became a lifelong pastime. Time and again when life became stressful, she would escape with paper and pencil and produce verse of admirable quality. About her summer in New York, she wrote:

New York 1945

We walked the sordid streets of the lower east side slums,
Past the outlawed push carts and the peddlers shouting wares,
Past the doorways filled with children who had never climbed
    a tree
Or felt the warm earth soft beneath bare feet.
And my heart was filled with shame,
So I could not lift my eyes to meet the weary eyes of women
    leaning on the sooty sills
Gazing past the pale green plants there that were striving
    toward the sun.
Bitter shame I'd never known—shame that I, a privileged one,
Could walk on by and out the end of the narrow, stifling street,
While they, whose hungry eyes followed after me, must stay,
Object, doubtless, of the next excursion.[19]

Rosalie may have intended to focus on student leadership and her sociology degree in 1945-46, but she could not avoid being caught up in the transition from war to peace that an entire generation was experiencing. Soldiers began coming home that fall, and thanks to the GI Bill, the next stop for many of them was a college campus. The University of Kansas quickly went from being female dominated to exuberantly co-educational, and romance was in the air.

Rosalie met Roswell Wahl during her first year at the University of Kansas. Aunt Sara provided the connection. As a member of the KU nursing faculty, Sara became a friend of Kay Bell Wahl, a medical artist and, as of 1940, the second wife of Dr. Harry Roswell Wahl, the dean of the university's medical school. During Rosalie's first year at KU, Kay and Sara saw to it that she met Kay's twenty-one-year-old stepson, whom everyone called Ross. They invited both young people to join them on a Sunday sailing outing that Rosalie described as "very exciting." The two established a connection sufficient for Ross to send Rosalie a Christmas card in 1943 after Eldon Peck's death, signed with only his first name. Like Eldon, Ross had left Kansas for military service. His years in the army included the miserable Battle of the Bulge in December 1944–January 1945. Only gradually and much later would he reveal to his family glimpses of what he experienced during that brutal winter in the Ardennes Forest, and even then he could not speak about it without shaking, his daughters said. For weeks, death was all around him. At least once, so were Germans, whom he narrowly eluded by hiding in a ditch. Soldiers would strip clothing—especially the most prized garment, socks—off corpses, in an often-futile effort to ward off frostbite. Ross spent Christmas Eve digging a foxhole, and in so doing lost a prized gift from his father, a gold watch. He was promoted to sergeant on the battlefield because he was one of only two surviving members of his company. Ross Wahl came home with a Bronze Star and what would likely be diagnosed today as post-traumatic stress disorder. He was sure of one thing: he wanted nothing more to do with war.[20]

For Rosalie, Ross had been out of sight and out of mind until he reappeared on campus in the fall of 1945. He enrolled in both premed and engineering classes, hoping to become a doctor but considering engineering his fallback plan. His bent toward pacifism drew him to the Young Men's Christian Association and friends who shared his desire for an alternative to war and to capitalism, which they held responsible for war. Some of those friends helped him renew his acquaintance with the president of the YWCA's KU chapter, Rosalie Erwin. Quickly, they were steady friends. They mused about what it would be like to be part of a community—a cooperative, as Henley House had become—that would allow members to earn their livelihoods together and live in common, without "having to go out and sell our souls to capitalist society." In what Rosalie called the "yeasty days" after World War II, idealism and passion burgeoned. "People thought there was going to be a better world," she said.

Rosalie earned her bachelor's degree in sociology in June 1946. She'd crammed four years of study into three. All that spring, she made plans to move to California and become a social worker. But when June came,

"I just couldn't go," she said. Instead of planning a trip, Rosalie and Ross planned a wedding. They were married in Danforth Chapel on the KU campus on August 19, 1946, with Rosalie's uncle, Ellis Patterson, walking her down the aisle and her two older sisters in attendance. A simple reception at Henley House and a brief honeymoon in Mexico followed the ceremony.

That fall, the newlyweds were back on the Lawrence campus—Ross still striving to become a doctor, Rosalie working as a teaching assistant in the undergraduate Western Civilization reading program. Her meager salary and his GI Bill stipend provided their only income. Their home was a tiny rented house at 320 Mill Street in North Lawrence, on the banks of the Kansas River. The house's distinguishing feature: a large billboard perched on the roof. That made the place easy for friends to find, the chipper couple told each other. Next door lived a budding young lawyer, Elmer Harvey, and his wife, Mary Alice. The Harveys were Quaker social activists who met at an American Friends Service Community work project to combat racism in Indianapolis in the summer of 1945. They were married a few weeks after the Wahls in 1946. Elmer and Ross had become best friends, brought together by their mutual interest in pacifism and cooperative living. Good news came with word that KU would launch a graduate school in social work, in which Rosalie could enroll in 1947. Bad news came when Ross applied to medical schools. His grades in his premed classes were satisfactory, but his engineering grades didn't measure up, dragging down his total grade point average. Ironically, that meant he was denied a place in medical school and felt compelled to turn to the field in which he had lesser interest and aptitude to make a career. He became an engineer. "So life goes," Rosalie would say decades later in a tone that still echoed disappointment.

News of a different sort also came in 1947. On December 12, their first child, Christopher, was born. Rosalie's graduate study ended. Six months later, Ross graduated from the University of Kansas. With a wife and a baby to support, Ross had to make a living. But he and Elmer Harvey weren't about to give up their vision of a new, humane way to work, live, and raise families.

Through the American Friends Service Committee, Elmer made connections with a new cooperative living project north of Minneapolis and St. Paul in Minnesota, a place called Circle Pines. It was a cooperative village of twelve hundred acres founded in May 1946. The Friends Service Committee had an internship program that employed young Quakers in projects to help establish the pioneering cooperative community. When Elmer completed law school in 1948, the Friends organization asked him to direct its activities in Circle Pines. He jumped at the chance to see firsthand what life could be like in a new shared-ownership village that aimed "to unite the habitation benefits of a functional and contemporary community with the economic advantages of a consumer's cooperative." Elmer was smitten by what he saw, so much so that he made a down payment on forty acres of land north of the emerging town. Those "Back Acres" would be the site of an "intentional community" that Elmer aimed to create of like-minded families. He urged his friends the Wahls to follow him and Mary Alice to Minnesota. Ross had been thinking about moving west, perhaps to California, as Rosalie had originally intended. Rosalie, confronting the demands of motherhood, was no longer eager to leave her support system of friends and family, but Elmer Harvey was a persuasive man.[21]

Ross went ahead to Minnesota in the fall of 1948 to look for a job. The Wahls gave up their tiny rented house. Courtesy of Ross's half sister Norma, Rosalie, baby Christopher, and the family dog, Tarz, were transported to Ross's parents' comfortable home in Kansas City—a situation that proved emotionally unsettling for Rosalie. She wasn't at ease in the orbit of her strong-willed stepmother-in-law. Fortunately, those living arrangements didn't last long. Ross found a job at Minneapolis-Honeywell Regulator Co., then bought a dubiously reliable 1934 Chevy. He named it "Fancy" and tinkered with it until he trusted it to make the trip from Minnesota to Kansas City and back. In early February 1949, Ross and Fancy pulled into Dr. Wahl's driveway to fetch his wife and fourteen-month-old son. As they drove north on two-lane highways, Rosalie watched the landscape turn progressively wintrier and more unfamiliar, and she thought wistfully about all she was leaving behind. The Wahls arrived in Circle Pines on February 7, 1949, at a small apartment Ross had rented for them while he and Elmer Harvey built permanent structures at Back Acres. A Scandinavian heritage made Minnesota an opportune place to start an "intentional community," she'd been assured. Whether it was also a place of opportunity for a sturdy young woman of intelligence and ambition was less clear.

Chapter Two

Feminism's Price

Despite its latter-day reputation for progressive politics, the Minnesota to which Rosalie came was not in the vanguard of American feminism. It never had been. The New England egalitarianism, Scandinavian communitarianism, and pioneer pragmatism that created the state's culture in the nineteenth century included strains of thought that had proven friendly to women's rights elsewhere. But Minnesota's advocates for women's participation in state governance endured six decades of frustration after statehood was granted in 1858. Minnesota was in no hurry to allow women to vote or hold elective office.[1]

The Minnesota Women's Suffrage Association agitated for the full enfranchisement of women for forty years before achieving success. During those years, only a handful of Minnesota women gained prominence in traditionally male-dominated professions, even though the University of Minnesota began enrolling women alongside men in 1858. In 1875, the state allowed women access to school board ballots and the opportunity to serve as school board members—but no more.[2]

The suffrage association faced formidable opposition. Politically potent liquor interests feared that the women's vote would usher in Prohibition. (Their fear proved right. Prohibition and women's suffrage arrived within months of each other in 1919–20, spurred by complementary reformist sentiments.) The wives of some of the state's most prominent business leaders abhorred the thought that their poorly educated servant girls would be allowed votes that would count the same as their own. Ironically, they feared that if all women could vote, their ability to sway state policy by swaying their husbands would be diluted.[3]

Despite that resistance to votes for women, the shared sacrifices of

World War I and improved public education for both genders spun popular opinion in favor of women's suffrage. By 1919, suffrage supporters comprised a clear majority at the Minnesota legislature and had won over the state's entire congressional delegation. Minnesota women, however, did not get to the polls until the Nineteenth Amendment to the U.S. Constitution was ratified the next year.

Almost overnight, the Minnesota Women's Suffrage Association morphed into the Minnesota League of Women Voters. But with the great battle finally won and longtime suffrage leaders ready to retire, the league's vitality was spotty around the state. Where chapters flourished— in Minneapolis, especially near the University of Minnesota campus and in affluent Kenwood, and in college towns and a few populist enclaves outstate—women took advantage of their newfound political muscle. Where the imprint of the League of Women Voters was faint or non-existent, political power stayed firmly in male hands.[4]

In 1922, the first year in which women could run for the Minnesota legislature, four of eight female candidates won. Two served only one term. Dubbed the "flapper legislator," Myrtle Cain of Minneapolis was just twenty-eight years old when she was elected. She had been a union organizer, a telephone operators' strike leader, and an activist in the National Women's Party, considered the radical wing of the suffrage movement because it pushed for the addition of an Equal Rights Amendment to the U.S. Constitution. (Cain lived long enough to testify in favor of the ERA before the Minnesota legislature in 1973.) Cain caucused with the Liberals during that nonpartisan period at the statehouse and was seen as too liberal even for some feminists, whose opposition helped doom her reelection bid in 1924. She lost by only thirty-nine votes, and despite a long lifetime of political activity, she never held elective office again.[5]

Sue Metzger Dickey Hough, the other one-termer among the first female legislative quartet, was a Republican from Hennepin County who studied at the University of Chicago Law School before marriage ended her legal aspirations. Her political pedigree included the fact that she was a great-granddaughter of John Quincy Adams, sixth president of the United States. Among the issues auguring against Hough's reelection was her outspoken support for handgun control measures—another matter in which Minnesota thinking belies the state's liberal reputation. After losing the seat in 1924, Hough tried for a comeback three times, to no avail.[6]

Mabeth Hurd Paige and Hannah Kempfer, 1941. *Minnesota Historical Society.*

The other two women in the legislature's class of 1922 made a larger impact. Hannah Jensen Kempfer of Ottertail County in northwestern Minnesota stayed in office for sixteen years, losing just one reelection bid, in 1930. She was a proud farm woman and former country school teacher with whom Effie Patterson and Rosalie Wahl could have identified. She sold eggs, raised pigs and turkeys, canned her own produce, and tanned animal hides for commercial sale. Although she had no children, her home became a haven for young people in need and a meeting hall for the many civic organizations that Hannah helped lead. As a young child, Hannah had been abandoned at an orphanage in Norway by her unwed mother, then adopted by a Norwegian couple before they emigrated to Minnesota when Hannah was six. Her experiences made her a legislative advocate for orphans, children born out of wedlock, and animal welfare. She survived constituent displeasure when she successfully sponsored legislation setting hunting and fishing seasons and limiting the number of animals that a single hunter or angler could harvest. A true political independent, she supported planks in both the Republican and the agrarian-progressive Farmer-Labor Party platforms.[7]

The most durable of the first four female legislators was Mabeth Hurd Paige. Alone among them, she established a pattern in her Minneapolis district sturdy enough to support subsequent election of female candidates. That feat required persistent effort by a person of exceptional ability. Paige was an established civic leader before her election. She had been president for twelve years of the prestigious Women's Christian Association (the city's oldest charitable institution) and had helped found the Minneapolis Urban League. She was a Massachusetts-born, Paris-educated art student who moved to Minneapolis to supervise art instruction in city schools. She gave up her art career in 1895 to marry James Paige, a professor and acting dean at the University of Minnesota Law School. Five years later, she graduated from law school herself and was admitted to the Minnesota bar. Paige yielded to her husband's opinion that it was "unwomanly" for her to appear in court, but that may have quickened her feminist zeal. She became involved in the suffrage movement at both the state and national levels and was three times a delegate to the International Congress of Women in the 1920s. Her legislative service spanned twenty-two years. That seniority and her affiliation with the dominant Conservative Caucus gave her a prominent voice in the house's welfare and judiciary committees. For six sessions she chaired a major committee, the House Welfare Committee, an achievement that no other woman legislator would attain for nearly a half century. Among Paige's legislative credits: improved working conditions for both men and women, stricter hospital regulation, more state support for dependent children, and successful opposition to a proposed major highway through the Superior National Forest.[8]

Kempfer and Paige gave their constituents a quality of representation that ought to have inspired voters in other parts of the state to send women to St. Paul. Rather than becoming the first of many, the two long-serving women in the class of 1922 found themselves increasingly isolated. That sense of isolation must have been heightened for them when the most prominent of Minnesota's early-twentieth-century feminist leaders, Clara Hampson Ueland, was killed on March 1, 1927, in a weather-related accident. She was on her way home to Lake Calhoun in

Clara Ueland, about 1921. *Minnesota Historical Society.*

Minneapolis after a day of lobbying at the capitol when she was struck by a skidding truck. Ueland had served as president of the Minnesota Women's Suffrage Association during its final push to victory, from 1914 to 1920, and was hailed in Minnesota and nationally as a highly effective organizer and spokeswoman for "the cause." Mabeth Hurd Paige had been her handpicked protégé in the crucial final months of the suffrage campaign. When that battle was won, Ueland had opted not to lead the new League of Women Voters, but to take charge of its lobbying at the capitol, at which she excelled. She made the league's case for legislation protecting the welfare of women workers, restricting child labor, and promoting public health. At the time of her death, Ueland remained the state's best-known feminist voice. She was granted the rare honor of a memorial service in the capitol rotunda. Today she is one of only two women commemorated inside the capitol with a permanent plaque. (The other, Dr. Martha Ripley of Minneapolis, was the founder of a hospital for unwed mothers in north Minneapolis in the 1880s.)[9]

Two other women joined Paige and Kempfer in the 1927 session; a third arrived in 1929. One was Laura Naplin of the Farmer-Labor Party, elected to complete the senate term of her late husband Oscar, who suffered a fatal stroke on the first day of the 1927 legislative session. Naplin was the first of a number of Minnesota women who found political opportunity in widowhood. But her service was brief. By the mid-1930s, Kempfer and Paige were the only women who held seats at the statehouse. When Paige stepped down after the 1943 session, the Minnesota legislature reverted to all-male status for the next seven years. The electorate's attitude about women in politics after World War II was characterized, one contemporary account explained, by "a resurgence of domesticity and motherhood."[10]

The 1950 election ushered two women into the Minnesota house. One, Sally Luther, a former newspaper reporter and Vassar College graduate, sprang from the Minneapolis district Paige had long anchored. She served for twelve years, four of them as the legislature's only woman. For future generations, the second woman's experience would be a marker of the deep-seated sexism that the Minnesota women's movement confronted in the middle of the twentieth century and would need to overcome. Her name was Coya Knutson.[11]

Cornelia "Coya" Gjesdal Knutson's story paralleled Rosalie Erwin Wahl's in several significant ways. Like Rosalie and her Aunt Sara, Coya was a smart, strong rural woman who chafed at conventional expectations. Just twelve years Rosalie's senior, Coya was born on a farm near Edmore, North Dakota, on August 22, 1912, to Norwegian immigrant parents. Her father, Christian, was active in the prairie-populist Nonpartisan League and instilled in his outdoorsy second daughter a passion for economic justice for farmers. Coya also exhibited a zeal for learning and considerable musical talent, which propelled her through Concordia College in Moorhead, where she graduated with a double major in English and music in 1934. She took a teaching job in tiny Penn, North Dakota, population ninety, while wondering whether she had enough talent for a career as a professional opera singer. A year in a prairie schoolhouse convinced her that she had to try. In June 1935, she bravely enrolled in a summer program at the prestigious Julliard School of Music in New York City and finagled an opportunity to sing a few bars of "O Sole Mio" on the popular *Major Bowes' Original Amateur Hour* on the CBS radio network. Her performance was not well received. At Julliard, she found that she was far behind other students in vocal training. Chastened, she returned to her teaching position in little Penn. She enjoyed teaching and singing at weddings, anniversary parties, and funerals—but she wanted more.[12]

In 1937, Coya took a high school teaching job in somewhat larger Plummer, Minnesota. Part of Plummer's appeal was its proximity to Oklee, Minnesota, and a farmer whom she had known since he worked as her father's farmhand in 1931. Andy Knutson was a shy, handsome fellow who, like Coya, was the child of Norwegian immigrant parents. Unlike Coya, he had been educated only through eight grades and had little interest in the world outside Oklee. He owned a 160-acre farm near his parents' place. Though Andy was three years older than Coya, she was his first girlfriend, and their courtship was slow and sporadic. They married on March 31, 1940, and moved into a farmhouse that lacked running water and electricity but boasted a new gas stove and washing machine. Her teaching career appeared to come to an end.[13]

But in remote northwestern Minnesota as in Rosalie Wahl's Kansas, World War II changed attitudes about women working. Coya signed on as a field agent for the New Deal's Agricultural Adjustment Administration in 1942. She also helped establish a local Red Cross branch, the Oklee Medical Clinic, and the Community Chest Fund. When the Farmer-Labor Party merged with the Democratic Party in 1944 to form the DFL, she got involved. That summer, she accepted a job at Oklee High School after the desperate school superintendent came to the farm twice to plead with her to join the staff.[14]

Coya was glad to teach again because her domestic life was not going well. Andy was often in town playing cards and drinking with his friends, and seemed to lose interest in the farm and in her. After two miscarriages, Coya was unable to become pregnant. She arranged for Andy to get a job as the high school's janitor, and the couple sold their farm and bought Oklee's only hotel, making a portion of it their home. Coya took her turn at hostelry chores, cleaning, washing linens, staffing the front desk, managing the hotel's small café, and waiting on tables. "The hotel was small, but at least I learned to count the change in the till," she would say of the experience. Andy functioned as the café's cook, assisted by his sister Anna and their widowed mother, who also lived at the hotel. Andy showed little interest in the business or in Coya's community activities. Coya begged Andy to agree to adopt a child, thinking that parenthood would draw them closer and compel Andy to accept more responsibility. In 1948, he relented. They adopted an eight-year-old son, Terrence, from the Lutheran Welfare Home in St. Paul. When Coya brought Terry home for the first time, the room she had carefully prepared for him had been torn apart by drunken Andy, whom they found passed out on Terry's bed. "We don't want you here," he growled at the boy. Terry would later describe his father as a "wonderful man" who would turn belligerent and violent when drunk. "He often told me that I took Coya's love away from him," the son said.[15]

That same year, Coya became chairwoman of the Red Lake County

DFL Party and a member of the county's welfare board. When the party sought a candidate for the Minnesota house in 1950, she did not need to be coaxed. She knocked out a three-term incumbent, conservative C. S. McReynolds, with a campaign distinguished by her musical talent—she sang and played the accordion at events—and her capacity for hard work. The latter trait was also evident in the 1951 and 1953 sessions of the legislature, as she pursued more state aid for education, funding for school nurses in public school, and fair employment practices legislation (which was finally enacted in 1955).

In 1954, with the hotel barely operating, its café closed, and her marriage little more than a financial arrangement—Coya supporting Andy— she was ready to move up the political ladder. But the DFL in northwestern Minnesota was not eager for her to do so. The party endorsed its congressional district chairman Curtiss Olson for the Ninth District seat held for six terms by Republican representative Harold Hagen, even though Olson had lost two previous bids for the seat. That didn't deter Knutson. She entered the DFL primary against Olson, as did three other

Coya and Andrew Knutson, Oklee, Minnesota, November 1954. *Minnesota Historical Society.*

men. Financing her campaign with the sale of land she had inherited from her father, she out-hustled the entire field. "She made every fair, every pickle festival, every corn festival, every market day that came along," the *Minneapolis Tribune* reported. "She greeted farmers in their dairy barns at 5 AM. She walked across fields to talk politics to men on tractors." Before the campaign ended, she logged more than twenty-five thousand miles on her car, crisscrossing the district's fifteen counties. Her message promoting higher farm commodity price supports resonated at a time when farmers were nervous about President Dwight Eisenhower's move to rein in federal agriculture spending. Knutson handily bested Olson in the primary and went on to squeak past Hagen by 2,335 votes out of more than 95,000 cast.[16]

Knutson was the first Minnesota woman elected to Congress, but that breakthrough was not much celebrated by other women around the state. If she had any campaign help, financial or otherwise, from women's groups outside her district, it went unreported. Some Twin Cities DFL women looked askance at Knutson's decision to take on the party's endorsed candidate to win. Coverage of Knutson's victory by the state's largest newspapers suggests that many Minnesotans weren't eager to see a woman in that traditionally male role. Two weeks after the election, the *Minneapolis Star* identified her as "Oklee housewife and lady legislator." A photograph accompanying a story in the *Minneapolis Tribune* showed her husband, Andy, who played little role in her campaign, overseeing the printing of campaign posters prominently displaying the title "Mrs." The Sunday *Tribune's Picture* magazine in January 1955 featured a photo of her frying eggs at a stove and seemed to imply that she belonged there. "Coya is an excellent cook, but during her campaign her husband (who used to cook professionally) and son had to take over in the kitchen," the caption reported. The theme would persist. In November 1956, after she won a second term, the *Tribune* told its readers, "Coya Knutson hasn't had time to cook a meal since Election Day."[17]

Knutson found more support from her new male colleagues in Congress. DFL representative John Blatnik from Minnesota's neighboring Eighth District coached her on winning a coveted seat on the House Agriculture Committee. There, she won public praise for her hard work from the committee's crusty chairman, North Carolina representative Harold Cooley. She championed higher prices for farm commodities, the school lunch program, and the use of surplus agricultural products as a foreign aid tool—a concept that, a few years later, President John Kennedy would rename Food for Peace. In her second term, Knutson enjoyed considerable lawmaking success, sponsoring the National Student Defense Loan Program and promoting the Food Stamp Bill of 1957. Her work to win a $1 million research grant to combat cystic fibrosis was the first of its kind in the nation and made her a heroine to those touched by the disease, including one family in Oklee.[18]

Knutson also became acquainted with Senator Estes Kefauver, a Tennessee Democrat with an economic populism akin to her own. When he announced his bid for the presidency in 1956, it did not matter to Coya that the Twin Cities–based DFL establishment preferred Adlai Stevenson, whom many thought could be persuaded to select Minnesota senator Hubert Humphrey as his running mate. Kefauver was for the family farmer, and that was good enough for Coya. She became one of Kefauver's most visible Minnesota supporters. On the night before the state's March 20 presidential primary, Knutson and former Farmer-Labor Party governor Hjalmar Petersen appeared on Twin Cities television to make a final appeal for the Tennessean. It worked. Folksy, glad-handing Kefauver upset the professorial Stevenson in Minnesota. Stevenson, however, ultimately won the Democratic nomination, and, in a break with tradition, he allowed the party's convention to choose his running mate. In part on the strength of the appeal he demonstrated in Minnesota, the delegates went for Kefauver, not Humphrey or up-and-coming Massachusetts senator John Kennedy. The Democratic ticket went down to defeat that year as popular Eisenhower won a second term, but that outcome did not ease the resentment Humphrey loyalists—including many DFL women—felt toward the congresswoman from northwestern Minnesota.[19]

Their resentment manifested itself in May 1958 in breathtakingly brazen fashion. Given the reality of Coya's marriage, it was also cruel. On May 5, a terse statement, dated May 4, was delivered to Ninth District newspapers signed by Andy Knutson. It announced, "I do not want her to file for reelection to Congress. I expect her to comply with this request." Released immediately after the DFL convention that endorsed Coya for a third term, the statement went on to urge DFLers to find another candidate for Congress.

That statement was followed by another delivered two days later elaborating on Andy's position: "Since her election four years ago our home life has deteriorated to the extent that it is practically non-existent," the statement said. "I want to have the happy home that we enjoyed for many years prior to her election." It implied that Coya's relationship with her executive secretary and campaign manager, Bill Kjeldahl, was inappropriate. "It is useless for her to be elected, as the decisions that are made are not hers," it said. Kjeldahl "dictates the policy of her office . . . [B]y his actions and dictatorial influence on my wife [he] has taken the close relationship and affection we enjoyed before." Two days later, yet another statement revised Andy's position on reelection but continued to paint Kjeldahl as a home wrecker. It said he would support Coya's third-term bid if she would fire Kjeldahl and "pay more attention to her home life."[20]

Andy's plea quickly became the stuff of national headlines. Reporters swarmed to Oklee and found the proprietor of Andy's Hotel happy to play the role of devoted-but-neglected husband—a portrayal sure to evoke sympathy in domesticity-centered 1950s America. "I didn't want her to quit Congress. I just wanted her to come home more often," he said in a story that moved on the International News Service wire. More telling about the real nature of their relationship was this admission: "I haven't seen her in almost three years. The last time I heard from her was in a three-line note, telling me how to handle the income tax return." He also informed reporters that he wanted Coya to deposit her congressional paychecks into their joint bank account in Oklee.[21]

That bit of information should have led reporters to ask harder questions about the yarn that was being spun. Had they done so, they might have learned that Andy had chronic trouble paying his bills, and Coya, whose household expenditures mounted when her mother moved in with her and son Terry in Washington, had cut him off financially. In January 1957, he wrote to her threatening to tell her detractors within the DFL Party about their estrangement unless she sent him money. The press pack might also have learned something revealing had they pressed Andy about who had put him up to the release of his statements, and who had actually written them. But those details would have undermined a juicy narrative of spousal neglect and possible infidelity by a power-hungry wife. That story had even become front-page news in London. Reporters weren't about to let go of "Coya, come home."[22]

"This has stirred up interest, and it has stirred up women," a seemingly chipper Coya said a few days later. She was voicing wishful thinking. The silence from Twin Cities DFL women was deafening. When Coya appeared in Minneapolis to receive an award from the Federated Women's Clubs for securing a statue of Minnesota educator Maria Sanford in the U.S. Capitol, some club women pointedly refused to speak to her. When reporters asked former U.S. ambassador to Denmark Eugenie Anderson of Red Wing, Minnesota, one of the DFL's best-known figures and a fervent Humphrey loyalist, whether Knutson should persist in seeking a third term, Anderson's "no comment" spoke volumes. Republican women were no help. A prominent one, former U.S. representative Clare Booth Luce of Connecticut, allowed that Minnesota was too far from Washington for a woman to succeed at both a congressional career and marriage and motherhood. Drawing any parallel between Knutson's life in Oklee and Luce's as a prominent playwright and the wife of Henry Luce, the publisher of *Time* and *Life* magazines, should have been impossible, but reporters let Luce rub it in: "I think it is easier for a man who is successful himself to adjust to a successful wife than for a man who is a failure."[23]

Coya could have responded to Andy's plea and insinuation by disclosing the facts about him. She refused to do so. "I didn't believe in pounding people when they were down," she would say much later. "He had lots of problems, and I knew the good Lord would take care of him." Neither did she publicly accuse the instigators of Andy's statements to the press, although she almost certainly knew their identities. Several Humphrey-allied DFL leaders in her district had tried to deny her the party endorsement that year and had criticized Kjeldahl in almost exactly the same language that appeared in Andy's statements.[24]

Coya's refusal to respond convicted her in the minds of many voters. She passed a primary challenge by one of her DFL critics with more than 4,100 votes to spare. But the general election was a different matter. She lost to Republican Odin Langen, a farmer and legislator from the state's far northwestern corner, by 1,390 votes. Langen did not cite the "come home" plea as he campaigned. Rather, the six-foot-five Republican rode to victory on a blatantly sexist slogan: "A big man for a man-sized job."[25]

Coya sought justice from a U.S. House investigative panel the month after the election. During testimony, Andy confessed that his wife's DFL political foes had originated and written his statements to the press.

He dropped an alienation of affection suit he had filed against Kjeldahl and publicly apologized for the pain he had caused Coya and Terry. But justice did not come, then or ever. "No matter how distasteful the interjection of the family life of a candidate into a campaign may be, it is something which must be left to the good taste of the electorate for correction," the committee's final report said. Coya failed in two comeback attempts, in 1960 and 1977, and never held elective office again. She divorced Andy in 1962. She lived until 1996, long enough to become an object of curiosity to a new generation that could not fathom the blatant sexism that ended her career.[26]

One long, eloquent essay in Coya's defense appeared in the *Minneapolis Tribune* under a byline that meant something to the surviving remnant of the feminist movement of forty years earlier. Brenda Ueland, Clara Ueland's daughter, said that Coya had endured "an excruciatingly painful experience to have everybody in the country believe something vulgar, utterly horrifying about you that is entirely untrue." Knutson's experience revealed the degree of animosity that existed in America toward "women struggling gamely into public life," Ueland said.[27]

Ueland's analysis hit home. Coya's painful experience showed her contemporaries and those who came soon after the high price they might pay if they sought to join men at the seats of power—especially if they happened to be women in troubled marriages. That may explain why only nine women served in the legislature in the 1950s and 1960s, and only two of them—Sally Luther and Helen McMillan—for more than two terms. Yet not many years later, some of the Minnesota women who had been mute witnesses to "Coya, come home" would throw themselves into an effort to break the all-male hold on government's levers of power. Coya's story makes Rosalie's all the more remarkable.[28]

 *Chapter Three*

More Useful

In later years, Rosalie frequently described the feminist epiphany that came to her while sitting in frustration outside a closed meeting of the all-male Washington County Board in Stillwater, Minnesota. The year was 1960, give or take a few months, and the issue was libraries.

As a lonely child, Rosalie loved the few books she had and craved the stories they told. Grandma owned a handful of books, but most weren't suitable for a grade-schooler. Birch Creek School had a meager few more. Rosalie borrowed one, *Legends and Myths*, over and over again.[1]

Her children would not endure such scarcity, she vowed. The Wahl household had no television until the 1960s, but the young mother insisted that it would have books. Some Minnesota public libraries had provided bookmobiles to rural residents since the 1920s. Why shouldn't a bookmobile stop near the Wahl place? That was the question she asked not long after the Wahls—Ross, Rosalie, and four children—moved in 1955 from Circle Pines in Anoka County to a former dairy farm atop a hill near Lake Elmo, east of St. Paul, in Washington County. Washington's county seat was Stillwater, a historic riverside lumbering town whose nineteenth-century success made it a proud, charming, and politically conservative location in the mid-twentieth century. The Stillwater Public Library was a handsome facility. Unlike its larger counterparts in Minneapolis and St. Paul, which had been dispatching bookmobiles into surrounding rural areas since World War I, the Stillwater library evinced no sense of duty to serve the rest of Washington County. Its governing board considered library services outside the city limits to be a county board responsibility, not theirs. One Stillwater library board member offended Rosalie by asking scornfully, "Where are all these people in the county who want to read?" We pay county taxes, Rosalie retorted. We deserve at least a bookmobile stop. She convinced like-minded neighbor Jean Lundquist, a future Stillwater Board of Education member, to join her in asking questions of the right people. The Wahls offered the end of their driveway as a location for a converted school bus to make a regular stop. In relatively short order, the women succeeded. A bookmobile was established and a stop at the Wahl place was arranged—but only once each month.[2]

That limited achievement only served to whet ambition for Rosalie and other library-loving mothers in rural Washington County. The bookmobile ought to be considered a stopgap on the way to establishing a true county library system consisting of several branch libraries, housed in buildings, not buses, they argued. Rosalie credited Stillwater librarians Vera Maunsell and Marvel Old with planting that idea in her mind and coaching her as she developed a plan. Rosalie shared it with a small network of friends who were willing to learn together how to petition their government for improved services. They rounded up allies and developed a formal proposal to take to the county board. It involved making the Stillwater library the central hub of a countywide system that shared materials and staff. The county budget was running a surplus that they reasoned was big enough to accommodate their plan without a tax increase. The library proponents talked their way onto the county board's agenda.

"We had people there from all over the county. We made a big presentation," Rosalie remembers. Then the advocates were ushered out of the meeting room. No state open meeting law had yet been enacted to compel the board to deliberate and act in public. The presenters were not allowed to hear the discussion or witness the vote. All they were told when the meeting was over was that their proposal had been rejected. Later, Rosalie heard that several commissioners who had promised her their votes reneged under pressure from a local foundation that feared an expanded library would be its rival for federal grant money under the county's control.[3]

"It was after that I decided to go to law school," she would say later. "I was tired of sitting outside of doors, with the doors shut, and them deciding." Her anger ran deep enough to swell in her voice fifty years later.

It says much about Rosalie that she would remember that moment as pivotal in her life. When she set a goal with the aim of benefiting others, she pursued it with intensity. She possessed a keen sense of democratic justice, and situations that offended that sense were highly motivating to her.

But like many epiphany stories, Rosalie's seems incomplete. It does not explain fully why this mother of four in her mid-thirties, a dozen years after moving to Minnesota, would think life-changing thoughts in response to local male functionaries doing what similar panels of men had been doing through her whole lifetime—closing the door on women and exercising power as they pleased. Something about that time in both her life and the nation's history emboldened Rosalie to head in a new, uncharted direction.

Rosalie with Great-aunt Lula Ellis Lake (Effie's sister) and four Wahl kids, vacationing in Spokane, Washington, 1962. *Wahl Papers, Minnesota Historical Society.*

The thought of going to law school sprang into Rosalie's mind as things were changing in the Wahl household. By the fall of 1960, her first four children were all in school. Christopher, born in Kansas in 1947, had been joined by Sara Emilie on December 1, 1949, Timothy Eldon on February 5, 1952, and Mark Patterson on January 20, 1955. When Mark started school, weekdays were suddenly quieter for Rosalie. She had time to ponder life's vagaries and options. How could they send four children to college on Ross's income alone? How could she cope with Ross's bouts of temper, discouragement, and depression—and how could she shield her children from the worst of his moods? How could she regain the sense of purpose she'd had at the University of Kansas, when she re-solved that she would "do something more useful" than be a teacher or a nurse? How could she become a decision-maker?

Grandma was no longer alive to be her sounding board. Effie Patter-son had died two weeks after Sara was born, during the bleak first winter that the Wahls spent on "Back Acres" north of Circle Pines. They shared a newly constructed basement with the Harvey family in what would be-come the Harvey house, then moved to a drafty old chicken coop of their own, while construction slowly progressed on permanent housing for the "intentional community" that the idealistic Kansans were establishing in Minnesota. A new baby, a toddler, and a lack of funds kept Rosalie from returning to Birch Creek for her beloved grandmother's funeral. Aunt Sara saw to it that nothing was removed from the Old Stone House until Rosalie, with baby Sara and toddler Chris in tow, arrived that spring to grieve and to distribute Grandma's few possessions. Rosalie was learning to drive at Back Acres in order to pull a trailer bearing a tank of water to housing construction sites that lacked plumbing. Never eager to get behind a steering wheel, she wasn't ready in 1950 for an interstate drive with two small children. They took a Greyhound bus to Kansas.

By 1960, the group of friends that had been Rosalie's surrogate family in Minnesota was also changing. Their "intentional community" had a core of four couples in the mid-1950s. Particularly close to the Wahls were Walter and Peggy Taylor, a couple they met in 1950 when they rented an apartment in Circle Pines after basement and chicken coop living on Back Acres became intolerable. Walt had been a conscientious objec-tor during World War II who had come to the University of Minnesota to participate in a self-sacrificing hunger research project. Peggy had been a social worker—the career Rosalie wanted—and was a fast friend. Also in the group were another World War II conscientious objector, Herb Crocker, and his wife Catherine, a nurse. For a time they counted among them Elsa Carlson, a native of Sweden and a divorced mother with one child whose Scandinavian communitarian values meshed with the Wahls'.[4]

A fifth couple that the Wahls had met at the Twin Cities Friends Meeting, Ed Stevens and his wife, Peg, became loosely associated with the community somewhat later. They were the Wahls' nearest neighbors when the community relocated to Lake Elmo. Peg and Rosalie became dear friends, but Ross and Ed, a 3M scientist with a German background, didn't click. Among the men in the community, Ross Wahl was the only one who had served in the military. That difference became a point of tension. "War never stops," Rosalie observed much later.

Meanwhile, the cooperative spirit that had inspired the Minnesota town that the Harvey-Wahl-Taylor-Crocker community chose had eroded. Just four years after its founding as a cooperative, Circle Pines was incorporated as a conventional village. Difficulty obtaining financing for shared-ownership housing and rifts among the original leaders led to the change. As if to punctuate the end of the original Circle Pines arrangement, its founder V. S. Peterson died of a stroke a few hours before the community's residents went to the polls to vote on incorporation.[5]

Like others in Circle Pines, the Wahls learned that the ideal of shared living is difficult in practice. The men in their group worked at conventional jobs by day, then pooled their money and non-work hours to build each other's homes, learning to be carpenters, plumbers, electricians, and landscapers as they proceeded. Sometimes they would work through the night. Mistakes and disagreements among them were unavoidable. They attempted to establish a jointly owned business that would permit them to give up their separate jobs and pool their disparate skills in a common enterprise. They went so far as to choose a name—Agworth— and to buy equipment, but the dream never materialized.[6]

The young mothers found more to like in their shared lifestyle than the men did. Their friendships were stronger. Their willingness to care for each other's children and share in the driving that rural childrearing required in the 1950s created a de facto early childhood education center, to the benefit of all. They collaborated on family-friendly weekend activities, including Saturday night potlucks and Sunday morning treks to Friends Meetings. At first, they carpooled to a well-established meeting in southwest Minneapolis. Then three of the couples—the Wahls, Taylors, and Harveys—shifted their affiliation to a silent-style meeting on the University of Minnesota campus. There the Wahls became better acquainted with a former American Friends Service Committee worker, Raquel Wood, who had helped build Back Acres housing, and her husband Frank. They would become dear friends. The campus group eventually took the name Twin Cities Friends Meeting; in 1969 it relocated to St. Paul.

Those shared activities kept the group's communitarian spirit alive. But the women were not equally skilled in the chores that rural living required, and that put a disproportionate burden on Rosalie. She knew how to cook for a crowd, milk a cow, raise chickens, tend a big garden, and "put up" its harvest for winter consumption. Those tasks fell to her. She loved cooking, and was very good at it, but she battled fatigue and resentment over too many chores.

While the Wahls lived in Circle Pines, Rosalie was instrumental in founding *Circulating Pines,* which began as the village's newsletter and later became its newspaper. Its publishers were Andrew and Grace Gibas, themselves veterans of cooperative living, first in Illinois, then in Minnesota. Andrew wore several hats in the community; he was also Circle Pines' first village clerk. Grace would relate twenty-five years later that a conversation between Andrew and Rosalie set the newsletter in motion. Andrew "was visiting at the Wahl home and complained that he couldn't get the whole agenda on a postcard when announcing community meetings . . . Rosalie wondered if the community shouldn't have a newsletter and further offered to edit one. That was how the *Circulating Pines* was born." Rosalie and Grace chose the publication's name, and Rosalie became its "first volunteer editor," an unpaid position that renewed the journalism skills she had acquired at the *Daily Kansan* in 1944–45. But the satisfaction she found in that work was short lived. In 1952 the yellow Wahl house at Back Acres was finally ready for occupancy, and another baby arrived. Rosalie was tethered to home once more.[7]

In 1954–55, first the Taylors, then the Wahls, sold their Back Acres houses, split the proceeds, and relocated to mostly rural Lake Elmo, southeast of Circle Pines. There, each family owned its own home. The

Wahl place originally had twenty acres, then downsized to twelve, still more than enough for a big garden and a menagerie of animals. The original four couples got together for Saturday night potlucks, sing-a-longs, and occasional barn dances (until one woman tripped on the old barn's rough floorboards and broke her arm), but the communal arrangement was shifting. The Lake Elmo move coincided with another addition to the Wahl family, youngest son Mark. "It was kind of hard," Rosalie would say of that period years later. Her complaints were rare, and always understated.

By 1960, the intentional community had dissolved. Having failed to find a way to make a living together, the men drifted apart. Attorney Elmer Harvey and his wife, Mary Alice, moved to the north shore of Lake Superior; he became a judge in Cook County and they operated an inn. Walt and Peggy Taylor, the first to depart, moved to eastern Wisconsin, where he began work with Native American bands there. The Wahls continued to live near the Crockers, and the Stevens family would soon join them in rural Lake Elmo, but the years of deep involvement in each other's lives had ended.

Unfortunately, the community's dissolution was hard on Ross Wahl, eroding his self-confidence. His bouts of depression and anger became more frequent and pronounced. Rosalie, on the other hand, drew on the lessons in adaptation that she had learned in the company of sturdy Kansas women. She chose to be philosophical about the change. "Those years weren't wasted," she would say. "I don't think something has to be successful for it to have been worthwhile." She saw the departure of the Taylors and the Harveys and the changed relationship with the Crockers not as a failure but rather as a time to let go of one dream and find another. She was ready to move on.[8]

Moving on to law school was a notion encouraged by someone Rosalie barely knew. The Wahls were involved enough in Democratic-Farmer-Labor Party politics to attend a spring 1962 dinner honoring U.S. representative Joe Karth of the St. Paul–centered Fourth District. Rosalie was seated next to a younger woman named Mary Louise Klas, a wife, the mother of young children, and a lawyer. Klas and her husband practiced law together. The conversation about Klas's work that evening left Rosalie thinking, "If she could do it, I probably could do it too."[9]

Law school would be a scholarly reach and a multiyear commitment,

both of which appealed to Rosalie. She craved the intellectual stimula-
tion she'd known at the University of Kansas. She also liked the idea of
easing slowly into a career after more than a decade as a stay-at-home
mother. "I wasn't eager to get out there in the world and have my ears
batted around," she would say later. Law school meant that when she
did finally go to work, it would be at a job that mattered and for which
she would be well prepared. She might have her own legal practice, she
thought. She could be a decision-maker, not an observer. She could be
inside the chambers of power, not outside.

William Mitchell College of Law on estimable Summit Avenue in
St. Paul was well suited to a thirty-eight-year-old woman who had been
away from college study for sixteen years. Named for a nineteenth-
century Minnesota Supreme Court justice, the school had been created
in 1956 after a series of mergers of five small law schools, one in St. Paul,
four in Minneapolis. Those schools, all founded in the early twentieth
century, had one thing in common: their students worked for a living.
Many of them were what today would be called non-traditional students, older and more varied in experience than the fresh baccalaure-
ate degree-holders who filled the more prestigious daytime law school
program at the University of Minnesota. William Mitchell offered night
classes and a curriculum tailored to adults who by day were bank tellers,
insurance agents, law-office clerks—and stay-at-home mothers. Assured
of her family's backing and with a loan from Aunt Sara to help pay tuition, Rosalie enrolled in the fall of 1962. A poem she wrote at the time
reveals the mixture of emotions that she took with her to classes at 2100
Summit Avenue:

On considering the advisability of studying law:

That one who would
Through thistles pass
Needs shoes,
Else barefoot,
Stay on grass.[10]

Rosalie fully expected to be taking classes alongside many younger
men. She did not expect that she would be the only woman in the room,
but that was what awaited her. Her class of about 125 students included

William Mitchell College of Law at 2100 Summit Avenue, 1959. *Minnesota Historical Society.*

only one other woman, Ellen Dresselhuis, who was assigned to a different class section. The male dominance that had been established at William Mitchell's predecessor schools in the early twentieth century continued in full force in 1962. Findings reported two years later by the state's first-ever Commission on the Status of Women explain why female law students were scarce: "The cost is high and there is a paucity of part-time and summer employment; the training is intense and rigorous; and there is a strong prejudice that the law is a man's field . . . It is felt that women have to be brighter than the average male student in order to compete equally in a field which is still a man's world."[11]

But that does not mean that Rosalie was in for a hard time, said longtime Mitchell professor Douglas Heidenreich, a Mitchell class of '61 alumnus who returned to the school as assistant dean in 1963. Then and now, the prevailing student spirit at "Billy Mitchell" is cooperative, not competitive, he said. "If you're a law student, you're a law student," not judged better or worse than any other by one's peers. Rosalie always said that her fellow students treated her well. But "they had study groups" either before or after the 6:30 PM classes, "and I was driving in at night from near Stillwater. I couldn't take advantage of that." Dresselhuis, younger, single, and inspired to study law by her father, a successful attorney in Iowa, recalled that she too was excluded from those groups. The male students' wives would have objected had they spent hours studying with a woman, she said.

After many fleeting encounters on the way to their separate classes, Wahl and Dresselhuis became friends. The older woman's example began schooling the younger in feminism. "She'd say, 'We need more women in law school,' and I'd say, 'But there aren't jobs for them,'" Dresselhuis said. Rosalie was confident that that would not always be the case. "She was always pushing women, always supporting women. She's a feminist to the core." Dresselhuis went on to found the Minnesota chapter of the Women's Equity Action League and to represent women in path-breaking gender discrimination lawsuits.[12]

Socializing among Mitchell students in the 1960s was relatively rare. Working by day and studying by night and weekend left little time to spare. But once per semester, students were invited to a party at a St. Paul hotel. The event's very name evoked masculinity. It was a "smoker." The school also offered monthly meeting space to the "law wives group." The wives of the male students would gather to learn a little about the law and current events, so they could be supportive of busy husbands and find a social outlet for themselves. The thought that the few female students at Mitchell might also be in need of domestic support evidently had not occurred to anyone.

Though Ross told the family he approved of Rosalie's decision to seek a law degree, her primary domestic support came from her children. She credits daughter Sara, who was thirteen in 1962, with taking charge at home on weeknights. Mother and daughter established a Monday through Thursday routine. Rosalie would start cooking the family's dinner in the afternoon and spend a little time with the children as they came home from school. At about 5:45 PM, she'd turn the stove over to Sara, get in the car, and drive to St. Paul. Sara would finish the meal preparation and get the food on the table, so that Ross and her brothers could eat dinner just as their mother was settling into her classroom for the evening. Brother Tim recalls that all four kids typically pitched in on after-dinner cleanup, then did their homework without much prompting from Ross. "Piano practice may have been another matter!" he said with a laugh.

Rosalie's most difficult day in law school likely came in the fall of 1963, during her second year. When school started that September, she was three months pregnant. A fifth child wasn't part of the plan she'd charted for herself when she enrolled in law school, but like countless women before her, Rosalie had been reminded that pregnancies often don't follow a schedule. Initially, Rosalie thought that she could cope with both childbirth and a full class load in the spring semester. But not long after registering for spring classes, maternal good sense won out over academic ambition. With more than a little trepidation, she went to see the assistant dean, Doug Heidenreich, to ask permission to drop a class.

When he asked her why, she told him as matter-of-factly as she could, "I'm expecting a baby."

Courtesy requires congratulations in response to such news, and Heidenreich might have uttered a few such words. But nearly fifty years later, both he and Rosalie remembered better what he said next. He warned that dropping one class in the spring of 1964 would mean adding an additional semester and maybe an additional year to her law school study. She would fall behind her peers. Even with a full year's delay in graduation, changes anticipated in the school's course offerings meant she might not be able to take all the courses required for the state bar exam. He urged her to reconsider.

Obviously, Heidenreich had never been a thirty-nine-year-old woman expecting a fifth child. He didn't know what he was asking. Rosalie did. She kept in check the emotions that must have welled inside her as this younger man faulted her decision. In as level a voice as she could muster, she told him that she understood the consequences for her legal education, and she would simply have to deal with them later as best she could.

On March 11, 1964, Jenny Caroline Wahl was born. Rosalie's "maternity leave" consisted of one missed week of classes. "At that point, I felt like I had a tiger by the tail and I couldn't let it go," she explained thirty-two years later. "I'm kind of stubborn about when you start some-thing, you should finish it." Her attendance was so good that classmate Dresselhuis remembers being surprised when she learned that Rosalie had given birth. Mitchell had a strict attendance policy, and Rosalie was determined not to run afoul of it. Ross and the older children quickly learned how to care for a newborn whose mother was absent for five-hour stretches several nights per week.[13]

Heidenreich, who confessed later that he expected Rosalie to drop out of law school after Jenny's birth, was impressed with what he saw. She remained a top student, worked very hard, and gave at least the outward impression that her life was under control. Several years later, Heiden-reich invited Rosalie to take sales law as an independent study with him. It was a crucial class for the bar exam that she otherwise would have missed because of her modified schedule. Heidenreich and Wahl became friends as they drank tea and discussed the Uniform Commercial Code during weekly Thursday evening three-hour meetings in his office.

Summer breaks from law school had to be precious to Rosalie, es-pecially after she became a mother of five. But rest and time with her children evidently were not her only needs in the summer of 1966. When an opportunity arose for a part-time summer job that would put her law lessons to lucrative use, she grabbed it—even though it would mean leaving toddler Jenny in seventeen-year-old Sara's care. Rosalie's love of a challenge and desire to serve certainly factored in her decision, but so did financial worries as her children reached college age and her hus-band's equanimity deteriorated. Christopher enrolled in the University of Kansas, his parents' alma mater, in 1965. Ross's electrical engineer-ing career had moved him from Honeywell to Remington Rand, which became Sperry Rand. He brought home a middle-class income, but he didn't feel secure about his prospects. "It wasn't a job with a future," one family friend recalls. His children remember him saying that he was glad Rosalie was pursuing a legal career because it would give the family "something to fall back on." Members of the family's circle of friends doubted the sincerity of his professed approval.[14]

Rosalie's 1966 summer job came by way of her constitutional law pro-fessor, C. Paul Jones. In November 1965, Jones had been tapped to head the state's first public defender's office. Its creation had been mandated by the 1965 legislature, nudged by the U.S. Supreme Court's 1963 *Gideon* decision requiring states to provide indigent defendants with legal counsel through appeal of conviction. Minnesota's two largest counties, Hennepin and Ramsey, had done as much for forty years. In other counties, courts appointed public defenders from the ranks of local attorneys as needed—a haphazard system that produced results of uneven quality. The legislature aimed for more consistency with the creation of public defenders' offices that would serve the state's other eighty-five counties. Its assignment was twofold: (1) organize and train a network of part-time, on-retainer public defenders in those counties, and (2) establish an appellate defense team to take the appeals of indigents convicted of felonies to what was then the state's only appellate venue, the Minnesota Supreme Court.[15]

In addition to serving as an adjunct professor at William Mitchell since 1953, Jones was a former Hennepin County and federal prosecutor who had lost a Minneapolis school board election in 1966 despite having Democratic-Farmer-Labor Party endorsement. He was also in the news in 1965 as the appellate attorney representing the convicted defendant in the state's most notorious murder-for-hire case, T. Eugene Thompson. (Thompson lost his appeal and spent twenty years in prison.)[16]

In his new role, Jones had a small budget, a big workload, and a bright idea. He'd observed at Mitchell that even the best of his female students seldom landed jobs in law firms or prosecutors' offices. "He saw that he could get really qualified women to work for not much money," said Esther Tomljanovich, a student at one of William Mitchell's predecessor colleges in the 1950s who would become Rosalie's judicial colleague and Lake Elmo friend. (Tomljanovich attributed the kindness of her male law school classmates to their recognition that "I would never be a threat to their careers. They knew I wouldn't even get an interview" when legal jobs opened, she said. "I could be the class pet." Tomljanovich started her post–law school career as a claims manager in the legal department of St. Paul–based Minnesota Mutual Insurance Co. "I was told I couldn't travel on claims trips because I was a woman. There was no question—I could never advance to general counsel." One boss told her, "Women do boring work so well.")[17]

Jones was a gentle, thoughtful man with a deep-seated passion for justice. Born in meager circumstances in North Dakota, he came of age in Minneapolis, going to work to help support his family after his father died. He lost fingers on his right hand as a result of an accident in a butcher shop where he worked as a teenager, giving him the lifelong nickname "Lefty." Also lasting was his empathy for people who struggled to overcome adversity. His sense of justice extended to women at a time when many other men in the legal profession seemed oblivious to sex discrimination. That may have been because his mother faced a lack of opportunity after his father died. She went to work as a bookkeeper and struggled to make ends meet. It may also have been because he was a devoted husband and the father of two daughters. "He was just good about women," said Emily Anne Tuttle, who, as a young woman, worked in New York City and roomed there with her University of Minnesota classmate Helen Fredel, Jones's future wife.[18]

Jones was allotted Ford Foundation funding for three full-time assistants when he set up shop in January 1966, and he chose three men. His hiring pattern changed soon thereafter, starting with the summer job Rosalie took in 1966. When Rosalie graduated from law school in 1967, she took a permanent position in Jones's office the next day. (She had taken the bar exam in February, earlier than most of her classmates, and learned that she had passed a week before Mitchell's 1967 commencement.) Then or soon after, other women lawyers—Roberta Levy, Doris Huspeni, Molly Raskind—joined her in working on appellate cases. Jones was making his office a training ground for future judges.[19]

He was also experimenting with more family-friendly workplace arrangements for women with children than would have been available anywhere else. Rosalie worked three days a week, Monday, Wednesday, and Friday, during her first two years in the defender's office. Her summer babysitter in 1967 was her daughter Sara, who graduated from high school the same year Rosalie finished law school. The family reasoned that Rosalie could earn more working in the summertime than Sara could at the summer jobs available to teens. When Sara enrolled at the University of Minnesota that fall, a family friend who was starting a home-based childcare business, Raquel Wood, took over Jenny's care in the mornings, and Jenny attended preschool at the University of Minnesota in the afternoons. The Woods and the Wahls had become good friends through their mutual association with the Twin Cities Friends Meeting. Raquel was a trained early childhood educator and had a daughter, Mina, nearly the same age as Jenny. The two mothers clicked

Rosalie and her children assembled on the farmhouse steps for this photo in 1972. Front, from left: Sara, Jenny, and Mark; rear: Tim, Rosalie, and Chris. *Courtesy Wahl family.*

as partners in childrearing and, eventually, as confidants about domestic life. "I never could have made it without friends," Rosalie would say of those stressful days.

Rosalie's marriage was deteriorating, and the struggles of two of her sons added to her pain. Ross was becoming increasingly erratic and psychologically abusive to Rosalie and their children. His behavior frightened her at times, and he was drinking heavily. When Rosalie asked him to move out, he lived for a time in a primitive shed on their Lake Elmo property, clinging to the notion of living off the land that he had harbored twenty years earlier. The Wahls' parting, years in the making, was legally final in 1972.

The eldest Wahl son, Christopher, was also troubled. He experimented with drugs in college, then left school to try to make it as a folk musician. He worked a stint on fishing boats in Alaska, then as an orderly in a hospital. He met a woman, fell in love, and had a son in 1972, moving his young family in with Rosalie and his younger siblings in an arrangement fraught with tension. Jenny, then age eight, spent several weeks during the family's difficult summer of 1972 with Patterson relatives in

Kansas. Eventually Christopher's sad diagnosis came: schizophrenia. Rosalie had to wonder whether genetics had anything to do with problems that appeared in her youngest son Mark's life at about the same time. He began abusing alcohol at age fourteen, in 1969. By the time his parents divorced, he was on his way to a lifelong struggle with chemical dependency.

For Rosalie, sorrow at home was mitigated by the satisfaction of establishing a meaningful new career. Constitutional law (con-law) had been one of Rosalie's favorite classes at Mitchell. Working on felony appellate cases, often involving constitutional questions, under the tutelage of her former con-law professor suited her well. The work involved a heavy load of research and writing, which appealed to a lover of language and ideas. Rosalie also had to present oral arguments before the state's highest court. In those years before the creation of the state court of appeals, the supreme court heard every appeal in the state system. Many lawyers practice for years without standing before the imposing array of supreme court justices. Rosalie found herself there within weeks of passing the bar exam, arguing on behalf of an impoverished, already-convicted defendant, knowing that her chances of prevailing were slim. After arguing that first case, she would recall later, "I felt as if I'd been thrown off a horse."[20]

During the next six years, she would play that role 109 times. Repetition increased her skill, comfort level, and positive reputation with the nine justices on the high court. She learned not to take it personally when Chief Justice Oscar Knutson turned his back on her while she argued her case. He was cranky with everyone, she discovered. She came to appreciate protocol and courtroom formality, but she could not hold her tongue on one occasion when an associate justice was dismissive of irregularities in a district court trial because the preponderance of evidence indicated that the defendant was guilty. "You mean to tell me that only the innocent get a fair trial?" she piped up. Word of her bold retort got back to the public defender's office on the University of Minnesota campus before she did.[21]

Rosalie also learned not to be discouraged by the frequency with which the appeals she brought to the court were rejected. Her clients were, after all, defendants who had already been convicted of burglary, rape, or murder. Under the guidelines established by the U.S. Supreme

Court, any indigent who wants to appeal a felony conviction must be granted that opportunity. "So many times, there wasn't a lot to argue. You might try lack of adequate counsel at trial level, or say there wasn't probable cause for the arrest or the search, or insufficient evidence, which is a hard thing to argue. You were always kind of arguing uphill."

She discovered that she could find satisfaction in the process of pursuing justice, regardless of the small number of cases she won. "One of the things I've just got in my bones from constitutional law is that you shouldn't take anyone's life, liberty, or property without due process of the law," Wahl would say later in life about what kept her going as a public defender. "It was my job to make the best possible presentation in regard to their case[s] with the facts you had and argue as hard as you could." She also took great satisfaction in representing those who, but for the state's provision, would not have access to the courts. In her view, equal access to the forum of justice was crucial to justice itself. She fretted about the legal system's shortcomings in this regard. "Even in the Twin Cities, where strong, viable legal assistance programs are operating, there have been times where only one in four requests for legal services could be handled . . . The implications in terms of unmet legal needs for this group alone are staggering," she told a Hamline University audience a few years later.[22]

More than once, Rosalie found herself wondering what happened among the justices when oral arguments ended and the nine robed men retreated into their private conference room to discuss what had transpired that day in the ornate capitol courtroom. "Wouldn't it be nice to go in there and sit with them and see what they talked about?" she recalled thinking. Years had passed since the day she sat with other women outside the Washington County commissioners' boardroom while men inside decided whether their hard work would bear fruit. Much had changed for her—yet she was still excluded from an all-male chamber of power. But instead of feeling angry and frustrated as she had a decade earlier at the courthouse in Stillwater, Rosalie was hopeful. By the early 1970s, she and other Minnesota women had reason to think that the doors of previously all-male quarters were cracking open for them.[23]

Chapter Four

"Libbers" and "Legalists"

E ven Minnesotans who spent years striving to open doors for women strain in hindsight to see exactly what made those doors budge in the early 1970s. They see not a single charismatic leader or pivotal moment, but a sudden, simultaneous emergence of a number of leaders, networks, and events. It was the same nationally. "It seemed that overnight, everything that America had taken for granted about a woman's role was being called into question," wrote *New York Times* columnist Gail Collins. "The apparent suddenness of it all was not due to the arrival of a great leader, although some of the leaders were amazing . . . There was something else—or a collection of something elses—buried deep in the social fabric."[1]

The "collection of something elses" Collins named pertained to the economy and women's role in the labor force. In 1970, Minnesota was positioned on those measures much like the nation as a whole. The postwar economic boom had been good to Minnesota. A state that had languished economically during the first half of the twentieth century took off in the second half, fueled by a well-educated workforce that could serve knowledge-dependent industries. State median household incomes that sagged below the national median in the 1930s and 1940s surged forward in the 1960s, exceeding the national mark by 3.6 percent in 1969. That trend would continue for the next three decades. The state's median family income would be 13.6 percent ahead of the nation's by 1999.[2]

Growing demand increased the value of the skills and work ethic that Minnesota women brought to their jobs. On average, women in Minnesota were better educated than other American women in 1970. Twenty-two percent of them had at least some college education, compared with 17.9

Activists hung a banner from Minneapolis's Foshay Tower, the tallest building in the state, to mark the nationwide women's strike called by the National Organization for Women on August 26, 1970. *Minnesota Historical Society.*

percent of American women generally. The share of Minnesota women who collected paychecks outside their homes rose apace with the national numbers in the 1960s. By 1970, 43.5 percent of Minnesota women past the age of sixteen were employed, nearly matching the 43.3 percent share of working women in the United States. Forty years earlier, women in both Minnesota and the nation had comprised just 22 percent of the workforce.[3]

Those statistics and the changing lives they represented are an essential backdrop to the women's movement that erupted in Minnesota and the nation in the late 1960s. The economy had become too dependent on women for them to remain confined to menial roles. Legions of women were ready and very able to do more, and employers needed their

contributions. Insulting women with substandard, blatantly discriminatory wages and working conditions was increasingly bad for business.

Yet it's likely that conditions would have improved more slowly than
they did had women not demanded change. Those who did drew inspiration and courage from a number of converging forces. By 1970, the mothers who raised the post–World War II Baby Boomer generation—Rosalie
among them—had launched their children at least partway toward independence. They had the time and talent for other work—and in many
cases, a financial imperative to bring home paychecks. Their sons and,
significantly, their daughters were rapidly becoming the best-educated
generation the world had yet produced. The cost of their children's college educations drove Rosalie and many of her peers into the workforce.
The arrival of "the Pill" in 1960 gave women better control over their
reproductive lives than ever before.

Two grassroots movements that came to the fore in the 1960s—civil
rights and opposition to the Vietnam War—produced enough positive
results to serve as models for other seekers of social and economic justice. Both movements served as training grounds for feminists. Minnesota was in the thick of national politics as the home of both 1968 Democratic presidential candidate Hubert Humphrey and that year's insurgent
antiwar candidate, U.S. Senator Eugene McCarthy. Minnesotans tended
to side with the Reverend Martin Luther King Jr. on civil rights, mourned
his assassination in 1968, and worked in the 1950s and 1960s to root out
racism in housing and employment.[4]

In the petite, vibrant person of Arvonne Skelton Fraser, Minnesota
women had a conduit to the women's movement that was brewing in the
nation's capital in the late 1960s. Fraser was the wife of U.S. representative
Don Fraser of the Minneapolis-anchored Fifth District and the mother
of six children. She also possessed one of the sharpest strategic minds in
the Democratic-Farmer-Labor Party. She had been a staffer in the 1948
U.S. Senate campaign that launched Humphrey's national career, a top
aide to future governor Orville Freeman when he chaired the state DFL
Party, and assistant manager of the 1960 Kennedy for President campaign
in Minnesota. She had been her husband's *de facto* campaign manager
in every race since his first, a successful bid for the state senate in 1954.[5]

When Don was elected to Congress in 1962, the Frasers moved
to Washington, and Arvonne chafed at the confining expectations for

"proper" congressional wives. She became an unpaid but indispens- able staffer in Fraser's congres- sional office. Before long, she met other frustrated women whose identities had been subsumed and talents underutilized due to their husbands' prominence. In early 1969, she invited some of them to a luncheon at her home. The "Nameless Sisterhood" was born. It was akin to hundreds, perhaps thousands, of informal feminist "consciousness-raising" and sup- port groups that were popping up

Arvonne Skelton Fraser, about 1970. *Minnesota Historical Society.*

all over the country. But this one was comprised of women with im- portant political connections. Within a year, the "Nameless Sisterhood" helped spawn the District of Columbia chapter of the Women's Equity Action League, or WEAL, with Arvonne as its president. She would go on in 1972 to be the group's national president, and WEAL would become the legal arm of the national women's movement—"legalists" focused on improving the lot of women through the law and the courts, rather than via the more visible rallies and protests associated with "women's libbers." WEAL's achievements include the far-reaching 1972 Title IX requirement of gender equity in federally funded collegiate activities, including athletics, and the Women's Educational Equity Act, which pro- vided $30 million—a jaw-dropping amount in 1974—to eradicate gender stereotyping in grade school curricular material.

In Minnesota, Fraser's accounts of what happened when Washing- ton women came together energized her large network of friends and admirers. They had been hearing about "consciousness-raising sessions" elsewhere in the country; some had begun organizing similar sessions of their own. "I was always talking to groups," Fraser related a quarter cen- tury later. "It was interesting how people in Minnesota responded to my interest in women's issues. Women would come up to me and whisper in my ear, 'I can't say anything publicly, but boy, am I proud of what you are doing.' I was as fascinated with the women's movement [in Minnesota] as they were with me." Among those inspired to start a Minnesota WEAL chapter was Rosalie Wahl's law school classmate Ellen Dresselhuis.[6]

Interest in Arvonne's reports may have run highest among the thirty-seven Minnesota women who, along with nine men, had served in the mid-1960s on the Governor's Commission on the Status of Women. Created in November 1963 by a less-than-eager governor Karl Rolvaag under great pressure from the state's Business and Professional Women, the commission was a response to President John F. Kennedy's similar action at the federal level in 1962. Kennedy's commission issued far-reaching recommendations about fair treatment for female federal workers and called for "new and expanded services that may be required for women as wives, mothers and workers." The services it listed foretold the women's movement agenda for the next half century: "education counseling, training, home services, arrangements for care of children during the working day," all to "enhance constructive employment opportunities for women." The Kennedy commission reported one month before an assassin struck down the president on November 22, 1963.[7]

Two pro-female changes in federal law followed within the next year. One, the Equal Pay for Equal Work Act for federal employment, was so riddled with exceptions and loopholes as to be nearly meaningless. The other would provide a lasting legal underpinning for those who sought to use the law to improve the lives of American women. It was the addition of "sex" as a category of prohibited discrimination in employment to Title VII of the 1964 Civil Rights Act. Ironically, that provision was added to the bill by an anti–civil rights congressman from Virginia who mistakenly thought that in so doing he was guaranteeing the bill's defeat.[8]

Against that backdrop of mixed federal messages, the state commission labored in 1964 and 1965 to make recommendations that might garner at least the attention of state lawmakers, if not their support. Commission members' expectations couldn't be high—not when they were reminded of Minnesota's habitual gender discrimination every time they gathered for working sessions at the Minneapolis Athletic Club. Female commissioners were told they were not allowed to walk through the front door but could enter the building through the kitchen. "I wouldn't do that now," commission member Edna Schwartz said nearly thirty years later. "But [then], we were so doggone ladylike."[9]

The commission called for an equal pay law to cover the large number of jobs that were out of reach of the new federal legislation. It made particular note of the need to root out pay discrimination at state colleges and universities, reporting in galling detail how male professors had been favored over similarly qualified females in the most recent distribution of salary increases at five state colleges. It also amassed private-sector data that pointed to rampant gender-based wage discrimination in Minnesota. For example: Women outnumbered men as sales clerks by eight to one but made an average hourly wage outside the metro area of $1.12 per hour, compared with $1.57 for men. At dry cleaning establishments, women were paid an average of forty cents per hour less than men doing the same pressing and finishing work. Women held 40 percent of retail supervisory and office jobs in the Twin Cities and were paid an average of $1.51 per hour, compared with $2.74 for men. Among registered nurses outstate—97 percent of whom were female—the few men were paid on average $2.82 per hour. The mean hourly wage for female RNs: $2.12.

Another notable recommendation: state government should "give increased attention to the appointment of qualified women to public office in policy making, executive and administrative posts and to judicial offices." The commission sent a questionnaire to the two major political parties probing their attitudes about "the participation of women in political matters."

The parties' immediate responses to that call are unknown, but they could not have been satisfying. To be sure, women were welcome in both political parties. The welcome mat appeared slightly larger in the Republican Party (GOP). Under the postwar leadership of former governor Harold Stassen, Minnesota Republicans initiated the practice of sending gender-balanced delegations to national conventions. In the 1950s, Republican women in the metro area were part of a nationwide network, the Women's Republican Workshop, devoted to teaching women the arcane protocols of precinct caucuses and Basic Political Organizing Units (BPOUs).[10]

But in both parties in the 1960s, women were largely relegated to menial tasks. Their increasing frustration inspired a group of DFL women to invite University of Minnesota social work professor Esther Wattenberg to prepare a report detailing the role of women in forty-seven legislative campaigns in 1970—all of them waged by male candidates. Five women filed for legislative seats that year; only one, three-term representative

Helen McMillan from Austin, was elected. While Wattenberg found women involved in all the campaigns she examined, in some cases in numbers larger than men, only two of the campaigns had female campaign managers; only five had female finance directors. Women were the "dedicated drones" of the campaigns, "making coffee, stuffing envelopes, 'manning' the phones and arranging coffee parties," Wattenberg wrote. The report's title summed up their status: *Women in the DFL: Present but Powerless*. The questionnaire response of a male legislator, recited in the report, would become infamous: "The women are the workers, not the planners. They addressed a hell of a lot of letters. This was their wish."[11]

No one seethed more at such comments than the chairwoman of the state DFL Party, Koryne Kaneski Horbal. The youngest child in a family with three daughters, Horbal was born in 1937 in blue-collar northeast Minneapolis into a union-allied household with Iron Range roots. She acquired her values at the family dinner table, where her electrician father often praised Eleanor Roosevelt, and her persuasive skill on the Anoka High School debate team, where she excelled. She was the homecoming queen who married the football captain, William Horbal. Bill became a water and sewer contractor; Koryne, who to her regret did not attend college, went to work at an advertising agency as a radio and television time-buyer. She made DFL politics a second vocation, building a strong bond with Minnesota favorite son Hubert Humphrey as he rose to the vice presidency. The Horbals' adoption of two children did not slow Koryne's rise through the "women's side" of DFL offices, from precinct captain to Hennepin County chairwoman to state party chairwoman in 1967 at the age of thirty. She was increasingly annoyed by evidence that those positions were of inferior status to those of their male counterparts. "It was like an auxiliary, not the real party," Horbal said of the meetings of state Democratic chairwomen she attended in Washington. "We had teaching camps about campaigns, at which the candidates would come and parade in front of us. They were all men. I thought, what is this? Why are all the women sitting here applauding all these men?"[12]

Horbal's questions persisted at home. Future Minnesota attorney general Warren Spannaus, DFL state chairman in the late 1960s, had a full-time position that paid an $18,500 annual salary. The "chairwoman" (she engineered a change to "associate chair") was unpaid, but was expected to travel as widely and spend as much time on party activities as the chairman. When she suggested that she and Spannaus carpool to party events around the state to save money, he resisted. He wanted to run for office one day, he explained, and he could not be seen traveling with a woman who was not his wife.

Nothing in Wattenberg's report came as a surprise to Horbal. Despite the report's discouraging assessment, Horbal seized upon it as "a breakthrough." It armed her with a tool for the strategy that was taking shape in her mind—old-style, person-to-person organizing to propel DFL women into positions of power. Even as she was plotting her own successful bid for election as Minnesota's allotted female member of the Democratic National Committee in 1971, she planned a series of meetings around the state to expose DFL women to Wattenberg's findings and enlist them as members of a renamed and repurposed group, the DFL Women's Caucus. The group had existed since the mid-1960s as the DFL Women's Federation, and functioned as a helpmate to the male-dominated party. "It's designed to keep women working but in their place," Wattenberg's report quoted Democratic National Committeewoman and former *Minneapolis Tribune* journalist Geri Joseph as saying. Horbal changed the group's name to the more forceful-sounding "Caucus" and urged it to embrace an ambitious goal—the full gender integration of every part of state politics and government.[13]

The first in Horbal's series of "women's awareness seminars" occurred at the Pick-Nicollet Hotel in downtown Minneapolis in late October 1971. Word of mouth was sufficient to draw a surprisingly large crowd—120 women and a smattering of men. Participants shared their stories of exclusion and underappreciation, of volunteer work that was scarcely rewarded with gratitude, let alone the invitations to fancy dinners or the offers of free tickets to an inaugural ball that male workers routinely received. By the time the seventh meeting in the series occurred in January, they had morphed into candidate recruitment sessions. Linda Hines, a twenty-eight-year-old Minnetonka housewife, told the *Minneapolis Tribune*'s Harley Sorensen that she was thinking about running for office. "We should stop being stamp-lickers, and we definitely should have some women candidates," she said. Within six months, the DFL Women's Caucus roster included four thousand names. Horbal assured a reporter that, had she tried a little harder, the list easily could have run to ten thousand.[14]

Simultaneously in 1971, another feminist organization was rising in

Washington, DC, that would leap across the country to Minnesota. Arvonne Fraser was among the dozens of Washington women who turned out in the Rayburn House Office Building one spring Saturday to consider a proposal by representatives Bella Abzug and Shirley Chisholm of New York and Patsy Mink of Hawaii to organize a bipartisan National Women's Political Caucus.[15]

One other Minnesotan was present, somewhat by accident. Republican activist Emily Anne Mayer Staples of west-suburban Plymouth was in Washington for a job interview with the Nixon administration. In 1971 Staples was forty-two years old, vivacious and brimming with leadership ability. She would have gone to law school after graduating in 1950 from the University of Minnesota but for her attorney father's discouragement. "Women aren't lawyers," he preached, tamping down her ambition. Instead, she channeled her considerable energy into raising four children, serving the Junior League as regional director, and working in the Republican Party, rising to assistant treasurer of the state finance committee. (Notably, the committee's treasurer was her friend and former college classmate Nancy Brataas of Rochester, who would also make Minnesota feminist history.) Staples didn't get the job she was seeking in the Department of Labor, but attending the caucus organizing meeting made her Washington trip worthwhile.[16]

Within weeks, the first meeting of the National Women's Political Caucus convened at the Statler Hotel in Washington, with 320 women from twenty-six states in attendance. Arvonne was among the event's co-conveners. Its keynoter was Gloria Steinem, a magazine journalist who had burst upon the national scene in 1963 as the freelance author of "I Was a Playboy Bunny," a first-person exposé of the shabby treatment of women in Hugh Hefner's Playboy Club. "This is no simple reform," Steinem told the assembly about their audacious aim: half of the elected officials in the country should be female. "It really is a revolution. Sex and race, because they are easy, visible differences, have been the primary ways of organizing human beings into superior and inferior groups, and into the cheap labor on which this system still depends," Steinem said. By contrast, feminists "are talking about a society in which there will be no roles other than those chosen and those earned." Not many Americans that day could imagine what such a society would look like, but a surprising share was eager to find out.[17]

Senator Emily Anne Mayer Staples with senate majority leader Nicholas Coleman, 1978. *Minnesota Historical Society.*

Six weeks after the national meeting, Arvonne interrupted her usual summer hiatus at the secluded Fraser summer house on the St. Croix River to join a kickoff rally for the new Minnesota Women's Political Caucus at NSP Plaza in downtown Minneapolis. The state caucus would be loosely linked to the new national organization, and it would be emphatically bipartisan. Its goals were all about increasing female participation in government and politics at all levels and via both parties. While "women's issues" were cited as a reason for women to take places alongside men in government, the caucus, in hopes of keeping its appeal broad, was not touting a particular policy agenda. Fraser became the first DFL co-convener and also headed the committee that wrote the national organization's constitution. Staples was the Republican co-convener in Minnesota and was elected finance director of the new organization. She confided to friends that she had her eye on running for the legislature.[18]

The notion of running for the legislature was lodging in a number of women's minds that year. Here are some of their stories.

‖ Minnesota Women's Political Caucus activist Phyllis Kahn of Minneapolis had been mulling a legislative bid since becoming a volunteer lobbyist at the 1971 legislature for a small, new organization called the Minnesota Council for the Legal Termination of Pregnancy. It was a fitting role for a Yale-educated biophysicist (PhD, class of 1962) whose career was stymied by the closed professional doors she encountered when her mathematician husband took a position at the University of Minnesota. She had encountered little sex discrimination earlier in

Representative Phyllis Kahn, about 1973. *Minnesota Historical Society.*

her career. In Minnesota, it was maddeningly blatant. She was allowed lab space in the university's department of genetics and cell biology to work as a post-doctorate research associate, provided she secured her own funding through National Science Foundation grants. When she filed a discrimination complaint in 1968 for being denied a faculty job, her lab arrangement was cut short. The dean who delivered that news didn't bother to hide the fact that she was being punished for filing the complaint. When the university's judiciary committee rejected the complaint, Kahn took it to the slow-moving federal Equal Employment Opportunity Commission, where it languished for more than a decade.[19]

Kahn had never set foot in any state's capitol until she and other local members of the five-year-old National Organization for Women went to St. Paul in 1971 to promote a bill sponsored by conservative senator George Pillsbury of Wayzata. It would have removed criminal penalties for abortions performed by licensed physicians and stiffened the penalties for abortions performed by anyone else. Her first assignment, to lobby Minneapolis representative Arne Carlson, gave her a fortuitous connection to a future governor and may have helped cement his support for abortion rights. Kahn attended a DFL precinct caucus in 1972 and soon thereafter was the only woman among five candidates running in

newly redrawn state House District 57A, which straddled the University
of Minnesota campus in northeast and southeast Minneapolis and had
no incumbent. The new Minnesota Women's Political Caucus had its
first electoral test.[20]

‖ An older women's organization was being put to a similar test in the
western suburbs. From the ranks of the League of Women Voters of Minnetonka came Joan Anderson Growe, a former teacher and mother of four
who had turned to the league as a source of more meaningful activities
than her local bridge club provided. Growe had been a mayor's daughter
in Buffalo, Minnesota, and was always more interested in politics than
was a brother who was forever being told that he could follow in his father's footsteps. Her life started conventionally enough, with marriage
and three children in rapid succession, but it took a consequential turn
when she and her toddler children left her alcoholic and abusive husband
and ventured to the Twin Cities. They survived on the low wages she
could earn as a parochial school teacher and, one summer, on welfare.
Growe married again in the mid-1960s and found middle-class suburban
stability, but she never forgot what it was like to be broke and alone with
hungry children at home, looking to the government for help.[21]

Redistricting changed the political landscape in the western suburbs
in 1972. Emily Anne Staples hoped the new District 43A map would give
her an opening to run for the legislature in Plymouth, but she wound up
in the same district as incumbent Republican state representative O. J.
"Lon" Heinitz, and deferred to a member of her own party.

By contrast, an open house seat had been created in District 40A, en-
compassing half of Minnetonka and all of Eden Prairie. The strong Minnetonka League of Women Voters promoted its president, Gwen Luhta, for
Republican endorsement, but the party nod went to auto repair businessman Richard Stranik. League members were furious. DFL chairwoman and league activist Nancy Wangen approached Growe to run
under the "Liberal" banner. (1972 was the state's last legislative election
without party designation.) It appeared to outsiders that Growe would
be a sacrificial lamb in the conservative (Republican) district. Growe's
fellow league members, however, didn't see it that way. One friend, future United Methodist pastor Gretchen Fogo, knew how a female Hopkins school board candidate succeeded with a campaign of intensive

door-to-door canvassing. Fogo preached the "Hopkins method" to the all-female Growe steering committee, drawn from league, church, and PTA ranks. It was to Growe's advantage that she had been president of Groveland Elementary School's parent-teacher association.[22]

Fogo found a Growe campaign chair for every precinct in the district and instructed those precinct chairs to call every person they knew to ask for help. Hosts were recruited for several dozen small coffee parties at which women could meet the candidate—a tactic that worked well because many suburban women in 1972 were at home during daytime hours. The steering committee drew up charts and maps to give each volunteer a daunting assignment—eighty homes to visit in person on Growe's behalf. Growe herself aimed to hit every door by Election Day, even though that meant campaigning seven days a week, rain, shine, or snow, during that year's unseasonably raw October. "I was told that I had to door-knock every single day, and I believed it," Growe said.[23]

‖ In solidly Republican Edina, former high school music teacher Mary Forsythe was just as determined to win a seat in the state house. Unlike Joan Growe, Forsythe did not face long odds after she clinched GOP endorsement in District 39A. "Mrs. Robert Forsythe" had to endure being constantly linked to her prominent husband, an attorney who had served a stint as state Republican Party chairman and ran unsuccessfully for U.S. Senate in 1966 and attorney general in 1970. But the list of party offices Mary had held was at least as long as his, and

Representative Mary Forsythe, about 1973. *Minnesota Historical Society.*

she had led workshops on the electoral process for Republican activists around the state for a number of years. She was also a volunteer leader in the Girl Scouts, PTA, United Fund, Guthrie Theater, Alpha House (a nonprofit organization for sex offender rehabilitation), and Bethlehem

Lutheran Church and the mother of five children—all activities providing rich but underappreciated preparation for elective office.

‖ A candidate recruitment meeting in Emily Anne Staples's living room early in 1972 clinched the candidacy of Ernee McArthur. A Republican, McArthur was executive secretary of the sizeable Brooklyn Center Chamber of Commerce, whose members included the stores of Brookdale Shopping Mall. Like Growe, McArthur had been an active member of her chapter of the League of Women Voters, which supplied her with an immediate base of support. Notably, Growe and Forsythe were at the same meeting—Forsythe to announce her intention to run, and Growe to applaud the candidates, without an inkling that she would be among them a few weeks later.[24]

‖ Linda Lee Berglin, a self-employed graphic designer, celebrated her twenty-eighth birthday a few weeks before Election Day. Shy, smart, serious, and extraordinarily determined, Berglin came to politics via involvement with Model Cities, a War on Poverty federal program that sought to create comprehensive strategies for improving blighted big-city neighborhoods. A factional dispute on the Model Cities governing board resulted in her rapid elevation to chair the thirty-member group in early 1972. Still, when she decided to seek a new open state house seat, she was denigrated for her youth as well as her gender. In both the primary and the general election, rival campaign literature scoffed, "Who is this girl?" and "Don't send a boy or girl to the Legislature to do a man's work." Her thirty-seven-year-old Republican general election opponent, Dick Rodenborn, took to prefacing his comments about her campaign positions with a patronizing

Representative Linda Lee Berglin, about 1973. *Minnesota Historical Society.*

smear: "My opponent is a nice girl, but I don't think she comprehends the effect of her financial position." Berglin countered the attacks with an aggressive door-to-door campaign. Her frequent companion as she trekked through south Minneapolis streets was the twenty-six-year-old owner of the all-female St. Paul public relations firm that was Berglin's graphic design client, Marlene Johnson of Split Infinitive.[25]

‖ Incumbent state representative Helen McMillan of Austin was seeking her fifth and final term at the age of sixty-three. A widow and past president of the state League of Women Voters, she had endured being one of three, then two, then the lone female among two hundred male legislators. She had been excluded from circles of power in the house. No Minnesotan was happier than she was to see more women's names on candidate rosters.

A record-breaking twenty-one other women's names were on the general election legislative ballot in 1972. Twelve more lost in the primary. Not since 1922 had the state seen such a surge in female candidacies. Many were long-shot DFL candidates, recruited and trained in Horbal's DFL Women's Caucus seminars and running "just to get exposure," Koryne explained. She was building for the long term.[26]

But these six—McMillan, Berglin, Forsythe, McArthur, Growe, and Kahn—made it to the state house on November 7, 1972, each by a comfortable margin. The surprise winner among them was Growe, who won with more than a 1,100-vote advantage and a core group of eight supporters whose lives would never be the same. Each of them went on to pursue professional or community service careers and would trace their change in direction to the Growe campaign.[27]

The 1973 legislature was comprised of six women—and 195 men. But six women in a chamber where there had been just one before was a sea change in Minnesota politics. No longer could male politicians count on victory over a female opponent or disregard women's concerns with impunity. If they did, these six were determined to protest—going so far as to rise to object during floor debates when anyone addressed the body as "gentlemen." These six new house members weren't planning to blend in. Their aim was institutional change. It was a good year for it: 1973 also saw the senate, house and governor's office all in Democratic-Farmer-Labor

hands for the first time in state history. Six decades without party designation at the legislature would come to an end in 1974. And for the first
time since the 1880s, the legislature henceforward would meet annually,
not biennially.

Horbal, the DFL's feminist general, put the new legislature to an immediate test. In Congress on March 22, 1972, nearly fifty years after a
version of it was first introduced, the Equal Rights Amendment to the
U.S. Constitution crossed the requisite two-thirds vote threshold and
was sent to the states for ratification. It said simply, "Equality of rights
under the law shall not be denied or abridged by the United States or
by any state on account of sex." It would be a bedrock guarantee of civil
rights to American women, and it would raise the legal bar against discrimination on the basis of gender. Congress allowed seven years for the
states to ratify the amendment; thirty-eight legislatures would have to
vote affirmatively for it to be added to the nation's charter. Before 1972
was over, twenty-two states had said yes. The Minnesota legislature's
first crack at ratification would come in 1973.[28]

Horbal wanted that vote cast as early as possible, before the ERA
could get tangled in the biennial battle over the state budget and before the rising chorus of spurious arguments against the amendment
could sink into public consciousness. While in Washington in 1972,
she met Carol Burris, a leading congressional lobbyist for the ERA and
the founder of the Women's Lobby, Inc. Burris warned that anti-ERA
organizing was taking a serious toll in southern states. Minnesota, a
midwestern state with a substantial Catholic population, could be next.
Conservative attorney Phyllis Schlafly of Alton, Illinois, was on her way
to national prominence with her Stop ERA campaign, which spread the
story that constitutional equality would lead to women being drafted for
military service, an end to single-sex public restrooms, and the loss of
widow's benefits under Social Security.[29]

Burris advised Horbal to act fast and coached her on how to proceed.
She gave Horbal a crash course in legislative lobbying—how to count
votes, how to research the backgrounds of legislators (for example,
knowing whether they had daughters), and how to prepare for committee hearings and floor fights. Burris's extra attention wasn't because of
any special tie to Minnesota. Rather, the Pittsburgh native recognized
Horbal as a rare feminist with genuine political party experience and

connections. She saw value in befriending a politically adept suburban Catholic homemaker who might be willing to lobby midwestern Catholic members of Congress.

Burris put Horbal in touch with some of the nation's leading feminists. From New York representative Bella Abzug, the boldest feminist voice in Congress, Horbal learned the importance of mastering legislative procedural rules and of preparing for any procedural possibility before floor fights. In Gloria Steinem, who had founded *Ms.* magazine earlier that year, Horbal found a lasting friend. Steinem admired Horbal's determination to work within a political party's structure to make gains for women. The Steinem-Horbal bond became a power line, transmitting feminist energy from the national scene to Minnesota and back for the next decade. When Steinem created the Ms. Foundation in 1973 to fund women's equality projects, she recruited Horbal for its founding board of directors.

National feminist leader Gloria Steinem, founder of *Ms.* magazine, took a particular interest in the women's movement in Minnesota and visited the state several times in the early 1970s. She stands in front, wearing her familiar aviator glasses. Other women who have been identified are Marlene Johnson (future lieutenant governor, second from left); Koryne Horbal, third from left; Linda Berglin, fourth from left; and Mary Pattock, holding the child on the far right. *Courtesy Mary Pattock.*

Back in Minnesota after the 1972 election, Horbal shared her new-found lobbying knowledge and sense of urgency with a cadre of devoted DFL volunteers. Among them: Yvette Boe Oldendorf, a volunteer at the state party office who helped Wattenberg prepare her pivotal report; Jeri Rasmussen, a spunky, tart-talking United Methodist housewife from suburban Shoreview with a passion for abortion rights; Mary Peek, a thoughtful former teacher and peace activist from the eastern suburbs; Cynthia Kitlinksi, Horbal's like-minded older friend from Coon Rapids, who would go on to serve on the state's Public Utilities Commission; Peggy Specktor, a Golden Valley housewife committed to stopping domestic violence; and Mary Pattock Bremer, a twenty-eight-year-old writer, progressive Catholic, and peace activist. Republican state chairwoman Luella Stocker, a former president of the Falcon Heights League of Women Voters and member of the Minnesota Women's Political Caucus, was a "wonderful ally," Horbal said. Stocker was the wife of a Land O'Lakes Corporation executive; her renown in GOP circles was her ability to recruit volunteers for any task. "She was a great person," Horbal said of Stocker. "We worked together all the time."[30]

A Minnesota Coalition to Ratify the ERA formed in the summer of 1972. It combined the established reach and reputation of the League of Women Voters and the Business and Professional Women with the upstart energy of the Minnesota Women's Political Caucus, the National Organization for Women, and the Women's Equity Action League. By January 19, the coalition boasted thirty-five member organizations—an impressive alliance sturdy enough to promote the ERA and much more. Catholics Horbal and Bremer were especially proud to add the Sisters Council of the Roman Catholic Archdiocese of St. Paul and Minneapolis to the list—especially after Archbishop Leo Byrne urged on January 16 that action on the ERA be delayed until lawmakers could "really try to learn the mind[s] of the women of the state." He said he feared that many women "will be in the position of being victims of its passage rather than being assisted by it."[31]

With the guidance of the ratification resolution's chief sponsors, Brainerd senator Win Borden and East Grand Forks representative Bill Kelly, both DFLers, coalition lobbyists fanned out to sell the ERA to legislators. (It must have stung representative Helen McMillan to be the fifth-listed co-sponsor of the resolution, not the chief author.) Their lobbying toolkit included a letter of endorsement signed jointly by the state's two U.S. senators, DFLers Hubert Humphrey and Walter Mondale. It also included offers to help legislators defend a "yes" vote to critics back home. "It relates to the core of American democratic philosophy—that all men and women are created equal, and have equal God-given rights," said the letter Mary Bremer drafted for DFL senator Roger Laufenburger, an insurance agency owner in southeastern Minnesota. "It applies only to the public, not the private, sector, and so will have no effect on our traditional values and customs concerning the family, which I know we all hold dear."[32]

The 1973 legislature's majority DFL leaders, senator Nicholas Coleman and house speaker Martin Sabo, saw the opportunity to ride the women's movement wave. They made the ERA ratification House Resolution Number One. They too must have sensed a need for urgency. The *St. Cloud Times* noted on January 8 that legislators "reported a heavy barrage of letters opposed to the proposal."[33]

The ratification bid was on the house floor on January 22, 1973, cruising to an easy 104–28 vote, when a political bombshell hit. The U.S. Supreme Court handed down its landmark ruling legalizing abortion, *Roe v. Wade*. In a 7–2 ruling, the high court said that state laws banning abortion in the first trimester of pregnancy, and most such bans in the second trimester, were an unconstitutional infringement on a woman's right to privacy. The states whose abortion bans dissolved that day included Minnesota—the home state of the Supreme Court justice who wrote the majority opinion, Harry Blackmun.

The state's women's movement was profoundly affected. A much greater measure of female control over reproduction had become the law of the land, to feminists' delight. But the new law and its origin in government's judicial branch faced immediate, fierce, and stubborn resistance that drained strength from the women's movement and put it on the defensive just as it was coming into its own. Minnesota's "pro-choice" feminists and sympathetic legislators of both parties had tried to use the legislative and executive branches to legalize abortions performed by licensed physicians in certified settings. Their efforts had foundered on opposition based largely within the state's large Roman Catholic establishment.

Catholic criticism of *Roe v. Wade* had particular political importance in Minnesota in 1973. Minnesota Catholics tended to identify with the DFL, the party that had just taken charge of the legislature for the first time. Officially, the party was neutral on abortion. The 1972 DFL state convention had removed from its platform the party's previous position favoring a relaxation of abortion restrictions. But neutrality wasn't the sentiment of DFL legislators whose political bases included large Catholic parishes. Within days of the Supreme Court's decision, a sizeable group of DFLers—all of them male—announced their support for a resolution asking Congress to send the states an anti-abortion "human life amendment" that would reverse *Roe v. Wade*.[34]

Horbal understood that, for ERA ratification to have a chance, she and her volunteer lobbying cadre had to steer clear of abortion, at least temporarily. That wouldn't be easy. The leaders of the ERA lobbying team had been regulars at the capitol in 1971 seeking a relaxation of the state's abortion ban. Until ERA ratification was final, "we pretended that we didn't even think about abortion," Horbal related years later. That did not mean she wasn't still quietly in charge of the feminist defense of *Roe v. Wade*. "We arranged for women around the state to send legislators small children's clothes hangers in the mail." Hangers had become well-known symbols of the back-alley operations to which desperate women turned in the absence of safe, legal abortion services. "We'd be meeting with legislators and they'd pull out these hangers and say, 'Have you seen what they're sending me in the mail?' We had to sit quietly and look surprised."

They struggled to keep masks of implacability in place on February 5, when the ERA came to the senate floor. Its most vocal opponent was DFLer Ed Schrom, an old-school, sixty-two-year-old farmer from heavily Catholic Stearns County. "Most of the proponents [of the amendment] hate men, and I think they hate themselves," he said, maligning most of the occupants of the packed visitors galleries above the chamber. He equated equality for women under the law with the dissolution of traditional households: "When a man goes away to be a wage-earner or a warrior, he needs to return home not to find a house in chaos and full of bastard children." Republican Jerome Blatz of Bloomington—whose daughter Kathleen would become the first female chief justice of the Minnesota Supreme Court twenty-five years later—urged senators to put the ERA "on a bumper sticker, not in the constitution."[35]

At one point during the debate, Republican Carl Jensen—a staunch ERA opponent—took the rare step of directing a question to the senate's presiding officer, DFL lieutenant governor Rudy Perpich, a dentist by profession. "Do you feel there was discrimination against women in dentistry at the University of Minnesota?" Jensen asked, expecting a negative response. Perpich surprised him. "I certainly do!" the lieutenant governor said. "How could that be?" Jensen asked, his skepticism showing. Perpich answered truthfully: "They just wouldn't let them in."[36]

The senate gave final approval to ERA ratification on February 8 with a 48–18 vote. On the same day, a resolution was introduced in the house asking Congress to overturn *Roe v. Wade* by launching a new amendment to the constitution, a "Human Life Amendment." To the chagrin of Horbal and Rasmussen, one of its cosponsors was Republican representative Ernee McArthur—one of the six female freshmen of whom feminists were so proud. The senate companion was introduced with Ed Schrom as its chief sponsor on February 12. That same day, one floor below the senate chamber, Governor Wendell Anderson hosted the ERA lobbying team in his reception room during a bill-signing ceremony that made Minnesota's ratification official. The special guest that day was former state representative Myrtle Cain of the house's class of 1922, one of the original four female members of the legislature.[37]

With that victory secured, DFL feminists could take their abortion-neutrality masks off. They took the gloves off, too. Horbal called a tough-talking press conference on March 21 and served notice to the party's male establishment that their kowtowing to the state's new anti-abortion lobby, Minnesota Citizens Concerned for Life, would meet henceforth with stiff feminist resistance. She pointed out that her get-out-the-vote efforts had helped engineer the DFL's historic 1972 victory and allowed that she was not inclined to do that work again given the positions taken by some of the legislators she helped elect. "DFL Feminists May Quit Party," the *Minneapolis Tribune* headline announced the next day. That option was among several that DFL Women's Caucus leaders and a few sympathetic legislators had discussed with Gloria Steinem when she had come to the state a few weeks earlier. The Minnesotans were keenly aware that the movement's national leaders were watching them.[38]

The DFL women drew inspiration from a smaller rebellion that had already erupted in the Minnesota Republican Party. Emily Anne Staples

Koryne Horbal and
Governor Wendell
Anderson, as the bill
ratifying the Equal Rights
Amendment is signed into
law, February 12, 1973.
Courtesy Mary Pattock.

was among the members of the 1972 GOP state convention's platform committee who went home from that biennial discussion angry and discouraged. The platform committee had unanimously recommended that the party support both legal abortion and the Equal Rights Amendment. Delegates disagreed, voting down both planks. Nine members of the platform committee, Staples among them, resigned their party positions in protest. Staples channeled her considerable political energies that fall into the Minnesota Coalition for the ERA. As she lobbied for the ERA and children's issues at the 1973 legislature, she announced to friends that she had switched parties. She was planning to run for the legislature in 1974 as a DFLer. This time, instead of deferring to Heinitz, she would challenge him in the general election. Republican women organized GOP Women for Political Effectiveness that summer without her.[39]

Both of the state's major parties had disappointed feminists at their 1972 conventions. The two parties seemed to be responding in tandem to the women's movement. But the actions of the Democratic national convention that summer would contribute much to a partisan realignment among feminists during the next two decades. Reforms engineered by Minnesota U.S. representative Don Fraser and South Dakota senator George McGovern, the 1972 Democratic candidate for president, ended winner-take-all delegation elections within the Democratic Party. A system of proportional representation that assured minority factions their due was put in its place, while also serving to perpetuate their minority status.

The new rules also required that state delegations to national conventions include equal numbers of men and women. That change reserved many more seats for women at the national Democratic Party's tables of power. The Minnesota delegation had been less than one-fifth female at the 1960, 1964, and 1968 national conventions—when all the while Minnesota Republicans were sending gender-balanced delegations to national meetings.[40]

Equal gender representation was seen by many observers as the big change in the Democratic Party in 1972. The unintended consequences of the move to proportional representation only became clear in hindsight. Dottie Rietow, a St. Louis Park Republican legal assistant who helped lobby for the ERA and went on to prominence in the National Women's Political Caucus, explained: "Abortion opponents recognized that they could do better in the Republican Party because it still had 'winner take all.' For the people for whom abortion was a primary issue, it wasn't enough to win only some. They wanted to take over a party," the prerequisite to controlling government policy.[41]

Republican winner-take-all rules combined with Minnesota's low-turnout precinct caucus format of party governance to offer an advantage to any well-organized, highly motivated special interest group. In 1972, the Democratic Party's new, complicated "walking subcaucuses" presented to outsiders the image of a chaotic, perpetually divided party. But it was also a party that had become resistant to takeover by a single-issue group. Conversely, that change made the state GOP more susceptible to transformation by a disaffected DFL minority.

As one steeped in party rules and their consequences, Horbal likely had a glimmer of the significance of that change. She also recognized that the feminist network she had built had acquired considerable influence within the DFL Party. They would surrender those advantages if they bolted from the party. She decided to take a different tack.[42]

In April 1973 Horbal and six other women formed the DFL Feminist Caucus, the first and, forty years later, still the only explicitly feminist permanent subcaucus within any state Democratic Party. This would not be a renamed DFL Women's Caucus. That organization would persist for many years to help any candidate wearing the DFL label. The new DFL Feminist Caucus would be more discriminating. It would reserve its blessing and exertions for those DFL candidates who adhered to fourteen (later thirteen) feminist principles. Support for the ERA and the U.S. Supreme Court's abortion decision were high on that list, as was access to contraception, childcare, and economic justice.[43]

The list's top billing went to the core American principle that the organization's "founding mothers" believed was being trampled by their opponents. The caucus would "support the Bill of Rights, especially freedom of speech, freedom of press, and separation of church and state." They sought the rule of law under the U.S. Constitution, trusting that, even without the Equal Rights Amendment, the law was their ally. Soon they began to seek qualified women whom they could recommend to the governor for appointment as judges. They wanted their trust in the law to rest in female hands.

Chapter Five

Ready to Soar

"Could I be a judge?" Gently but persistently, that question bubbled inside Rosalie at gatherings of the DFL Feminist Caucus, which she joined not long after its formation in 1973. Electing pro-choice women to the legislature and statewide executive offices was the new group's highest priority, but its members spoke often about their desire for more women on the bench to secure their legal rights.[1]

Judicial ambition had been tugging intermittently at Rosalie for several years. Being a lawyer in the state public defender's office gave her more frequent exposure to the Minnesota Supreme Court than the vast majority of practicing attorneys had. She also came to know and admire the state's first female district judge, Hennepin County's Susanne Sedgwick, through Minnesota Women Lawyers, another organization founded in 1972. Rosalie noted how Sedgwick got to the trial court bench. It wasn't via the customary gubernatorial appointment. Since statehood, the names on governors' judicial appointment lists had been uniformly male. Republican governor Harold LeVander's list in 1970 was no exception. So that year, Republican Sedgwick became a judge the unconventional way: she filed for election as a municipal judge, ran against an incumbent, and won. Four years later, she would become the first woman appointed to the district court bench.[2]

Rosalie was a moderately active DFLer, participating in precinct caucuses and occasionally attending fundraisers. She wasn't inclined to run for office, nor did anyone approach her to suggest that she should. Yet watching Sedgwick's electoral leap into the judiciary kept the question rolling in Rosalie's mind: "Could I do that? Could I be a judge?"[3]

That question was not the inspiration for Rosalie's next career move,

Minnesota Women Lawyers meeting at the Minnesota State Bar Association convention, June 24, 1974, in Duluth, MN, two years after the group's organization under that name. Left to right: Irene Scott, Mary Louise Klas, Judith Oakes, Susanne Sedgwick, Corrine Lynch, Charlotte Farish, Mary Walbran, Rosalie Wahl, Patricia Belois, (unknown), Nancy Olkon, Sue Halverson, Camilla Reiersgord, and Cara Lee Neville. *Courtesy Minnesota Women Lawyers.*

however. In the spring of 1973, Rosalie's former professor Doug Heidenreich, dean of William Mitchell College of Law, called her with an intriguing offer. Mitchell was establishing a new kind of elective for senior-year law students. It would be a "clinic"—a chance for students to practice law in the service of low-income civil litigants and criminal defendants, under the supervision of professors who would function as attorneys of record on their cases. It was the kind of legal work that was bound to appeal to an idealistic Quaker who had personally felt poverty's pinch. But it would put its founding professors on the cutting edge of something new and unconventional in legal education. Academic purists scorned it as "trade school stuff." Launching a law school clinic would be exhilarating, but it would be a step off the customary path to the judiciary.

Plans for a clinic at William Mitchell had first taken root when a group of William Mitchell students and a young charismatic professor, Roger Haydock, established a relationship with Legal Aid Society of

Minneapolis and Legal Assistance of Ramsey County in 1972. It allowed student volunteers to represent their indigent clients under the supervision of an attorney. The project greatly appealed to Haydock. A graduate of DePaul University Law School in his native Chicago, Haydock was a Roman Catholic with a calling to service and social justice strong enough for him at one point to consider becoming a priest. Instead, he came to St. Paul to work for Legal Assistance in 1969, having won a competitive national Reginald Heber Smith Fellowship for lawyers willing to spend a year working with the poor. Within a year Haydock was also a part-time instructor at Mitchell; in 1972, he was hired to teach full time, with the understanding that he could explore ways to continue providing legal services to the poor.[4]

The extracurricular program Haydock established quickly became popular with Mitchell students. Some were drawn to an opportunity to help the disadvantaged. Others recognized that the study of law and the practice of law are not one and the same. Many found that academic work alone was insufficient preparation for the tasks they would perform after passing the bar exam and taking their first jobs. Students thought the clinic valuable enough to belong in Mitchell's course catalog. They petitioned Heidenreich to make the clinic a for-credit experience. The dean agreed. "In class, we deal with solved problems," Heidenreich said years later. "The only way to learn what those problems are really like is to deal with someone who's actually living through that problem. That's what happened in the clinic. There's really no substitute for it."[5]

The more prestigious University of Minnesota Law School led the way the year before with a small clinic of its own. Heidenreich recruited that program's director, Robert Oliphant, to consult with Haydock and a student committee designing Mitchell's version. Oliphant and Heidenreich agreed that they wanted two clinical divisions, civil and criminal, each with its own professor. Haydock would head the civil practice. Heidenreich said thirty-eight years later that it was Haydock's idea to call Rosalie to lead the criminal program; Haydock credits Heidenreich for knowing "just who he wanted." Oliphant contributed to the decision. He knew firsthand how suited Rosalie was for Mitchell's venture. In 1972, while still employed three days a week in the state public defender's office, Rosalie also worked part time as an adjunct professor in Oliphant's program. It was a logistically easy gig, since the defender's office was housed at Fraser Hall, the University of Minnesota's law school building. Oliphant could attest that, though thirty years had passed since Rosalie's Birch Creek School days, she had not lost her knack for teaching.[6]

That first taste of working with law students evidently whetted Rosalie's appetite for more. She jumped at the chance to return to her alma mater and start something new. The fact that her daughter Sara had enrolled at William Mitchell in 1972 and could be one of her students undoubtedly sweetened the prospect. Rosalie's enthusiasm for the task was clear when she spoke about it decades later: "What days those were! Wow!" she said in 2009. "It was exciting, because it would be the first time a law student would appear in court."

It was also a chance to collaborate with other lively minds to create something that had not existed before. "Roger and Rosalie made up the program as we went along," said one of the 1973 students, Sandra Neren, who would become a prominent state capitol lobbyist. She was one of eight "student directors" who initiated the program with Haydock in the spring of 1973 and continued as its co-designers and implementers that fall. "We class members had a lot to say about what happened, too, and we appreciated that very much," Neren said. Unlike faculty at many other American law schools, William Mitchell professors were open to the new program and genuinely supportive. At Mitchell, clinical faculty members were not adjuncts, but full-fledged professors eligible for tenure. "Mitchell had always been kind of a school where people worked and went to school . . . so they were a little bit closer to practice," Rosalie observed.[7]

Rosalie was not completely without a template for the program she was creating. In the summer of 1973, William Mitchell sent her to a National Institute for Trial Advocacy training and to a national clinical legal education conference in Buck Hill Falls, Pennsylvania. It was Rosalie's first introduction to a nest of law school reformers intent on making a practicum experience an integral part of law school curricula, not a specialized or secondary subject. Among the emerging leaders she met at that conference was Rose Bird, who would go on to be the first female chief justice of the California Supreme Court. Rosalie came home with an address book full of professional connections and heightened awareness of the significance of her new venture.[8]

Rosalie's law school days were recent enough for her to remember well the emotions associated with beginning to practice law. She identified with her students and they bonded with her. "Rosalie was a great leader," remembered another student in the first cohort, St. Paul attorney and lobbyist Ross Kramer. "The students loved her. She was one of us, and worked with us in that fashion. She had a lot of trust in all of us and wasn't afraid to delegate to us. That trust was what we craved."[9]

By happy coincidence, a small house at 2093 Grand Avenue, across the alley from Mitchell's 2100 Summit Avenue headquarters, had been bequeathed to the college by John Webster, a neighbor and admirer of the institution. It came into the school's possession just as decisions were made about how to accommodate the twin "law firms" that Haydock and Wahl would head. This house became the clinic's headquarters. Heidenreich called it "a facsimile of a small law office." Rosalie's afternoons and many evenings were spent there, consulting with students about their cases. Two nights per week, she led seminar-style classes.[10]

Most mornings, including Saturdays, started at 8 AM at the Ramsey County Courthouse, for the arraignments of those arrested the previous night on misdemeanor charges. As permitted by the state supreme court and by arrangement with the Ramsey County Public Defender's Office, senior law students could represent indigent defendants accused of those lesser crimes under the supervision of an attorney who had been admitted to the bar. Felony cases were reserved for non-student public defenders. Rosalie would be on hand "in the pit" to assist her students as they met their new clients and learned enough about them to decide on a plea. Ramsey County used two arraignment courtrooms, so she enlisted the public defender on duty to help supervise students in one while she shifted to the other. "I always felt that I needed to be there, both to help them learn what to do but also to see what they needed to know, to see what they needed to learn in class and to see how they used or misused what it was that they were learning," Rosalie said years later in explanation of her long hours.[11]

"They would bring into the bullpen all these people who had been taken into custody overnight, and there would be Rosalie," remembered clinic student Tom Miller, a member of Mitchell's class of 1974. "She was this sweet middle-aged woman who looked like somebody's mother. And she'd be talking about cases involving prostitution, disorderly conduct, assault, many things related to public drunkenness. She knew how to work that courtroom and showed us how to handle a variety of different

In a classic demonstration of her willingness to get her hands dirty, Rosalie joined students in painting signage on the building that was to house the clinic. *Courtesy William Mitchell College of Law.*

characters. She taught us how to make the pleas and how to handle ourselves in the courtroom."

The students did more than appear at arraignments and enter pleas. They investigated cases, prepared trial memos, plea-bargained sentences, and participated in trials. A separate clinic was established to provide legal defense for indigent defendants appealing felony convictions, the sort of cases Rosalie had handled at the state public defender's office. Rosalie gave her students ample opportunity to make decisions. "She let us make mistakes without choking us," one former student said— provided those mistakes did not damage the client's case. "The welfare of the client has the highest priority," she wrote in a 1975 memo to public defenders in the Ramsey County Municipal Court system about how to lead a law school clinic. "The educational value of the experience to the student comes next, and in that regard you are serving as educators . . . Don't stand aloof and let the student make mistakes to the client's detriment on the one hand, or do the work for him or her on the other." Haydock would tell years later about a comment Rosalie made in conversation with him that became part of the Mitchell clinics' philosophy: "We don't have problems for clients. We have clients with problems." Haydock added: "To Rosalie, what we did as lawyers was not just to resolve problems, but to serve people. That's what she did. She taught us all how."[12]

Rosalie's first encounter with Harriet Lansing, a young lawyer who would figure prominently in her later story, came in connection with Rosalie's work with Mitchell students in Ramsey County's arraignment court. The year was about 1976, and Lansing was the newly appointed city attorney—the first woman in that post not only in St. Paul, but in any major city in the country. Rosalie was supervising a student whose client's eligibility for a public defender had been questioned by someone in Lansing's office, who had told the judge that the defendant was wearing expensive shoes. The shoes had been borrowed, unbeknownst to the judge and prosecutor, because the client wanted to look presentable in court. Rosalie navigated the situation in the courtroom so that the client's representation by her student was not interrupted. Afterward, she marched up the stairs to Lansing's office and reported to the new city attorney what had transpired. It had been an assault to the dignity of the client, in the very place in which respect for human dignity should be upheld, Rosalie said. Lansing, then thirty-one years old, was moved by the older woman's indignation. "For her, the courts were a sacred place and everyone entering them was to be treated with respect and dignity," Lansing would say years later. "She was willing to act on that principle in any way she could."[13]

Rosalie's respect for clients rubbed off on her students. They saw, and developed strong views about, the human consequences of insufficient court funding, and they developed genuine empathy for the people they represented. One student in the 1975 fall semester summarized a key lesson he had learned: "Confidence is something very difficult to build, and until that is achieved, the public defender should not really try to convince his client to 'take' the consequences of his act. Equally important as obtaining the best results for the client is leaving him with a feeling that he did get the best results, and not that he was given a fast shuffle into a deal." That student was Eric J. Magnuson, who would become chief justice of the Minnesota Supreme Court in 2008.[14]

Rosalie often related another student's version of respect for the clinic's clients: "He came in one day and was so outraged. His client was a prostitute. But when she was arrested, she was just walking to the store. He said, 'She didn't even have her white boots on!' He was pretty offended!" Laughter was part of the chemistry that made Rosalie a professor for whose classes students would stand in registration lines for hours in hopes of securing one of thirty spots. "She was the best teacher and mentor I've ever seen," said Miller four decades later as a Wayzata-based bankruptcy specialist. "She was classy, low-key, very, very smart, and extremely good at getting her point across."

One instance of Rosalie's plainspoken directness became legendary. Nadine Strossen was a Minnesota Supreme Court law clerk in 1976, fifteen years before she became the first female president of the American Civil Liberties Union. In 2003, she related the memorable day in 1976 when Rosalie's opening salvo in oral arguments before the state's all-male, gray-haired high court was, "What's so special about the penis? The penis does not kill. The penis does not maim. The penis is not a deadly weapon." Her point: state law erred by punishing male-female rape much more harshly than other sexual crimes. It certainly got the justices' attention. They "were almost hiding under their bench" before she finished, Strossen related. Strossen was directed to draft an opinion that avoided use of "that word." She told the court's other law clerks, all of them male, about her assignment, and they cheerfully spent the rest of the day compiling a list of eighty euphemisms she might use instead of the biological name for the male sexual organ.[15]

For the women in the clinic, Professor Wahl was one thing more—a role model. "She was my only female professor," said Neren. "She was the first female attorney role model any of us ever saw. Her just being there made a big difference." Professor Wahl showed no favoritism to the female students, Neren added. "She was never offensive about asserting her feminism. She was just competent and persistent, in a nice way. You trusted what she said."

Mitchell's class of 1973, like Rosalie's in 1967, included only two women. But Neren's class of 1974 had ten, and more were coming in subsequent classes. Female enrollment gains were being reported at law schools around the country as the baby boomer generation came of professional school age. As a Minnesota-born troubadour sang, the times were a-changin'.

Minnesota's 1974 election would be remembered not for the advancement of women, but rather for the triumph of the Democratic-Farmer-Labor

Party. Coming in the wake of the Watergate scandal in Washington and Republican president Richard Nixon's resignation, 1974 would be the left-of-center state party's twentieth-century high-water mark. Governor Wendell Anderson returned to office with a whopping 62.8 percent of the vote, carrying all eighty-seven counties. DFLers captured 104 of 134 state house seats.[16]

The ranks of women in the legislature grew in that election from six to seven, but their lineup had changed considerably from the previous session. Only three of the 1972 six returned: DFLers Linda Berglin and Phyllis Kahn and Republican Mary Forsythe. New to the house were four DFLers: Shirley Hokanson of Richfield, Peggy Byrne of St. Paul, Janet Clark of Minneapolis, and Claudia Meier Volk of Rice. DFLer Helen McMillan retired. Republican Ernee McArthur had been swamped in the DFL wave, replaced by an ambitious attorney and future congressman, Bill Luther. And Joan Growe gave the state's feminists their best reason to cheer. She defeated Republican Arlen Erdahl to become secretary of state.

Secretary of state Joan Anderson Growe at the podium of the Minnesota House of Representatives, about 1975. *Minnesota Historical Society.*

It was the first time a woman had been elected to any statewide office "in her own right"—that is, not by first being appointed to the office as the widow of the office's recently deceased occupant. Those were the circumstances in 1952 that landed the first woman in one of the state's "constitutional" offices. Virginia Retta Holm's Swedish-born husband Mikael Hansson Holm was Minnesota's longest-serving secretary of state, making the name "Mike Holm" synonymous with election administration for more than a generation of Minnesotans. Republican Holm had been in office since 1921 when he died at the age of seventy-six on July 6, 1952. Twice-widowed Holm married Virginia in 1946. For public and political purposes, she was "Mrs. Mike Holm" from that year forward. She was an active Republican and had reason to think that Governor C. Elmer Anderson would appoint her to her late husband's seat, but in the days after Holm's death, Anderson abruptly gave that nod to assistant secretary of state H. H. Chesterman. The spurned widow wasted little time responding. The filing period for the 1952 GOP primary was still open. She paid the filing fee and put the name "Mrs. Mike Holm" on that ballot, and rode a wave of sympathy to victory in the September 9 Republican primary.

Anderson, himself in a tough general election fight with the DFL state chairman, up-and-comer Orville Freeman, saw a chance to correct his perceived slight to the widow Holm. On September 15, he announced that he was un-appointing Chesterman and replacing him with the GOP primary winner, Mrs. Mike Holm. The outraged DFL candidate for the seat, Koscie Marsh, had no legal grounds for complaint about the governor's action. But by early October, Marsh decided on a different legal tack. On October 6, he went to the state supreme court to argue that the name on the November ballot should be Virginia, not "Mrs. Mike." The court ruled that Marsh's complaint was too late in coming and tossed it out on that basis, leaving unaddressed the question of whether a female candidate has an obligation to file for office in her own name instead of her husband's. Virginia Holm won the 1952 election, served one term, and lost her reelection bid to DFLer Joe Donovan in 1954, when Freeman finally won the governorship. Virginia Holm's name choice helped her become the first woman elected to statewide office, but it diminished her achievement in the eyes of Minnesota's next generation of female politicians.[17]

Growe's husband Glen was a factor of a different kind in her decision to seek statewide office. Their marriage was not happy. In early 1974, she was headed toward divorce. Although she enjoyed representing the Minnetonka area in the state house and thought she could win reelection, even though the district was considered politically perilous territory for a DFLer, she needed full-time employment at a better salary and decided to try for a public-sector job before exploring private-sector opportunities. Secretary of state offered the best opportunity, she concluded, and its focus on election administration fit nicely with her League of Women Voters work. After four years in Republican hands, the office looked ripe for return to the DFL. Arlen Erdahl had not won over the group that comprises any secretary of state's most important constituency, the eighty-seven county election administrators that actually make elections happen. Over Erdahl's relatively mild objections, the 1973 legislature had created a new opportunity for voters to register to vote at the polls on Election Day. "Same-day registration" was a major change that required timely outreach to county officials to establish and explain new rules and procedures. From her League of Women Voters network, Growe learned that county officials were not pleased with Erdahl's handling of that change. Thanks to them, she had her campaign theme, and was off and running.

In that first statewide campaign, Growe displayed an independent streak that served her well and would make her a model for female candidates a generation later. Advised that she should seek permission from DFL governor Wendell Anderson before announcing her candidacy, Growe paid the governor a visit—but only to inform him that she was running. She would not play the supplicant role. Word that male party regulars preferred St. Cloud mayor Al Loehr for secretary of state only made Growe work harder. She also chose to keep some distance between herself and the new DFL Feminist Caucus. The caucus asked candidates to respond to a lengthy questionnaire and to promise to ally themselves only with other candidates who favored the U.S. Supreme Court's *Roe v. Wade* decision. Growe was pro-choice but refused to be so confined. "I was working with DFL legislators who were not pro-choice but were right on every other issue. I wasn't going to shun them," she recalled years later. She would take orders from neither the party's men nor its feminist leaders.

The rift between the DFL Feminist Caucus and the party's first female statewide officeholder would be patched over time. But in 1974, the
caucus's failure to support Growe was cited by those who argued that
the new caucus was "too extreme" to be trusted with legitimacy and
power. Its Republican counterpart had a different problem. GOP Women
for Political Effectiveness, formed in the summer of 1973, seethed with
considerable frustration over the small effect it had in the winner-take-
all Republican Party structure. That year's state party platform called
on the legislature to rescind its ratification of the Equal Rights Amendment. What's more, Republican feminists watched with concern as the
DFL outstripped them in putting female names on the ballot. "Unlike
some of my friends . . . I stayed with the Republican Party—it was where
I had some political strength," Kathleen Ridder, a state and local Republican and civic activist, would later write about that period. "At every
opportune moment, I pressured the party to recognize the importance
of women's issues because it needed the women's vote to win elections."[18]

Some Republican feminists preferred to channel their political energy
into the bipartisan Minnesota Women's Political Caucus, which predated
the GOP group by two years. It was growing rapidly under the leadership of a vigorous and visionary chair, Marlene Johnson. Twenty-seven
years old in 1973 and the owner of an all-female public relations firm, Split
Infinitive, Johnson was schooled in DFL politics as the eldest daughter
of an early activist in the rural electric cooperative movement in Minnesota, Beauford Johnson, and as the friend and business associate who
helped Linda Berglin win a south Minneapolis legislative seat in 1972.
(Feminism was a signature element of Split Infinitive's identity in a lit-
eral sense: Berglin was the graphic designer who created its commercial
logo.) Johnson agreed to become caucus chair at a time when partisan
DFL feminists were questioning the need for a bipartisan organization to
promote women in politics. Johnson disagreed with them. Given the GOP
Party's drift to the right and the fascination of some in that party with the
anti-ERA movement, "it felt safer for them to be in a bipartisan organization then," Johnson said. Other Republican feminists joined Emily Anne
Staples in switching parties. Seven Republican women sought Minnesota
house seats in 1974, but only Edina's Mary Forsythe was elected. Staples
was on the ballot that year as a new DFLer, losing to representative Lon
Heinitz but netting a respectable 48 percent of the vote.[19]

Despite feminists' struggles within the GOP, the next Minnesota women's "first" was scored by a Republican. The state senate had been an all-male preserve since statehood, with just one exception. On February 7, 1927, Laura Emelia Johnson Naplin won a special election to complete the term of her husband Oscar, who suffered a stroke on the day he was sworn in for the 1927 session and died eleven days later. Though Naplin won a second and final term in 1930, her "widow woman" status diminished that achievement in the eyes of latter-day feminists.[20]

Nancy Brataas won her Rochester senate seat with no such familial tie, although she too came by way of a special election. Rochester's seat fell vacant when its previous occupant, Harold Krieger, was elected a district judge in 1974. A special election was set for February 1, 1975—a rare Saturday election. The GOP leaders who recruited Brataas likely figured that if anyone could turn out the vote for that oddly timed election, she could. Crafting winning campaigns by improving turnout had been Brataas's avocation as GOP state chairwoman in the 1960s, then her professional specialty. She was the founder, owner, and genius behind Nancy Brataas Associates, Inc., a political consulting firm so highly esteemed in Republican circles that it was hired to handle voter identification and turnout efforts in ten large industrial states for President Richard Nixon's 1972 reelection campaign.[21]

Senator Nancy Brataas, about 1981. *Minnesota Historical Society.*

It wasn't the career one might have expected of an art history major at the University of Minnesota or the wife of a Mayo Clinic administrator and Chamber of Commerce president. But Brataas was competitive, politically strategic, and seemingly fearless. She and politics seemed made for each other. Applying her direct-mail savvy to her own race, she rolled over two male opponents in the January 19 primary—demonstrating a phenomenon political parties were slow to realize: when a woman runs against two men, the woman often has an advantage. In that February 1 special election, Brataas garnered an impressive 58 percent of the vote, even though her DFL opponent was himself a former state representative. The fact that Brataas was an outspoken defender of the 1973 *Roe v. Wade* abortion decision was no impediment to her acceptance by the GOP—not yet, anyway.[22]

The 1976 election brought two developments that may have seemed of relatively minor consequence to Minnesota feminists at the time, but in retrospect loom large in their quest for their rightful share of state power—and in Rosalie's story. The first was the decision of Second Congressional District DFLers to choose an untested but unusually gifted woman as the party's customary sacrificial lamb for the U.S. House. The conservative Second District, then reaching from Lake Minnetonka south through Mankato to the Iowa border, was firmly in Republican U.S. representative Tom Hagedorn's hands, even in a year in which Democratic presidential candidate Jimmy Carter was favored to carry Minnesota. In tony Tonka Bay lived Gloria Griffin, a fifty-year-old former New York City art director for *Good Housekeeping* and *Harper's* magazines and a committed feminist. Her husband Jack's job transfer landed Griffin and their four children in Minnesota in 1967. After the move, she attempted to keep her career alive as a freelancer and plunged into volunteer activity with the League of Women Voters, the DFL Party, and the nascent Minnesota Women's Political Caucus. Griffin played a minor role in the team that launched Growe's political career in 1972. She came into Koryne Horbal's orbit at about the same time and soon was a regular volunteer with the new DFL Feminist Caucus. ("Koryne could express what most of us really couldn't put into words that early. Every woman who is active owes a lot to Koryne," Griffin said many years later.) Mature and professional, Griffin's style was cooler than Horbal's, but her commitment to improving the lot of women ran as deep.[23]

In 1976, Griffin opted to try for the DFL nod for Congress. She had become annoyed with the Second District's clubby DFL men—some of them state party kingpins—who had "passed the nomination around" for years. She tapped Marlene Johnson, the leader of the Minnesota Women's Political Caucus, to manage a campaign aimed more at cracking the DFL Party's glass ceiling than at winning the November election. "We have run middle-aged men in this district for 36 years and they have never won," Griffin argued publicly. It was time to try a woman. Her opponent for DFL endorsement was John Considine, head of the Mankato Area Catholic Board of Education. He declined to say—publicly anyway—that he and Griffin differed on issues, though the abortion question was clearly a subtext in their contest. Instead, he told *Minneapolis Star* political journalist Betty Wilson, "I don't think the district is quite ready for a woman candidate." He could not have chosen more motivating words. Feminist indignation propelled Griffin to an easy first-ballot endorsement with 73 percent of the vote. Considine considered continuing his campaign in the DFL primary but abandoned the idea a few weeks later, giving Griffin and her female-dominated campaign team a clear shot at Hagedorn in the fall.[24]

Those DFL women soon learned that the aggressive door-to-door campaigning they had used to propel Growe to the legislature four years earlier was not suited to a large and mostly rural congressional district. While Griffin made a strong impression on those who met her, she was not well known and lacked the resources required to build name recognition. "She couldn't win down there if she were the Virgin Mary herself," gubernatorial chief of staff Tom Kelm, a resident of the district, was quoted as saying. On Election Day, Griffin performed no better than most of her middle-aged male predecessors had. She wound up with just shy of 40 percent of the vote. But the drubbing didn't send her into retreat. Instead, it sent her to the governor's office. When a man runs for Congress and loses, a governor of the same party typically helps find jobs for that candidate's newly unemployed campaign staffers, she said. Griffin went to make the case that her mostly female staff deserved the same consideration.[25]

The office she visited was in the throes of a dramatic transition, which hindsight reveals as the second notable feminist development of 1976. The election of Minnesota's Walter Mondale as vice president left vacant a U.S. Senate seat that the state's governor was empowered to fill. Heretofore politically surefooted governor Wendell Anderson, forty-three years old and a rising star in national politics, opted to take a fateful risk. On November 10, one week and one day after the election, Anderson announced that he would resign in late December to become a U.S. senator. Lieutenant Governor Rudy Perpich of Hibbing, "bright, honest, and dedicated to the people of this state," in Anderson's words, would succeed him in office. While Anderson's statement to reporters did not say so explicitly, it was plainly predicated on an understanding between the two men that Anderson would resign, making Perpich governor and allowing him immediately to appoint Anderson to complete the remaining two years of Mondale's Senate term. The move was popular with Anderson's most devoted fans, but it was described from the start as a "self-appointment," and widely decried as a brazen display of raw ambition. When the idea was first floated a month before the election, the *Minneapolis Tribune*'s Minnesota Poll found 55 percent of respondents opposed to Anderson making himself a senator.[26]

Minnesota's politically active feminists watched the maneuvers of the men in the governor's office with detachment and not a little disdain. In Anderson, they were losing a governor who was not hostile to the women's movement but had never evinced much interest in it either. In Perpich, they were getting someone they did not know well, but of whom they were wary. The son and grandson of Croatian immigrant mineworkers and labor organizers, Perpich was the state's first governor from the Iron Range and the first with eastern European roots, ending eighty years of Scandinavian hold on the office. Tall, handsome, and full of energy, Perpich spoke in clipped sentences, with an accent that revealed that English was not his first language, and at a pace that often suggested that his thoughts were outrunning his tongue. He had a herculean appetite for work and little respect for convention. He had been a dentist, a school board member, and a state senator before becoming lieutenant governor in 1970. He was known as a friend of working people and the environment, and was given to voicing contempt for the mining companies that had been the villains of his childhood. It was not widely known that, as a new Hibbing school board member in 1956, he rocked the local boat by urging equal pay for female teachers and allowing married women to teach full time, an opportunity then limited to single women and widows. Perpich was forty-eight years old in 1976, married, and the father of two gifted teenagers. He would be Minnesota's first Roman Catholic governor, an affiliation that worried feminists. When pressed—but only then—he would say that he opposed legalized abortion.[27]

As they watched Perpich take the oath of office in the capitol rotunda on December 29, 1976, little did Griffin and other feminists realize that a champion for the advancement of women had arrived. But they must have been intrigued by his choice of a judge to administer the oath of office. He tapped St. Louis County judge Gail Murray, the first woman judge in northeastern Minnesota and a friend from Hibbing, to play the ceremonial role often reserved for the chief justice of the state supreme court. Journalists wrote profiles detailing the new governor's populist sympathies and identification with working men. What the state would learn was that, more than most of his male contemporaries, he also identified with working women. Joan Growe would later say of Perpich, "He got it."[28]

Perpich's thinking about women's rights was much influenced by his deep bond with two women—his mother, Mary Vukelich Perpich, and his wife, Delores "Lola" Simic Perpich. In his mother, he saw someone of considerable intelligence and ability who was denied an education and confined to a life of hard physical labor by the expectations and financial limitations of her time and place. Mary Vukelich was the third child and the eldest surviving daughter of Croatian immigrants Jura (George) and Ana Vukelich. She was born in 1911, the year after the young married couple reunited in Minnesota after a long separation. Jura had spent several years before 1910 seeking a new life as a miner in far-flung South America, Central America, and Arizona, after the economy in his home country collapsed. His sojourn had intensified his desire to work through the budding labor movement for a better life for working people. As he settled into the Iron Range and his family grew to four children, his responsibilities at the mine increased, and his assignment kept him in relative safety above ground. But his desire for higher wages and better working conditions didn't lessen. The Vukelich home became a de facto union hall, the site of impromptu meetings and the place where young, single, pro-union miners could find a home-cooked meal or temporary lodging. In about 1925, Jura organized what amounted to a wildcat strike. It didn't last long. The mining company pressed men with young families to abandon the strike and come back to work. Consequently, Jura was reassigned to more dangerous underground work. In 1926, he was injured on the job and developed an infection; he died in January 1927.[29]

Mary was a bright, sensitive girl who was fluent in both English and Croatian, loved literature, and quoted poetry with ease. She was close to her father, who often told her of his dream to see her become a teacher. Jura's dream died with his death. With no workers' compensation or Social Security benefits yet available, the Vukelich family was in dire straits, not unlike those Effie Patterson and her granddaughter Rosalie Erwin experienced in rural Kansas in 1932. With great reluctance, Mary went to work at age fifteen for a dollar a week cleaning the houses of well-to-do people in Hibbing. For her part, Ana took in boarders, including twenty-seven-year-old Anton "Tony" Perpich, another immigrant who had known Jura before coming to Minnesota and supported Jura's efforts at labor organizing. Though nearly twelve years separated them in age, Mary and Anton fell in love and married on August 14, 1927. Their first son, Rudolph George, named after Tony's brother and Mary's father, was born on June 27, 1928. They lived in a tiny three-room, second-story apartment for several years before moving into a company-owned, not-much-larger house in the mining village of Carson Lake. The humble house lacked both an indoor toilet and hot water. Mary was alone with her children through long days as Tony worked ten-hour shifts in the mines and walked many miles to and from work. The Perpiches did not own a car until Rudy was a late teen.

The young family experienced an early tragedy that deepened the emotional bond between mother and eldest son. A year after Rudy was born, daughter Marion arrived. Called Bunnie and adored by her young mother, the toddler was severely burned by scalding water at the age of fourteen months. She was taken to the hospital, developed pneumonia there, and died. Devastated, Mary clung all the more tightly to her son, who, even as a three-year-old, understood that he was her surest source of solace. He was also keen to share her workload. Mary's chores increased as three more sons arrived in the Perpich family—Anton John (Tony) in 1932, George Frank in 1933, and Joseph George in 1941. Rudy's ability to shoulder responsibility increased proportionately. At a tender age, he was taught to milk the family cow and water, weed, and harvest the large garden that the family was allowed to cultivate on land owned by the Great Northern Railroad near Grandma Vukelich's house. While still small, he could capably chop wood for the tiny house's cooking and heating stoves. His aunt Ann Vukelich Brown, five years younger than Mary, remembered how cheerfully Rudy did chores like washing dishes or laundry alongside his mother. "Most kids, when you tell them to do this or do that, they're not too happy about it. Rudy seemed to enjoy doing it," Brown said.

As he grew, so did Rudy's awareness that his mother's girlhood dreams had not come true, even as he heard her impress the importance of education on him and his brothers. He also became aware that Mary was not the only mother in his community who had been denied opportunity. Some were deprived the simple justice of safety in their homes. Rudy took a job in a Hibbing grocery store at about age fourteen. His duties included delivering groceries to households occupied by ill-clad, housebound mothers and broods of children. Years later, he would relate to his own children the scenes he would encounter of distraught, bruised women crying at their kitchen tables. Anton Perpich was strict with his boys. He did not hesitate to inflict corporal punishment when he deemed it warranted, but, to his son's knowledge, he never lifted a hand against Mary. She was not only the mother of his children but the teacher who taught him English and prepared him for the citizenship exam he passed in 1931. By example, he taught his sons to treat a wife and, by extension, all women with respect.[30]

The prime beneficiary of that lesson in Rudy's life was a seventeen-year-old malt shop waitress from nearby Keewatin whom Rudy met in the summer of 1948. Delores "Lola" Simic (pronounced *Simich*) was two and a half years Rudy's junior, a tall, strikingly beautiful brunette of Croatian descent whose father John worked as an oiler for the Great Northern Railroad. Their marriage on September 4, 1954, inaugurated a life of deep companionship. They had the kind of marriage that friends envied and mere acquaintances noticed as something special. "It was one of the most genuine love matches I have ever seen," Gloria Griffin said.[31]

Lola was at his side as Rudy set up shop as a Hibbing dentist, ran for school board and the legislature, moved to St. Paul during legislative sessions, then ran for lieutenant governor. She was his driver, door knocker, fundraiser, volunteer recruiter, surrogate, and most trusted sounding board. Lola did not like to give speeches, and Rudy did not press her into that service. She was reluctant to give interviews to all but a few journalists whom she knew and trusted. But in every other respect, "Mom was his partner politically," their son Rudy Jr. attests. "They discussed everything." When son Rudy Jr. (born in 1959) and daughter Mary Sue (1960) arrived, they were either left in the care of grandmas Mary Perpich or Anna Simic or included in the action as their parents campaigned. The whole family moved to the Twin Cities during the winter and spring of odd-numbered years beginning in 1963, Rudy's first year in the Minnesota senate. (The legislature met biennially prior to 1973.) Only briefly, when the children were students at Hibbing High School and Rudy was governor, did the family live apart during the work week.

When Griffin called on soon-to-be Governor Perpich in December 1976, jobs for her top five congressional campaign staff members were on her mind. Perpich dashed cold water on her appeal. "I don't do 'plums,'" he told her. He had a different idea. He asked her to head a search effort for a new head of the state's relatively new environmental watchdog organization, the Pollution Control Agency. Griffin allowed that she had no particular expertise in environmental protection. He countered that she was acquainted with the DFL's most talented women, and it was his intention to put a woman in that role. He and Lola had watched Griffin in action in the 1976 campaign, he told her, and they had decided that she possessed sound judgment. If Griffin was surprised to learn that she had made such a positive impression so quickly, she would soon learn that making quick, sound judgments about people was Perpich's knack. She took the assignment. It resulted in a promotion for a thirty-year-old Pollution Control Agency staff attorney, Sandra Gardebring, launching a career that in time would bring Gardebring into Rosalie Wahl's orbit. It marked the beginning of a fruitful Perpich-Griffin collaboration.

Two weeks into his governorship, Perpich was the featured guest at a DFL Feminist Caucus meeting on January 15, 1977. The meeting had the dual purpose of wooing the new governor and intimidating him with a show of considerable size and political strength. Perpich wasn't easily intimidated, and he never went into such a setting unprepared. He had a winning strategy of his own. He announced that evening that he had appointed Griffin head of something new, an Open Appointments Commission. It would be an eight-member screening panel for gubernatorial appointments, with one member from each congressional district. They were charged with replacing political patronage with a merit-based selection system for the scores of executive branch appointments a governor is obliged by law to make. Their marching orders also included Perpich's directive to find a woman or a person of color whenever possible. "I hope that by the end of my term—and hopefully long before that—the numbers of women and minorities in state government will increase dramatically, and I'll work very hard to see that that happens," he told the Feminist Caucus that night. "We aren't doing this because it's the political thing to do but because it's the right thing to do."[32]

Although that remark was met with cheers, it wasn't the comment that made headlines in the next day's St. Paul and Minneapolis newspapers. The headline-grabber came moments later, when Koryne Horbal asked whether the new governor was willing to promise that he would appoint a woman to fill the next vacancy on the state supreme court. It was a question that already had been put to him in private conversations with DFL feminist leaders, who bluntly told him that such a move was crucial to winning their support in the 1978 election. But some in the audience thought Horbal's question was an overreach. Their jaws dropped and applause ensued when Perpich smoothly answered, "Yes."

Perpich was utterly sincere in making that vow. He had already told several people in his inner circle that he meant to put a woman on the supreme court as soon as the opportunity presented itself. But it was a promise so unexpected, unvarnished, and uncharacteristic of most male politicians that many DFL feminists who heard it that night refused to believe it. Perpich had a reputation for being impulsive and mercurial. His listeners tucked his promise into their portfolios, expecting that they would need to pull it out one day to remind him—and, if necessary, other Minnesotans—of the vow.[33]

Their portfolios also included a list of women lawyers deemed ripe for judicial appointment. Developing that list had been an early project of Minnesota Women Lawyers, which Rosalie helped found in 1972. The group periodically sent a questionnaire to all of its members inquiring about their interests, ambitions, and willingness to serve in a number of voluntary and appointive capacities, the bench included. When Rosalie's questionnaire arrived not long after she began teaching at William Mitchell, it renewed the question that she had mulled as an appellate public defender: "Would I be willing to be a judge?" With the question put to her in black and white, Rosalie did not take it lightly. She didn't have an immediately clear answer. She was not like any of the judges she knew, she told herself. But she had not shied away from being a pioneer before. The questionnaire sat on her always-overflowing desk for months before she felt ready to reply. She checked "yes" to putting her name on the list for judicial appointment. "I just thought, well, you know, there comes a point when if you are urging the appointment of women, you just have to put up or shut up," she would say years later.[34]

That list, sent to the new governor soon after he took office, and the record of Perpich's promise were at the ready in mid-May when opportunity arrived. Word came from the White House of President Jimmy Carter's intention to appoint Minnesota Supreme Court associate justice Harry MacLaughlin to the federal bench to succeed retiring district judge Earl Larson. The state's legal community had been expecting that appointment. MacLaughlin was a well-respected, well-connected jurist. He had been a law school chum, law firm partner, and U.S. Senate campaign chairman of Vice President Walter Mondale, who remained his friend and fishing buddy. With the U.S. Senate in Democratic hands, MacLaughlin's eventual confirmation was not in question. The president's announcement in May was sufficient for the governor's office to swing into full-tilt judicial appointment mode.[35]

Minnesota feminists and their allies in the press did the same. *Minneapolis Star* courts reporter Gwenyth Jones wrote a column reminding the governor of his promise to appoint a woman to the high court. Her editors published it on the newspaper's front page. Feminists peppered the governor's office with phone calls and letters, asking that he keep his promise. "The feeling was that[,] unless the high court included a woman, women lawyers would always be struggling at the bottom rung of the profession," recalled Rahn Westby, who in 1977 was a twenty-five-year-old St. Paul attorney, co-chair of the Ramsey County Women's Political Caucus, and a recent graduate of William Mitchell Law School, where her criminal law clinic professor was Rosalie Wahl.[36]

It was a time when the state and nation were keenly aware of both the drive for women's legal equality and the backlash it had generated. After Florida's state senate rejected the ERA by just two votes in April, national pundits declared that the drive to amend the U.S. Constitution had failed, though it had two more years to run before its deadline. The ERA had won approval in thirty-five states, three fewer than necessary for an amendment's ratification. In the two states where it was put to a popular vote, New York and New Jersey, it failed, largely because female voters bought opponents' arguments that married women would lose economic security if it passed.[37]

Meanwhile, in Minnesota and other states, plans were being made for mass meetings of women interested in learning more about the women's movement and participating in developing a policy agenda to be forwarded to a National Women's Conference in Houston, Texas, that November. Congress had supplied funding for the state and national meetings in the wake of the International Women's Year conference held in Mexico City in 1975. The state-level meetings provided a chance to put the flowering of the women's movement on display around the country. Planners envisioned them as organizational stepping stones to the enactment of state and national policies that would assure women a greater measure of economic justice and control over their lives. Minnesota's meeting was set for the campus of St. Cloud State University on June 2–5. Any Minnesota woman was welcome to attend. The conference planners expected that attendees would have a feminist bent and drafted a set of thirty-two resolutions to set before attendees that, if affirmed, would be sent to the national meeting. Those resolutions had a strong equal-rights component and included support for keeping abortion legal. But the state's ERA opponents and anti-abortion activists were also planning to make their presence felt. Conflict makes news. News organizations latched onto the narrative that Minnesota women were gearing up to battle over abortion in St. Cloud.[38]

Griffin was closely following the run-up to the Minnesota Women's Meeting, and she made certain that her boss was, too. She wanted the meeting to signify much more than an abortion fight. She knew that Perpich loved surprise and had a flair for drama. It isn't known whether he originated the idea of announcing the appointment of the state's first female supreme court associate justice at the St. Cloud meeting, but it was the kind of brainstorm he often had, and thoroughly enjoyed

The Minnesota Women's meeting at St. Cloud State University's field house, June 1977. *Minnesota Agriculture*, June 9, 1977.

executing. He would not be in St. Cloud on Friday, June 3, personally to make the announcement; that was Hibbing High School's graduation day. He was the scheduled commencement speaker at his alma mater, and Rudy Perpich Jr. would be among the graduates. But what if he could make history in both places? A plan took shape. He would announce his court appointment in Hibbing that Friday evening and tap his friend secretary of state Joan Growe, the Women's Meeting plenary session chair, to share the news moments afterward with the several thousand women expected to be on hand in St. Cloud. He gave his ad hoc team of judicial advisers a tight timeframe. He wanted a DFL female attorney chosen for the high court by June 3. He said as much to anyone who asked, including the capitol press corps.

What ensued was likely the most transparent gubernatorial judicial selection process in state history. An initial team of three Perpich advisers reviewed the Minnesota Women Lawyers' list and other recommendations. Eighteen names were considered. The team included University of Minnesota labor historian Hyman Berman; William "Bill" Kennedy, head of Hennepin County District Court's Public Defender's Office; and Ramsey County district judge Joe Summers, known for his wit and warmth. Rosalie credited Summers for changing her impression of judges for the better and quickening her own judicial ambition. "He would greet the defendants when they came in and would talk to them as if they were people," Wahl said. All three screeners were trusted personal friends of the governor. Plainly, none of them was female. Griffin, head of the governor's Open Appointments Commission and a well-connected political feminist, would seem an obvious choice for inclusion. Her commission was on its way to a groundbreaking first year, in which fully half of Perpich's appointees would be either women or minorities. The fact that Perpich did not tap Griffin for this particular kitchen cabinet and turned instead to longtime male friends suggests that some distance existed between the governor and his appointments chief. That gap would become more evident in ensuing months.[39]

When the initial screeners gave a list of names to the governor, they might as well have given it directly to the press. Perpich was his own worst "leak." On May 25, in almost beauty contest fashion, the *Minneapolis Star* published the photos of six semifinalists for the high court nod. They were Hennepin County district judge Suzanne Sedgwick; state revisor of statutes Esther Tomljanovich; Delores Orey, a St. Paul attorney and adjunct professor at Mitchell; Roberta Levy, an associate professor at the University of Minnesota Law School; Diana Murphy, a judge at Hennepin County municipal court; and Rosalie Wahl. Knowledgeable readers likely had little trouble guessing which of the six were leading contenders. Sedgwick was highly regarded, but had been a Republican before her election to the bench in 1970. Perpich had seen former Republican governor Elmer L. Andersen vilified by his own party for appointing a known DFLer to the supreme court. Perpich, who admired Andersen, was not likely to make the mistake of giving a plum appointment to someone from the opposite political side. Tomljanovich, also much respected, was linked too personally to the Perpiches for political comfort. Her mother-in-law and Anton Perpich came from the same small town in Croatia and had been lifelong friends. Murphy was brilliant, and would go on to be a federal appellate judge, but in 1977 she was only three years out of University of Minnesota Law School and was considered too junior for the state's high court. The three finalists summoned to interviews with Perpich and his advisory team, according to Berman, were Orey, Levy, and Wahl.[40]

None of those three were sitting judges or prosecutors, from whose ranks high court appointments had traditionally come. That was the way

Perpich wanted it, Berman said. Perpich's desire to break the judicial mold involved more than gender. He also valued "humaneness" and empathy for the disadvantaged. He intentionally did not seek the advice of the Minnesota Bar Association, whose leaders were accustomed to consultation with governors on high court appointments. "He didn't want some cigar-smoking, fat-cat corporate lawyer telling him who to appoint," Berman said. Instead, in addition to his initial screening team, he sought the counsel of Arvonne Fraser, who in 1977 was working at the U.S. State Department on women's economic development and who could attest to which candidates were participants in the feminist movement. Of the three finalists, Wahl was the most involved in feminist activities.[41]

When Summers bowed out of the screening panel, aware that, as a district judge, his involvement might be perceived as currying favor with a future appellate judge, he was replaced by state senate majority leader Nicholas Coleman, another close Perpich friend. Coleman's involvement raised the stakes for a member of Perpich's senior staff, Ronnie Brooks, who was a former researcher for Coleman's senate caucus and a friend of the gregarious senate leader. Brooks was among the feminists who had concluded that Rosalie ought to be Perpich's choice. She worked from within the office to position Rosalie first among the finalists for interviews with the screening panel and the governor, believing that that would give her an advantage.[42]

Other Wahl admirers were also going to bat for her. When Rahn Westby saw the list of finalists, the young Women's Political Caucus activist quickly concluded that Wahl was "the only plausible appointment." A successful candidate not only had to win over Rudy Perpich in 1977 but win statewide election in 1978. Minnesota Supreme Court justices typically arrive in office by midterm gubernatorial appointment and then stand for election at six-year intervals. The MacLaughlin seat would be up for election again in 1978. Of the finalists, Wahl possessed the compelling life story, passion for human rights, advocacy for the downtrodden, maturity, and demeanor that would sell most readily both to Perpich and the voters, Westby concluded. In Wahl's favor was that she was divorced and her children were nearly all grown. (Only Jenny, age thirteen, remained at home in 1977.) No one could accuse Wahl of neglecting her husband and small children, or of being too much swayed by an influential spouse—a problem for Roberta Levy, whose husband

Robert was a well-known University of Minnesota law professor. As a recent Mitchell graduate, Westby also knew that she could obtain the names and addresses of other students who had taken Wahl's clinical class since its establishment in 1973. She had an ally in the clinic's secretary, Alberta Dowlin, who kept meticulous records and was fond of Professor Wahl.

The young lawyer decided to make an extraordinary investment in Wahl's candidacy. She took a brief unpaid leave from her job at a legal defense firm in St. Paul. Then, in systematic fashion, Westby set out to telephone each attorney on the student list and ask that a personal letter urging Rosalie's appointment be sent to the governor's office. Knowing Perpich's Iron Range roots, Westby made an extra effort to solicit letters from newly minted Mitchell graduates living outside the Twin Cities. A hard sell was not necessary, Westby said. "Many of her students were really fond of her." Westby also got out the word via the Women's Political Caucus network. As a result, hundreds of women sent postcards to the governor's office touting Professor Wahl.

Rosalie was unaware of the extent of the effort on her behalf until June 2, when her lunch was interrupted with a call requesting that she come to the capitol as soon as possible to meet with Perpich and his

Rosalie in her office, 1977. *Courtesy Minneapolis Star Tribune.*

screeners. She was surprised when she was shown a thick file of mail urging her appointment—and judging from the screeners' comments, they were surprised and impressed too. After a brief session with them, she was ushered into the governor's office to meet Rudy Perpich. It was their first encounter. She was surprised by his height (six foot four) and impressed by his warmth. He asked her about two issues in particular. What were her views on the death penalty? Like Perpich, she opposed it. And what about abortion? Rosalie said she supported the *Roe v. Wade* decision of the U.S. Supreme Court. Perpich was nominally anti-abortion, but "he understood how women felt. He was for the downtrodden," Rosalie would say later. He made clear to her that her abortion views were not an impediment to her appointment. Perpich often said that he applied a personal test to every major appointment he made. As he chatted with a candidate, he would ask himself, "Would I feel comfortable walking to the other side of the table and hugging this person?" At age fifty-two, with hair streaked gray and a ready smile, Rosalie could have been a model for a Norman Rockwell illustration depicting American motherhood. She evidently struck Perpich as quite huggable.

When the interviews ended, Perpich asked for written votes from four screeners—Coleman, Kennedy, Berman, and Montgomery—and prepared a ballot himself. The tally was 4–1 in favor of Wahl, with Montgomery casting the only dissenting vote for Roberta Levy. (She would go on to be the first female chief judge of Hennepin County District Court.) Perpich was sold on Wahl, and the vote sealed his decision. He later gave the written ballots to Rosalie as a keepsake.[43]

A few hours later, the irrepressible Perpich telephoned Westby. She was having dinner in a St. Paul bar and restaurant, McCafferty's, with feminist friends including Carol Connolly, a St. Paul antiwar and DFL activist married to attorney John S. Connolly, who was part of Nicholas Coleman's political orbit and well acquainted with Perpich. Connolly would soon become co-chair of the Minnesota Women's Political Caucus. At the restaurant, a message arrived for Westby that she should call the governor's office right away. Excitedly, she and Connolly went to a pay phone in the hallway to place the call. To their disappointment, Perpich wasn't ready to reveal his choice, but he had a question that tipped his hand: if he chose Westby's favorite, Wahl, would she and other Women's Political Caucus activists aid Wahl's election campaign the following year? Like Westby, Perpich was thinking ahead to 1978. He knew that if his appointee did not survive the election, it would be a long time before he or any other governor would feel comfortable putting a woman on the high court. He also knew that he himself would be on the 1978 ballot, and that winning election in his own right would be a challenge. He would have little or no time to lend his appointee a campaign hand. Connolly took the phone and promised Perpich that she would manage Wahl's campaign. Although Connolly had been an active DFLer, she was also the mother of seven children. She had never managed a statewide campaign before. She was making a major commitment. Nevertheless, she was good as her word, and her word satisfied Perpich.[44]

Perpich was also good as his word, but the leaders of the DFL Feminist Caucus did not trust him. They believed that, before making a decision, he was susceptible to being persuaded by the last person with whom he spoke. With that in mind, Koryne Horbal, Jeri Rasmussen, and Cynthia Kitlinski paid him a visit at the governor's residence that same evening. "We came to give him a pep talk," Horbal said—one that evidently was not brief. The session ended with Perpich advising the women that he needed to go to bed, and with them hearing once more his promise to appoint a woman to the high court. The evidence is strong that Perpich didn't need their persuasion. But the visit nevertheless underscored how much feminist passion was attached to this appointment. Perpich knew that he would be making history. The DFL feminists made clear to him that thousands of Minnesota women knew it too.[45]

After their phone conversation with Perpich, Connolly and Westby called Rosalie. They told her that she was the leading candidate and advised her to plan an acceptance speech. But Rosalie's phone remained frustratingly silent all day June 3, until she and daughter Sara could stay home no longer. They had to leave for St. Cloud if they were to be on hand for Friday night's plenary session of the Minnesota Women's Meeting. They gave the governor's office their hotel's name and phone number and made the drive. (Daughter Jenny, still in school that day, arrived in St. Cloud separately, driven by Sara's law school friend Lisbeth Nudell.) Rosalie and Sara had just arrived in their hotel room when the phone rang. It was Ray Bohn of Perpich's staff, checking to make sure she was there and asking her to stand by for a second call. Perpich was on his way to Hibbing, but (twenty years too early for cell phones) he had access to a telephonic radio in the state trooper–driven car that governors use. Neither Rosalie nor Bohn remembered thirty-five years later whether Perpich himself made the second call, or if Bohn did on his behalf—though Bohn said, "I've got to believe that he called her. He understood better than anyone what a big deal this was."[46]

Anyone, perhaps, except Rosalie. She quickly finished preparing her acceptance speech, shared the news with Sara, Jenny, and Liz—and no one else, as the governor's office requested—then made her way to the St. Cloud State University arena, at which an estimated four thousand people waited. News reports that day advised the participants to expect word of a judicial appointment. Rosalie and her party were escorted to an anteroom, where Joan Growe met them. She, too, had received a call from the governor informing her of Wahl's appointment, and of his decision to name Esther Tomljanovich, the legislature's chief revisor of statutes, to a district court vacancy, making her only the state's second woman on a district court bench. Growe was prepared to announce the news to the assembly as soon as she had word that Perpich, speaking at his son's commencement in Hibbing, had uttered the words himself. Rosalie's tingly wait didn't last long. She and her daughters were ushered to the stage in time to hear Growe announce that Minnesota's next supreme court associate justice would be Rosalie Wahl.[47]

No one present that night is likely to forget the jubilation of that moment. The auditorium erupted in pure joy. Laughter, tears, hugs, cheers, and applause rocked the room. An uninitiated observer might have believed that everyone present had a personal tie to Rosalie or was personally affected by her elevation to the bench. In fact, relatively few had even heard of Rosalie Wahl before Perpich's screening process began. But everyone present knew that society would not be fair to women unless the judicial branch of government was. The Wahl appointment was a breakthrough and a long-overdue victory, as well as a moment of unity in a conference otherwise fraught with division over abortion.

For most in that audience, their first exposure to Rosalie came moments later, when the arena finally fell silent enough for her to speak. Her carefully chosen words and masterful delivery left an indelible impression, and those words were so highly praised that they were published in their entirety in the *Minneapolis Star* on June 7. Here's an excerpt:

Men are not the enemy. Men are our brothers, our husbands, our sons, our fathers, our friends.

The enemy is fear—fear that by being all of what we are, by realizing our full potential, we will somehow jeopardize what little security we have attained for ourselves and our children.

A good many years ago, when my then-four children were in school and I had gone with some trepidation to law school to prepare myself to help share the economic burden of supporting those children, a poem came to me which expressed my feeling at that time of what it meant to be a woman:

> Foot in nest,
> Wing in sky;
> Bound by each,
> Hover I.

Now I know it is not necessary to hover. Now I know it is possible to soar, to know the vastness of the sky and then come back, fully, to the nest, enriched by the vision of the whole and by the exercise.

Now I know it is possible to extend the nest to include our children wherever they are—in the factories, at the switchboards, in the mines, the shops, the halls of finance and commerce and government—and nourish there the values which were sprouted by the hearth—a sense that every individual in the human family is a unique and precious being, a sense of justice and fair play, a sense of compassion where justice ends or fails.

I pledge to you and ask your pledge that wherever we are, we will never cease to work for these goals.[48]

Chapter Six

Wahl for Justice

"I just happened to be standing in the right place at the right time in history," Rosalie told a Minneapolis reporter shortly after the tumult at the St. Cloud State University arena had died down. At that triumphant moment and always thereafter, she assigned credit for her professional success to lucky timing and the assistance of others, especially other women. She rode the "second wave" women's movement of the twentieth century that was washing over Minnesota, she often said. If she saw herself as a new leader of that movement, she didn't make that claim.

But those who had been doing the leading welcomed her to their ranks. Koryne Horbal, the DFL feminist general, approached Rosalie at a reception shortly after her appointment, took her hand, and said words Rosalie never forgot: "Thank you for being ready." Another DFL Feminist Caucus founder, Yvette Oldendorf of Lake Elmo, made a similarly lasting impression when she told Rosalie, "I used to wonder on those cold winter nights when I would drive thirty miles alone in the dark to speak to five or six women, why I was doing it. Now I know."[1]

Rosalie keenly felt the weight of being a standard-bearer for her gender. "The only concern I have is not to fail the people who share my concerns," she told one Minneapolis reporter in the days after she returned home from St. Cloud. She told another: "Probably there were many women before me who were eminently more qualified than I. And probably in the future, women won't have to wait as long" for such posts.[2]

Rosalie herself still had four months to wait. Perpich had announced his choice well in advance of the U.S. Senate's confirmation of Harry MacLaughlin to the federal bench. MacLaughlin finally got that nod on September 16. Rosalie's swearing-in ceremony was set for October 3 in the ornate supreme court chamber that dominates the east wing of the capitol.

That delay gave Rosalie one last, sweet summer of comparative leisure, but not of privacy. She had become an object of curiosity to many Minnesotans and a target of resentment by some ambitious male attorneys who deemed themselves more deserving of gubernatorial favor. Those sentiments swirled around the Twin Cities' courts-covering beat reporters, who kept calling Rosalie for interviews.

"On the surface, Rosalie Wahl is that soft little Quaker woman, but there's a fiery core there," reported Gwenyth Jones of the *Minneapolis Star*, quoting an unnamed Wahl friend. The quotable lines she got from Rosalie are the careful words of a committed but politically prudent feminist. Rosalie allowed that a female could have something to contribute to a court's outlook that males don't have—and vice versa. "I'm sure men would think there was something missing if there were a court sitting up there made up of nine women," Rosalie told Jones. The reporter noted that among the eight male justices with whom Rosalie would be seated, two had been criminal prosecutors, but none had Rosalie's background as a defense attorney. A consummate beat reporter who was herself a gender pioneer in her profession, Jones had undoubtedly picked up comments about Rosalie's atypical supreme court qualifications from courthouse sources—men more willing to suggest that Wahl was unqualified than to openly disparage her gender or lament the fact that the state's judicial candidate pool had just been significantly enlarged.[3]

An editorial in the June 9 edition of the *Circulating Pines* weekly newspaper—the publication that Rosalie helped found in 1951 as a "volunteer editor"—revealed a bit more about the "fiery core" to which Jones alluded: "Even 25 years ago people who knew Rosalie Wahl recognized she had more than ordinary strength and ability. Hers has not been an easy life. There have been sorrows and disappointments as well as singing and recognition. But all the experiences she has had have been preparing her for this important job on the highest court in the state. We are confident she will bring not only knowledge of the law but compassion into her decisions."[4]

Interest in Rosalie and her appointment also brought her a wave of speaking invitations in the summer of 1977. Those invitations stirred the teacher in her. They were her chance to explain to average Minnesotans why representation of both genders in the halls of civic power mattered. She wasn't yet comfortable enough at a podium to speak without a text before her. She wrote out her planned message in large, scrawling script, often on inexpensive legal pads or the backs of previously used paper. But she delivered those words with a sincerity and steady cadence that disguised any nervousness and won over audiences. She would be in demand as a public speaker for the next quarter century.

"Perhaps you've never noticed that there are virtually no women on the benches of our courts of justice," she said on July 7 to a St. Croix Valley School District audience. "For all intents and purposes 51 percent of our population is unrepresented on the benches of our courts. And yet those courts make simple and complex decisions which affect our lives, our taxes, our property, and all the precious rights which keep this a free and open society. Women want only to contribute their experience and their considerable talents to the solving of our common problems. It is adding the second lens to a pair of binoculars—the depth and breadth of our vision of the whole is thereby increased."[5]

Affirmations outweighed criticism that summer and fall. But there was enough of each to make Rosalie—and Perpich—aware of many watchful eyes as they stood together on October 3 in the well of the capitol's court chamber. News cameras clicked and whirred nearby as the audience in the small elegant chamber strained to hear. Others watched via closed-circuit television in an overflow room elsewhere in the capitol. Among them, to Rosalie's delight, were the spouses of the other high court justices, eager to show their support. Perpich officially presented Wahl to Chief Justice Robert Sheran, who administered the oath of office. In the audience were Rosalie's family members, including Aunt Sara Patterson, by then an energetic seventy-five-year-old whose devotion had been the one constant through Rosalie's fifty-three years. Rosalie's vision of justice for all shone through her brief inaugural remarks:

> I will endeavor with the other members of the court to
> make equal justice under the law a reality for all, for every
> person. I have been deeply moved by the messages you
> have sent, you who hunger and thirst after justice; you who
> hold that to be able to go to a judge or a court with your
> disputes with your fellow man or the government with the

assurance that that one will decide fairly and with wisdom, is the consummation devoutly to be wished. You who want only that your voice be heard, and your case decided on the merits, regardless of your position of power or power-lessness. In order that justice finally be done, it will be necessary that everyone who has a right to be asserted or a wrong to be redressed have a channel through which to

Governor Rudy Perpich helps Rosalie Wahl don the robe of an associate justice of the Minnesota Supreme Court while Chief Justice Robert Sheran looks on, October 3, 1977. *Courtesy Minneapolis Star Tribune.*

assert that right or redress that wrong, and the services of able, effective counsel.

. . . The work of this court cannot rise above the level of the practice of law throughout the state. High as that level is, we know it can be higher and we will make it so. The bell of justice may be here, in this high court, but the rope which rings it—like the grapevine rope that rang the bell of Atri—is among you, and it must be long enough for even a child to reach. My thanks to you, Governor Perpich, for your trust in me, your trust that I can hear that bell when it rings.[6]

Rosalie deeply believed that courts belong to the people, not to the legal or political establishment. That was more reason for some members of the establishment to resent her new position. Rosalie knew what their resentment could portend for her first election, scheduled just thirteen months after she donned judicial robes. But she was also confident that the state's feminists were in her corner. That assurance allowed her to focus in the ensuing weeks on learning her new job rather than on winning an election to keep it.

She was joining an exceedingly busy court, so much so that calls were increasing to add a new appellate tier to the state's judicial structure to screen initial appeals and dispense with most of them. But formation of the Minnesota Court of Appeals was nearly six years away in the fall of 1977. Rosalie immediately had her hands—and overnight briefcase— full of cases. Chief Justice Sheran was warm and welcoming, but he did not hold back in assigning the new associate justice—"Number 9" in court reckoning—her share of the workload. Sheran reserved the most important decisions for himself, but otherwise divided writing assignments among his justices. "I just took my turn," Rosalie said. "I began to understand and relish the collegial process." The give and take reminded her of Quaker congregational meetings—courteous, formal, respectful, but forthright and at times outspoken.[7]

She quickly developed warm associations with all eight of her male colleagues on her first court. They were "some of the finest men I have ever known," she would say years later. Associate Justice James C. Otis was the feminist in the bunch, she discovered; his wife Connie was active

Rosalie takes her seat after being sworn in. *Wahl Papers, Minnesota Historical Society.*

in Republican politics, and his son Todd was planning his first bid for a state house seat, as a DFLer. She formed a particular friendship with Associate Justice Walter Rogosheske and his wife Dorothy. Rogosheske was ten years Rosalie's senior and had interrupted his political career in the Minnesota house to join the U.S. Army in 1943. He was reelected in 1944 despite his military absence—a political feat attesting to his ability and appeal. In a poem of tribute Rosalie wrote for his retirement in 1980, she described Rogosheske as a

> Gentle, steely presence
> On the court
> Binding
> In one
> Justice and mercy
> As none else
> Has done.[8]

At the entrance for justices. Some of the accommodations for the court had to be rethought. *Courtesy Wahl family.*

One question of some delicacy immediately arose for her, as it had for newly elected female legislators a few years earlier: where to go to the bathroom in the capitol? Architect Cass Gilbert's elegant statehouse design did not anticipate the need for facilities for both genders in the judicial or legislative suites. A public women's restroom stood just outside the second-floor court chamber. Rosalie made use of it, but was soon advised that it wasn't fitting for a justice to "mingle" in this way with attorneys who had come to the court to plead their cases, as well as with the legislators, lobbyists, reporters, and tourists who happened by. A third-floor bathroom, one floor up from the justices' suite, was designated for her use.

Rosalie's days were packed. They often included three or four hearings in the morning, a working-lunch conference with her colleagues to sort and decide cases, writing opinions in the afternoon, and reading in the evening to prepare for the next day's hearings. She had little time for much else, but she loved the work. "It's the job I always wanted, though

I didn't know [it] existed" for much of her adult life, she told friends and, later, audiences. She wouldn't consider moving her home closer to the capitol. Retreating each evening to the quiet and natural beauty of her twelve acres in rural Lake Elmo calmed and recharged her. She loved the Wednesday evening fellowship of the small, tight-knit Quaker group in the east metro area that she had helped form at about the time she joined the high court, and which would shift to Sunday meetings and take the name St. Croix Valley Friends Meeting in 1983. Besides, Rosalie still had a teenager at home, as well as three dogs, a cat, a pet rat, and two horses, one for Jenny and one for a visiting friend to ride. The need to feed the horses before leaving for work in the morning meant that the newest associate justice sometimes took her seat with a telltale strand or two of hay in her increasingly white hair.[9]

Though her days were already full to overflowing, Chief Justice Sheran had a special assignment for the court rookie—one too near to her heart-strings to turn down. Within days of her inauguration, Sheran tapped Wahl to serve as the supreme court's liaison to a new Commission on

Rosalie and Jenny feed the family's horses before heading to the capitol and to school, respectively. *Courtesy Minneapolis Star Tribune.*

the Mentally Disabled and the Courts. The chief justice knew of Rosalie's "interest and concern for the problems of mentally disabled persons," the commission's report would acknowledge. Her ex-husband's and two sons' struggles with mental illness and chemical dependency were evidently not lost on Rosalie's colleagues. Her immediate task was to help select commission members along with its chair, Hamline Law School dean Richard C. Allen, a former consultant to President Lyndon B. Johnson's Committee on Mental Retardation, and vice chair Gerald Ronning, a psychiatrist and medical director of the Crisis Intervention Center at St. Paul's Bethesda Lutheran Hospital. The project director they chose was Lisbeth Nudell, an attorney with Legal Assistance in Ramsey County—the same family friend who drove Jenny Wahl to witness her mother's appointment announcement at the Minnesota Women's Meeting. A project lasting eighteen months was charted—one that would occupy Rosalie throughout tumultuous 1978.[10]

Nothing in Minnesota's political history or tradition would have advised Wahl to make her election an immediate priority. Her timing was unlucky in one sense. Minnesota statutes provide that if a judge takes office more than a year before the next general election, that judge must stand in that election to keep his or her seat. An appointment less than a year before the next general election delays that judge's appearance on a ballot for another two years. Rosalie's tenure was just one month and four days too long to allow for postponement of her reckoning with the voters until 1980. She had less time to gain recognition by the voters than many other judges were granted.

Minnesota had applied for statehood in 1857 in the months immediately following the U.S. Supreme Court's infamous *Dred Scott* decision denying citizenship to African American slaves and their descendents. The state's anti-slavery pioneers insisted that voters retain an opportunity to elect—or, more to the point, unelect—their judges. But the state's constitution also gave governors the power to appoint judges when vacancies occur between elections. That option quickly established the state's normal sequence for judicial selection. Only twice in the half century prior to 1977 did a non-incumbent become a supreme court justice by appealing directly to the voters for election to an open seat. Most judges were first appointed by governors. With similarly rare exception, most judges ran unopposed when their turn came for election to a constitutionally prescribed six-year term. Judges generally served until retirement, which could occur voluntarily but was compelled by state statute at age seventy. Only once in the twentieth century, in 1946, was an incumbent justice ousted by the voters, and then after less than a year in office.[11]

But, as Perpich had warned Rosalie's backers, Justice Wahl's election would be different. The governor told Carol Connolly that one would-be challenger, former attorney general Robert Mattson Sr., had come to the governor's office and said, "If you appoint a woman, I'll run against her." It was no idle threat.[12]

Rosalie's first written opinion for the court's majority put her at odds with another potential challenger. In *State v. Hugh Edward Flowers*, the court's majority overturned a decision by Ramsey County district judge J. Jerome Plunkett in a case involving an aggravated assault charge against a defendant who had been previously convicted of criminal sexual assault with a minor. That previous conviction was the subject of a Rasmussen, or suppression, hearing and order before the trial. That meant that references to the previous conviction were to be omitted from the new prosecution. But prosecutors repeatedly made references to the defendant's prior conviction at trial, and Judge Plunkett overruled the defense's objections and rejected its motion for a new trial. That much disregard for the original suppression order was erroneous, the high court majority deemed. It warranted a new trial. "The state's proper remedy, if it disagrees with a pretrial order of this nature, is not to violate the order but rather to exercise its right to appeal," Rosalie wrote. She cited ample precedent to back that judgment. If it pained her that her first opinion led to a retrial for a convicted rapist, her careful prose revealed no such emotion.[13]

That opinion was issued on December 2, 1977. Soon after, Rosalie heard rumors that Plunkett was mulling a bid to unseat her—though he denied that her reversal of his rulings in the *Flowers* case was a factor in his thinking. In April, Plunkett went public with his intentions. The son of the solicitor general for James J. Hill's Great Northern Railroad, Plunkett was fifty-four years old in 1978—the same age as Rosalie. Like Ross Wahl, he'd suffered through the Battle of the Bulge. He also was among the GIs who stormed ashore at Normandy in action that earned him a Purple Heart and Bronze Star. Law school immediately followed military service for him, and a brief stint as an assistant St. Paul city attorney led to his appointment to the municipal court bench in 1954, at the precocious age of thirty. Republican governor C. Elmer Anderson gave Plunkett his first judicial job, and Republican governor Harold LeVander promoted him to the district bench thirteen years later. In 1978, he figured he was due for another promotion.[14]

Rosalie vowed an active campaign against the St. Paul judge. "I didn't take this job to get beat the first time around," she told *Minneapolis Tribune* reporter Nick Coleman, the son of the state senate DFL leader by the same name who had counseled Perpich on the Wahl appointment. Allies advised Rosalie that Plunkett had evinced no feminist tendencies on the bench. In 1970, Plunkett tried without a jury the case of Dr. Jane Hodgson, a Minneapolis obstetrician who quite openly performed a then-illegal abortion with the intention of testing the constitutionality of the state's ban on the procedure. Plunkett obliged her, finding her guilty and sentencing her to jail. But her sentence was suspended pending appeal, and that appeal was tossed out after the January 1973 *Roe v. Wade* ruling changed the legal status of abortion nationwide. More recently, Plunkett had sided with critics of the proceedings at the Minnesota Women's Meeting in St. Cloud. He ordered secretary of state Joan Growe not to submit to National Women's Meeting organizers some thirty-five resolutions approved on the meeting's final day in sparsely attended workshops, rather than by a quorum of participants in a plenary session.[15]

Rosalie and her supporters soon had another rival to worry about, this one with a DFL pedigree. On May 11, Judge Daniel Foley of the Third Judicial District in southeastern Minnesota announced his candidacy. Foley, a fifty-six-year-old native of Wabasha and resident of Rochester, was the son of an attorney and a member of a large family that took Democratic politics seriously. Like Plunkett, he was a World War II veteran who plunged into law school when the war ended, enrolling in Fordham University in New York City. He also became active in the American Legion, rising to national commander in 1962–63—the only Minnesotan to hold that post. The name Dan Foley was known in every American Legion post in the state, giving him a ready-made political base. The Foley name's familiarity in DFL politics didn't hurt either. Foley's son Tom was on the 1978 ballot in Ramsey County for the first time, seeking the county attorney's post. (He would win, and go on to serve four terms.)

Brother Patrick was U.S. attorney for Minnesota during Lyndon Johnson's administration; brother Eugene was director of the Small Business
Administration under President John F. Kennedy; brother John had been
a member of the U.S. House for one term, 1959–60, representing a district in Maryland. Dan Foley had been in private practice when DFL
governor Karl Rolvaag put him on the district bench in 1966. After twelve
years shuttling between courthouses in the Third District's eleven counties, he too considered himself ready to move to the top judicial rung.[16]

Then there was Mattson, who waited until the last day of the filing
period, July 18, to make good on his promise to run for Wahl's seat. His
move came as a surprise to the capitol press corps, but not to Rosalie's
campaign team, who remembered what the former attorney general had
told Perpich months before.[17]

Of the three men challenging Rosalie, Mattson was the best known
and most clearly identified with socially conservative traditionalists in
the DFL Party. Born on Minnesota's Iron Range exactly one day before
Rosalie's birth in 1924, Mattson too had served in World War II, receiv-
ing a Purple Heart for wounds sustained in France. His early legal career
landed him a position as a staff attorney in the state highway department. His political mentors included federal judge Miles Lord, for whom
Mattson had served as chief deputy while Lord was attorney general
in the 1950s, and governor Karl Rolvaag. The latter appointed Mattson in
December 1964 to complete a political transition begun that year when
Minnesota U.S. Senator Hubert Humphrey was elected vice president.
Rolvaag filled Humphrey's Senate seat by tapping future U.S. vice president Walter Mondale, who had served as attorney general for four years.
Mattson was practicing law in Minneapolis and living in Bloomington
when he got Rolvaag's nod to return to the attorney general's office. He
left that post two years later without seeking reelection, telling reporters
that with four children—one a son and namesake, Robert Mattson Jr.,
about to enter Harvard University—he could not afford to serve in the
$18,000-a-year post. Rosalie's job paid $49,000 in 1978, a sum he evidently considered sufficient.[18]

The Mattson name stayed familiar to voters in the 1970s through the
repeated candidacies of Robert Mattson Jr. In 1978, he was seeking reelection to a second term as state auditor. But the name recognition that
the son gave the father that year was not entirely positive. Mattson Jr.

had alienated DFL party regulars by running against party-endorsed candidates three times—in 1970 for secretary of state, 1974 for state auditor (his one successful bid), and 1976 for the U.S. House from the St. Paul–based Fourth District. He lost the latter race to state representative Bruce Vento, who would spend the rest of his life in Congress.

In 1978 young Mattson was in a tough fight to hang on to his auditor's post. He had acquired a reputation as a reckless, shoot-from-the-hip character. In 1975 he charged Hennepin County officials with impropriety in building the Hennepin County Government Center. A year later, a special grand jury not only found no criminal wrongdoing but also castigated Mattson for drawing incorrect conclusions, failing to follow recognized audit procedures, and using inflammatory language. The DFL state convention had opted for no endorsement for auditor after eleven ballots, despite the withdrawal of two other candidates from the contest. The Republican Party had found a smart, scrappy, centrist candidate for the post in Minneapolis state representative Arne Carlson. Within weeks of the conventions, Minnesotans learned that young Mattson had been "extremely intoxicated," chased by police, and handcuffed during a late-night incident in Minnetonka in February. He then sought to keep the police report secret, which he succeeded in doing for five months. Not long afterward, the state AFL-CIO endorsed Carlson for auditor. It was the first time that big labor had backed a Republican for statewide office in Minnesota. Rather than thinking he could ride his son's coattails, Mattson Sr. may have decided to file for the supreme court in the hope that his lingering positive reputation from the 1960s would add some luster to the son's tarnished image—or at least create confusion about which Mattson was running for what office. The son accompanied the father to the secretary of state's candidate's filing desk on July 18, signaling their intention to stump the state as a team.[19]

Rosalie had a teammate of her own. Standing at her side when she filed for election was her colleague from Edina with a Republican pedigree, Associate Justice C. Donald Peterson. He too had an election challenge that year, albeit a much less formidable one than Rosalie faced. Jack Baker, a former University of Minnesota student body president and early gay rights activist, filed against Peterson, who had written the supreme court's unanimous 1971 opinion that Minnesota law does not permit same-sex marriage. Baker was a plaintiff in that case.[20]

It's not clear who originated the notion that Wahl and Peterson would run as a team. But Peterson was "on board early" and committed to seeing his colleague reelected, Connolly recalls. He was uniquely qualified to help. He had served two terms in the legislature and run unsuccessfully as the Republican candidate for lieutenant governor in 1962, losing to a future Minnesota Supreme Court chief justice, A. M. "Sandy" Keith. Peterson was also one of only two justices in the mid-twentieth century to arrive on the high court via election as a non-incumbent—and he got there by defeating the son of the other one.

Born in Minneapolis in 1918, Carl Donald Peterson was the youngest of ten children in a clergyman's family. He honed his verbal skills in the exceptional speech program at Minnehaha Academy, attended junior college at his father's alma mater in Illinois, and became the debate team partner of future U.S. Senator Hubert Humphrey when he enrolled at the University of Minnesota in 1937. He returned to Illinois for law school. Then he spent five years in the military, first in the U.S. Army Air Corps, later as a military judge advocate during the Korean War. He married Gretchen Palen, a great-granddaughter of Minneapolis pioneer Ard Godfrey, and they settled in Edina to build a life rich with civic and political involvement.[21]

Peterson often claimed that the political lessons he had learned as the losing lieutenant governor candidate in 1962 helped him seize the 1966 opportunity for direct election to the bench. Associate Justice Thomas Francis Gallagher, first elected in 1942, had indicated early that year that he would seek another six-year term. As the July filing period drew to a close, however, Gallagher abruptly withdrew. Filing in his stead was his thirty-one-year-old son, Thomas Patrick Gallagher, a former head of the consumer protection unit in the Minnesota attorney general's office who had moved into private practice. Conveniently for young Gallagher, the law did not require the use of middle names or initials on the ballot. That, plus his father's twenty-four-year tenure, gave him an immediate name recognition advantage in what swelled overnight to a six-way race. Joining Peterson and Gallagher on the primary ballot were Rosalie's future rival Daniel Foley, future supreme court chief justice Peter Popovich, Hennepin County district judge T. B. Knudson, and Ramsey County district judge Harold Schultz. Foley, Popovich, and Schultz successfully pleaded with the state supreme court to require, at the minimum, the insertion of Gallagher's middle name on the ballot to distinguish him from his father. Still, Gallagher led the primary ballot with nearly 107,000 more votes than Peterson, who came in second and advanced with Gallagher to the general election.[22]

Gallagher's electoral strength in the primary roused the state's Bar Association and editorial writers. The Gallagher father and son had engaged in a "form of legal nepotism which is not good for Minnesota or the Supreme Court," scolded the *New Ulm Daily Journal*. The Bar Association surveyed its members and released lopsided results: 1,958 for Peterson, 763 for Gallagher. Meanwhile, Peterson applied campaign tactics he had learned in his previous campaigns. He enlisted friends in both law and politics to send cards and letters to their friends and to place local newspaper ads on his behalf, over their signatures. He met with the president of the state AFL-CIO, an organization allied with DFLers, and elicited the best promise a Republican could hope to receive: "We will not help you, but we will not hurt you." He toured the state, calling on newspaper editors and radio stations, where he was often invited for impromptu on-air interviews. Peterson didn't hesitate to bring up Gallagher's youth as he touted his own assets. "Bluntly, is a 32-year-old man quite ready to be a judge on the highest court of Minnesota?" asked the candidate who had achieved the ripe old age of forty-eight.[23]

Those were the winning ways Peterson described twelve years later to Rosalie and her campaign aides as they talked about how to secure her election. Those tactics had yielded a sixty-five thousand–vote margin of victory for Peterson in 1966. They would work again, he told Connolly when he paid a surprise early-morning visit to the tiny downtown Minneapolis office that had been donated to Rosalie's campaign. "When I arrived at the office, Justice Peterson was quietly sitting in a desk chair," Connolly recalled. "He wanted to let us know that he would campaign in any way he could to help Rosalie, and also that we could use his name in any way that was helpful. He was a lovely, humble gentleman." The fact that he was a well-known Republican and thus could add a bipartisan purple tint to Rosalie's DFL blue didn't hurt either.[24]

Wahl and Peterson had the benefit of backing from what today would be called a political action committee that had been formed earlier in the 1970s to give incumbent supreme court justices the wherewithal to defend themselves from political attack. Donors to the Minnesota Lawyers

Volunteer Committee to Retain Incumbent Judges included some of the state's most prominent lawyers. A leader in the group was Leonard Lindquist, a nationally known labor lawyer who, along with future federal judge Earl Larson, founded the Minneapolis law firm that would provide a professional home for DFL luminaries including Governor Orville Freeman and U.S. representative Don Fraser. Lindquist arranged for his young niece to spend her summer days as the Wahl campaign's sole office staffer.[25]

True to her vow to Perpich, Connolly was the political general of the Wahl campaign. Officially, she was its co-chair, a title she shared with Rosalie's former professor and boss, Douglas Heidenreich of William Mitchell College of Law. But Heidenreich's participation was largely confined to lending his name to the effort. Not so for Connolly. She was forty-four years old in 1978. Like Rosalie, she was a political liberal, a peace activist, the mother of a large brood (the Connollys had seven children), and the female half of a struggling marriage. Connolly would divorce her husband John, an attorney and future Ramsey County district judge, one year later. She and Rosalie shared one more thing—poetry. Both women habitually retreated from stress-filled lives long enough to pen lines of heartfelt verse that inspired others while refreshing themselves. A poet's spirit connected them even before each knew the extent of the other's writing.[26]

Connolly was better politically connected and more campaign savvy than the candidate she served. Connolly had been appointed the year before to the St. Paul Human Rights Commission, a post that became a tough political proving ground. To the new commissioner's great regret, St. Paul voters repealed on April 25, 1978, what had been a groundbreaking municipal ordinance banning discrimination against homosexuals. Connolly was quicker than Wahl to recognize the political peril Wahl faced as two sitting male judges mounted campaigns to unseat her, and she grew nervous as Wahl insisted on focusing on her judicial duties rather than her election threat. But Connolly took heart when the filing period closed on July 18 and she saw that Rosalie had not one or two but three male challengers in the September 12 primary. Two candidates would advance from the primary to the nonpartisan general election ballot. Dividing the primary's anti-female vote among three men likely assured that Rosalie would be among the primary's top two finishers, Connolly reasoned.[27]

That thought did not diminish the campaign's zeal. Connolly knew she had a major challenge just to make voters aware of the judicial race, let alone familiar with the case for Rosalie's election. Wahl was running in a remarkable political year in Minnesota. U.S. Senator Hubert Humphrey's death in January 1978 meant that all three major statewide offices, governor and two U.S. Senate seats, would be on the November ballot. Out of a desire to break ground for women—and to make a safe political call—Governor Perpich appointed Humphrey's widow Muriel to fill his Senate seat until the fall general election. On both counts, Perpich misjudged. Feminists typically did not rank appointed widows among gender pioneers. Furthermore, Muriel Humphrey's appointment permanently damaged Perpich's relationship with senate majority leader Nicholas Coleman, whose longing to serve in the U.S. Senate was an open secret. Coleman's clout made him someone no governor could afford to alienate.

The new Senator Humphrey announced soon after taking office that she would not run for election in her own right. On the heels of that announcement came word of the candidacies of two DFL men who were opposites in philosophy, temperament, and background. U.S. representative Don Fraser was a quiet, principled intellectual, the son of the dean of the University of Minnesota Law School and an attorney who had spent sixteen years in Congress. He was a national leader in the effort to end the war in Vietnam and make the United States a force for human rights around the world. By contrast, Robert Short was an outspoken businessman who grew up on the hardscrabble Minneapolis North Side and briefly practiced law before buying a trucking company. He had become wealthy as a buyer and seller of sports teams, downtown hotels, and apartment complexes. The patriarch of a large Catholic family, he opposed legal abortion and was willing to give the tourism industry considerable latitude to bring motorboats and other modern amenities into the Boundary Waters Canoe Area Wilderness. Fraser, by comparison, was the U.S. House sponsor of a bill to keep motorboats, mining, and logging out of the entire BWCA. The Boundary Waters issue erupted just as the 1978 campaign season dawned, splitting DFLers into hostile north-south camps. Short was the darling of northern Minnesota pro-gun, anti-abortion, anti-feminist populists. Fraser was the most liberal member of the state's congressional delegation; his wife Arvonne was among the state's best-known feminist activists. The Fraser-Short primary was the state's marquee political event in the summer of 1978.

"Do everything we can think of" became Connolly's motto as she tried to draw attention to her candidate on a laughably limited campaign budget. Well-heeled feminist allies paid for a personal wardrobe and hairstyle makeover for Rosalie at upscale Dayton's department store. Following Peterson's advice, personal letters were sent to feminists, lawyers, friends, and Friends—that is, members of Rosalie's Quaker congregation. They appealed for donations and asked supporters to send postcards and letters urging their friends and acquaintances to vote for Wahl. A volunteer with graphic arts skills, Joe Huttie, was enlisted to design a billboard bearing both Wahl's and Peterson's names. The simple design—gray on black, featuring a line drawing of a column resembling courthouse pillars—was also used as the campaign's stationery letterhead and on signs on Metro Transit buses. The billboard sparked a brief tussle between Connolly and Nancy Dreher, the young attorney at the Leonard, Street and Deinard firm in Minneapolis who was treasurer and the de facto manager of the Committee to Retain Incumbent Judges. Dreher summoned Connolly to her office to object to the billboards, arguing that they were a waste of money. Connolly disagreed, arguing that billboards were cheap; these were particularly legible, and they nicely underscored a connection between Wahl and the better-known Justice Peterson. What's more, Connolly was in charge. The billboards stayed.[28]

But another campaign staple—pin-on buttons—was rejected by Rosalie herself. Campaign volunteer Josie Corning had come up with a similarly simple black-on-gray design reading "WAHL for JUSTICE/justice for all." The buttons made their debut at the campaign's first major fundraising event, at the large Lake Minnetonka home of James and Laura Miles. Many at the party praised the buttons. Rosalie did not. To her, they represented a kind of advertising she considered unseemly for a judge. In addition, "justice for all" came too close to making a campaign promise about how she would perform on certain cases. The Minnesota canon of judicial ethics then barred judicial candidates from discussing specific cases before the court. Rosalie was a stickler about the principle of judicial impartiality, and she insisted that her campaign observe it to a fault. The buttons were never again distributed, becoming instead collectors' items.[29]

The hosts of that first fundraiser in many ways typified the people who were drawn to Rosalie and her campaign. They were liberal, not intensely partisan, well educated, and believers in the power of diversity and the

The campaign button rejected by the candidate. *Courtesy Carol Connelly.*

rule of law to improve society. James Miles was an electrical engineer and lawyer who contributed to the founding of Control Data, becoming the computing pioneer's vice president. He was also the chairman of the governing board that built the Minneapolis Children's Hospital. In 1974, he ran for governor as a nonpartisan independent, adopting the campaign tactic of a grassroots idealist. He walked the state, from little Lyle on the south-central Iowa border to International Falls, the state's gateway to Canada. Laura Haverstock Miles was trained as an attorney and worked briefly in a bank trust department before surrendering her career for the sake of marriage and motherhood, as Rosalie and many other young women did after World War II. She had been active in the grassroots effort to end the war in Vietnam and was an early adherent of the Minnesota Women's Political Caucus, which was vigorously backing Wahl. "We women who were supporting Rosalie knew that if we could get this first woman justice through the election, it would become easier to get other women appointed," Laura Miles would say thirty-four years later. "Besides, she was in considerable jeopardy." In addition to inviting several hundred potential Wahl donors to her home, Miles said, she and other Women's Political Caucus members called "all the friends we could think of, especially outside the Twin Cities." Gloria Griffin, who in late

1977 had parted with the Perpich administration, orchestrated that effort as head of the Hennepin County Women's Political Caucus. Of Wahl, Griffin said, "We consider her an absolute must to retain."[30]

By 1978, Minnesota feminists had identified a lot of friends. The organizing done to pull off the Minnesota Women's Meeting in June 1977 had substantially lengthened the rosters of the Minnesota Women's Political Caucus and the DFL and GOP Feminist Caucuses. (GOP Women for Political Effectiveness had adopted that more realistic name in 1975.) Taken together, their contact lists numbered into the thousands. The thirty-five Minnesotans who comprised the state's delegation to the National Women's Conference in Houston in November 1977 also provided Rosalie with an informal but reliable base of support.[31]

A leader in that group was Rosalie's good friend Mary Peek of Grey Cloud Island Township, in the southeast metro exurbs. Two years Rosalie's senior, Peek had met Rosalie years earlier through school improvement work. Their friendship was understandable to anyone who knew them. They were sisters in spirit, interests, intellectual heft, and verbal ability. Peek was the wife of psychologist Roland Peek, a mother of three, and a journalist, teacher, DFL activist, unsuccessful legislative candidate, and consultant to school districts on the implementation of the landmark Title IX requirement for gender equality in federally funded public education, enacted by Congress in 1972. She had been badly injured in a senseless bombing at the St. Paul Dayton's department store in August 1970, giving her more than a few moments of fame and admiration as she emerged from weeks in critical condition to say, "I don't think I'll ever again lack compassion for the helpless." Like Rosalie, she expressed herself in a way that compelled attention.[32]

The two women were close enough for Rosalie to recall details of Mary's family story and include them in her remarks to the Minnesota Women's Meeting: "I am remembering Mary Peek's grandmother—Kari Sougstad Anderson—as a young woman in Norway, refusing to marry the man chosen by her father, asking for her dowry, coming to the New World alone, knowing no English—as an old woman, 78 years old, being the first person in line to vote at the first election after the ratification of the 19th Amendment."

Peek was in the political and feminist thick of things in 1978. She had been a delegate to the National Women's Conference in Houston and was one of seven Minnesota women appointed to the conference's Continuing Committee, working to implement its twenty-five recommendations. But she made time to lend both a campaign hand and a private shoulder to Rosalie. Among her gifts was an introduction to Nina Rothchild, the executive director of the Council on the Economic Status of Women and, along with her mortgage-banker husband Kennon, the frequent host of fundraisers for DFL and feminist causes in her Mahtomedi home. Kennon had run unsuccessfully for the state senate in 1970; Nina had managed Peek's unsuccessful state house bid two years later.[33]

The council was itself a gift to gender-equity seekers. It grew out of state house hearings in 1975 headed by Minneapolis representative Stan Enebo, a labor-allied liberal legislator who, as head of the House Labor-Management Relations Committee, was moved by compelling testimony about women's unfair pay, benefits, and working conditions. Governor Anderson liked the idea and promoted it in the 1976 session. If the council's backers thought they were sending feminist agitators away to conduct research quietly, they were mistaken. The council was chaired for its first seven years by state representative (after 1980, state senator) Linda Berglin who, since her 1972 election, had matured into a formidable policy-minded legislator.[34]

Berglin had an exceptional teammate in Rothchild, a Smith College math major who brought feminist principles to bear on her service as a Mahtomedi school board member from 1970 to 1978. On the heels of the enactment of federal Title IX requirements, she had written the booklet *Sexism in the Schools: A Handbook for Action*. By 1978, Berglin and Rothchild were well along in achieving their vision of the council as a data-rich toolbox for anyone seeking to give women a fair shot at work and fair treatment in the workplace. They made the council a unique hybrid body—a cross between a legislative study commission, a governor's advisory task force, and an independent lobbying group. "We are problem-finders and process-starters," Rothchild told a reporter in 1979.[35]

Rothchild, Peek, and Wahl were made-for-each-other allies. But such was the developmental level of the Minnesota women's movement in 1978 that, while Nina knew well who Rosalie was, and Rosalie had met Kennon when he was Washington County DFL chair, Rosalie and Nina had not met before Mary asked Nina to host a fundraiser for the new justice. Nina's response also says something about the spirit of the

movement. Without seeking further introduction, Nina agreed. Invitations to a ten-dollar-per-person party on August 24 went out to many
people the Rothchilds knew and to more whom they did not. "We were
always having fundraisers to which nobody came," Rothchild recalled.
"To this one, a lot of people came—a lot we didn't know."[36]

What Nina remembered clearly thirty-five years later was the warmth
of the response to Rosalie's considerable rhetorical power. "People absolutely loved her," Nina said. At that event and dozens of other opportunities to address audiences in the summer and fall of 1978, Wahl made the
case for keeping on the high court the kind of diversity she represented,
not only of gender but also of legal and personal experience. Of the nine
justices then on the court, only she had a background in criminal defense, she noted. "I've looked at the system from the bottom up." Only
she had recent experience as a law professor. "I know at least 450 young
lawyers around the state in whom I have great confidence," she said. She
frequently told a spare version of her life story, carefully omitting the
painful parts. She would describe life as a rural Kansas girl, loving language and learning; of early career dreams giving way to marriage; of deciding at age thirty-seven to go to law school. "I still don't know what I'm

Ken and Nina Rothchild host Rosalie at a campaign fundraiser, August 24, 1978.
Courtesy Nina Rothchild.

going to be when I grow up," she told one audience. "Although I promise you that for the foreseeable future, my opposition notwithstanding, I will be on the Supreme Court!"[37]

Her opposition held back little in their efforts to foil her resolve. Plunkett, Foley, and Mattson gave Minnesota voters a judicial election unlike any they had witnessed before or would see again in the twentieth century. Before it was over, it would include the negative ads, innuendo, and smear tactics associated with recent campaigns for executive and legislative branch offices, not judicial ones. The 1978 campaign to unseat Rosalie Wahl rebuts the notion that Minnesota has never witnessed the rough-and-tumble judicial electioneering that erodes respect for the courts and is in no danger of falling into that pattern. Precisely this sort of campaign was waged against Rosalie. Nothing in Minnesota's judicial election process has changed to prevent its recurrence or it from becoming the norm. The supreme court election battle of 1978 illustrated the need for Minnesota to give its judges a sturdier shield against electioneering excesses.[38]

Each of Rosalie's challengers denied that her gender had inspired his candidacy, but each argued that in experience, training, and perspective she was unqualified for the high court—an argument sure to resonate with those who doubted that women belonged in judicial robes.

Plunkett and Foley claimed that their experience as trial judges was greatly superior to Rosalie's in criminal defense and legal education. "An appellate court should consist of people who have had extensive experience at the trial level, either as a trial judge or a trial attorney," Plunkett said during an August 27 KQRS radio debate involving himself, Wahl, and Foley. It was believed to be the first such broadcast meeting of three supreme court candidates in state history. (Mattson had told the station that he too would participate but was "called out of town on legal business" and declined shortly before the broadcast, program host Bill Tilton announced.) Plunkett dismissed as inadequate the kind of diversity Rosalie was bringing to the high court. "If we're going to have diversity, we should have someone who's had experience as a trial judge, particularly, because a trial judge has had to see both sides, not just the prosecution or the defense," Plunkett said.[39]

Foley piled on. While "sex or gender should have nothing to do with whether one is seeking this office," the fact that Rosalie alone on the high court was not at one time a trial attorney was troubling, he said—disregarding her work as a defense attorney in the William Mitchell legal clinics and at the state public defender's office: "Those other individuals on the court were trial lawyers. That's a significant matter to take into account." What's more, he said, district court judges were due for another seat on the nine-member supreme court: "The last trial judge to succeed to the Supreme Court was in 1961. We are a proud part of the bench and bar. We like to feel that we, after an abundance of trial experience in a wide variety of [cases], that we can make an input on that court."

Foley also argued that non-metro Minnesota was underrepresented on the court—and that Rosalie's exurban Lake Elmo address did not qualify as "greater Minnesota." Two of the nine justices in 1978 hailed from outstate places, both of them north of Hennepin County. Foley lived in Rochester and grew up in the Mississippi River town of Wabasha. "No judge should be a regional candidate, but if we're going to talk about diversity, I think that's an element that comes to me," Foley said.

When a radio caller asked Foley why he chose to run against Rosalie rather than C. Donald Peterson—who also had not been a trial lawyer before his 1966 election—his answer marginalized Rosalie. "It would have been foolish for me to run against him because I think he is more than qualified," Foley said. "There's general consensus among trial judges and trial lawyers that Judge Peterson is an excellent judge."

The two men in the radio debate called each other by first name and bantered in a friendly way that served to isolate Rosalie. "You can tell Dan and I have been discussing these things for many years," Plunkett said with a friendly chuckle. When Rosalie described her philosophy of criminal sentencing, striving to speak in generalities to avoid making comments related to specific cases, Foley chided, "We're dealing with the real world, we're not dealing with the idealistic world."

During the run-up to the primary, Plunkett was the most outspoken in minimizing Rosalie's accomplishments. News reports picked up his claim that she was not shouldering a full workload at the high court, something radio moderator Bill Tilton asked her about. "As far as I'm concerned it's an unfounded accusation," Rosalie said. "My timing on the court is about par for the course," noting that the workload on the high court ramps up over time for all new justices.

More damning, and inaccurate, was Plunkett's comment that in founding and directing William Mitchell's criminal law clinics, Rosalie had done little more "than showing students where the criminal court was." He said he had checked with people familiar with the program and that "nobody recalled her supervising people doing trial work."[40]

Rosalie's former students numbered more than four hundred in 1978. Many of them were practicing law in Minnesota and following their professor's election closely. Plunkett's comments stirred several of them to respond to Plunkett via letters to the editors of the state's newspapers. "The fact is that in Wahl's program, students were presented with perhaps their most demanding set of experiences in law school," wrote attorney Larry Purdy. "Each student was required to represent numerous indigent clients in actual legal proceedings involving the possibility of both incarceration and/or a substantial fine. The proceedings included bail motions, arraignments, pre-trial hearings and trials both before the court and before a jury . . . For Judge Plunkett to so casually dismiss the dedicated efforts of Justice Wahl and her former students is to do a disservice to an effective and indeed much-needed program." Wahl's own rejoinder showed her skill at verbal jousting. "I like to think judges are a little better informed when they make decisions," she said.[41]

While Plunkett and Wahl sparred openly in the press, another opponent attempted a covert strike. KSTP-TV reporter Marcia Fluer—a former teacher and entertainer new to the political beat, the first female broadcast journalist with a regular post at the state capitol—was contacted with information about the mental health history of Rosalie's eldest son, Christopher. The Foley campaign was its source, Fluer would recall thirty-four years later. (Another source attributes the tip to the Mattson campaign.) Fluer said she was told that "there was a family issue that might get in the way" of Wahl's service on the high court. The schizophrenia with which Christopher Wahl struggled was poorly understood in the 1970s and was thought by many ill-informed people to result from defective parenting. Only six years earlier, Democratic U.S. Senator Thomas Eagleton had been forced to step aside as a vice presidential candidate because of a history of mental illness. A diligent reporter, Fluer called Connolly to check out the accuracy of what she had been told. Connolly told Fluer about Christopher's mental health history, then waited anxiously to see what Fluer would do with the information. No story ensued. Fluer decided that Rosalie's adult son ought not be dragged into her campaign. "I was new at this game—but I knew I was being manipulated. I knew this was wrong. I thought about Tom Eagleton, and decided, 'This is none of anybody's business.'" Fluer gave Connolly the papers about Christopher that had been given to her. She didn't tell her editors about the tip—a courageous and potentially career-damaging decision. She feared that if she had shared the information with them, she would have been compelled to air the story.[42]

In early August, with the primary election about a month away, Rosalie was under pressure to spend every spare moment campaigning. Yet she kept a promise to host at her home the gathering of a regional Friends singing group, the Nightingales, for a weekend-long campout and song-fest. Rosalie had been among the group's founders about a dozen years earlier at semi-annual weekend gatherings of Friends Meetings in Minnesota and Wisconsin. It started when mothers would put their young children down for the night, then gather to sing lullabies, favorite hymns, and folk songs, always a capella, often from memory, as Rosalie preferred. The fun and spiritual connection was such that the women, and the men who eventually joined them, would keep harmonizing until the wee hours of the morning.

"She would come seeking sustenance, and finding it," Raquel Wood of the Twin Cities Friends Meeting said of Rosalie's involvement in both the Nightingales and the Friends. The Nightingales were well aware of the demands on Rosalie that intense summer. They divided the chores, some coming early and others staying late to help with preparations and cleanup. The 1978 Nightingale campout was the start of a twenty-seven-year summer tradition at the Wahl farm. "Rosalie just loved seeing the tents pop up in her yard," reported Gail Lewellan, a younger attorney, Friends member, and Nightingales singer who shared the hosting chores as Rosalie's upstairs tenant in the 1990s.[43]

While Rosalie sang with and drew strength from the Friends, her campaign team huddled. That team included Carol Connolly, Mary Peek, Rahn Westby, Gloria Griffin, and state senator Emily Anne Staples, who in 1976 had finally achieved her goal of a seat in the legislature, becoming the first DFL woman elected to that body in her own right. By August, it also extended to a small but growing cadre of politically savvy, well-heeled feminists who were capable of contributing and raising campaign funds on short notice. Among them: Marilyn Tickle Bryant of Wayzata, the first Republican chair of the bipartisan Minnesota Women's Political Caucus and an executive in her family's construction business, Adjustable Joist Co.; Barbara Forster of Minneapolis, a pioneering woman in the banking industry who would go on to be a founder of the Women's Foundation of Minnesota; and Kathleen Ridder, whose husband Robert was part of the publishing family whose newspapers included dailies in St. Paul and Duluth, and who that spring had lost her bid for GOP endorsement for a state house seat to Art Seaberg, a white, middle-aged, abortion-opposing attorney. The experience served to stiffen Ridder's feminist resolve. That summer, Ridder was a Wahl campaign volunteer, stuffing envelopes in the basement of the home of two St. Paul attorneys, Carolyn and John Cochrane.[44]

The Wahl strategists concluded in early August that their candidate needed more visibility. They collaborated with Minnesota Women Lawyers to host a large ice cream social fundraiser for the Wahl campaign at Gloria Griffin's Lake Minnetonka home on Sunday, August 27—Rosalie's birthday. A brand-new attorney who hoped to run for the legislature one day, Ember Reichgott of New Hope, did much to organize the event. (Among its featured guests was Alan Page, a star defensive tackle for the Minnesota Vikings and, in 1978, a newly minted graduate of the University of Minnesota Law School. He would go on to distinguished service and partnership with Rosalie on the Minnesota Supreme Court.)[45]

Proceeds from that event helped pay for a chartered airplane two days later for something Minnesota voters had not seen before—a supreme court justice campaigning with a "fly-around," in the manner of candidates for governor and U.S. Senate. The campaign team had concluded that filling Rosalie's noon hours, evenings, and weekends with speaking engagements wasn't enough to assure a primary victory. The haphazard schedule of those events was also straining the campaign's volunteer capacity, Connolly recalled. "After the third trip to Marshall in two weeks, we insisted that she had to let us assign her a scheduler." Rosalie had been reluctant to leave work to spend entire days campaigning. Often, she took legal briefs for the next days' cases with her to read in the car as volunteers drove her to events. She rejected the suggestion that she should shake hands in shopping malls or ride in parades. That would be undignified for a judge, she said.[46]

But as August waned, she yielded to her team's judgment that keeping her job required spending more time away from her job. One of her former law students, J. Thomas Mott, took time off as an assistant public defender in Ramsey County to serve as an aide-de-camp for the August 29 Wahl for Justice campaign tour and as her scheduler for the duration. Also on board were Connolly and campaign aide Deborah Fisher, a freelance journalist and neighbor of Rahn Westby who had written a profile of Rosalie for *Twin Cities Woman* magazine that summer.[47]

The long, warm, late-summer day started with an early-morning flight to the Fargo, North Dakota, airport and a drive across the Red River to a Moorhead, Minnesota, hotel, where a press conference had been arranged. Rosalie was in feisty form. "They may think a woman may be easier to defeat, a pushover," Wahl said of her competition. "They're in for a surprise." Her plane then hopscotched to the southeast, making stops with similar press conference arrangements in Alexandria, Rochester, Austin, and Mankato before heading back to the Minneapolis–St. Paul airport. The Rochester stop worried Rosalie, since it was Daniel Foley's home base. But women's organizations in the city saw to it that the chairs at the airport press conference were filled with her supporters. At her home stop, twenty women bearing hand-lettered signs greeted her: "Women salute Rosalie E. Wahl." After five press conferences and a lot of small-airplane bounces in one day, she had earned their salute. Her exertions netted press coverage at every stop that day and throughout the primary campaign's remaining two weeks.[48]

Of the three men running against Rosalie, Robert Mattson was the least combative before the primary. But having served a dozen years earlier as attorney general and with a son and namesake as the sitting state auditor, Mattson had a name-recognition advantage over the two district judges and Rosalie herself. That was true particularly among the state's DFL voters, who turned out in force on September 12. The Don Fraser–Robert Short contest for the party's nomination for Hubert Humphrey's Senate seat had mushroomed into an intra-party fight of epic proportion. Unusually high DFL turnout on Mattson's native Iron Range, where many vehicles wore "Dump Fraser" bumper stickers, assured Mattson of a strong showing. Some veteran political observers predicted that he would be the top vote-getter in the four-way race.

That may explain why the primary's result got strong second billing on the *Minneapolis Tribune*'s day-after front page. Right under the unfortunate September 13 headline "Fraser Apparently Beats Short" (he hadn't) was "Wahl Tops 3 Opponents for Supreme Court." Her large smiling photo was prominently displayed in early editions. Rosalie led the field with unexpected ease, capturing 41 percent of the vote to Mattson's 23 percent. Foley and Plunkett trailed with 19 percent and 16 percent, respectively, and were eliminated. Wahl and Mattson advanced to the general election ballot. An elated Elin Malmquist Skinner, chair of the Minnesota Women's Political Caucus, summarized the realization that was dawning on the state's political establishment: "You shouldn't underestimate the importance of the feminist movement in politics."[49]

But Wahl and her backers were about to experience how vicious judicial politics could be—even in a "Minnesota nice" state in which judges do not wear party labels. Beginning three weeks after the primary, Mattson launched a series of newspaper ads criticizing Wahl's opinions in selected supreme court cases. They portrayed her as "soft" on rape and drug trafficking, insufficiently respectful of police work, and at odds with state law. The ads bore a resemblance that could not have

Rosalie on primary election night, 1978. *Courtesy Minneapolis Star Tribune.*

been coincidental to those being aired in California that year against that state's first female chief justice, Rose Bird. Mattson also picked up where Plunkett and Foley left off, arguing that Wahl was not qualified for a seat on the high court. He embellished that argument by claiming that she had a poor record as a public defender. She succeeded in less than five percent of the cases she represented, his ad said.[50]

Mattson was seriously distorting Wahl's record. When he said she "was the *only* justice out of nine who voted to reverse the conviction of a rapist who held his victim at knife point," he was referring to a dissent that was not about rape. Rather, it concerned the rightful bounds of warrantless searches conducted by police when making an arrest. She was calling on the state's police to respect the search limitations articulated by the U.S. Supreme Court in its 1969 decision in *Chimel v. California,* a landmark ruling about police search powers. In a similarly styled ad, Mattson claimed Wahl was "the only justice to vote to suppress evidence necessary to convict an alleged drug trafficker." But drug trafficking was not the issue in the case to which he referred. The actual charge was possession, not sale, of marijuana. When reporters asked Mattson to explain his ads' contention that her "vote" in those cases "is inconsistent with Minnesota law," he responded that every dissent from the court's majority opinion is inconsistent with the law, because the majority opinion is the law until the decision is reversed or modified. He was voicing stunning hostility toward dissenting opinions.[51]

Rosalie's former boss at the state public defender's office, C. Paul Jones, put into proper context Mattson's claim about Wahl's record as a public defender. He noted that her defenses at the municipal court level, working with William Mitchell students, resulted in acquittals in about half of the cases. Appellate criminal defense is a different matter. Jones explained that the U.S. Supreme Court requires taxpayers to allow indigent defendants to appeal their convictions at public expense, leading to a large number of appeals that are unlikely to lead to a reversal. Rosalie's "success" rate of less than five percent was typical for such cases, he said.[52]

Mattson didn't stop with negative ads. He and Robert Mattson Jr. campaigned together that October, conducting their own fly-around and revving up the rhetoric against Rosalie. Mattson flatly told the *Worthington Daily Globe* that Wahl was incompetent, lacking in fair-mindedness, and "extremely biased" in favor of criminal defendants. He described her career as one entirely spent making futile appeals to the supreme court. On September 29, he filed a complaint against Wahl with the Minnesota Ethical Practices Board, which had been created in 1975 to enforce the state's post-Watergate public campaign finance laws. He complained that Wahl had designated more than one campaign committee as her principal committee and that she failed to disclose contributions of more than a hundred dollars. The complaint was promptly examined and dismissed by the board on October 16 as lacking merit—but not before generating the damaging headlines against Wahl that appeared to have been Mattson's goal.[53]

Mattson had gone too far. The harsh tone and dubious veracity of Mattson's critique rallied the state's legal and political establishment to Wahl's defense. "As a lawyer who has practiced 40 years in the various courts of our state, I deeply resent Mattson's departure from the high road of campaign tactics traditional for candidates for high judicial office," prominent Minneapolis attorney Si Weisman wrote in a letter to the *Tribune* that was typical of those that began to appear in all of the state's newspapers soon after Mattson's ads surfaced. "My resentment is not based solely on the fact that Mattson's self-serving advertisement is demeaning to the judiciary, but because it is an intentional misrepresentation of facts to the public and a serious disservice to voters." In Fergus Falls, Bill Johnson's letter to the *Daily Journal* said, "'I am sure that Her Honor is not without fault and shortcomings. But who among us is not? But heaven help us if we swallow the rhetorical poppycock of her opponent! I submit that there is absolutely no place on the bench for a cheap shot artist who, in my opinion, is apparently willing to stretch fairness and reasonableness to the very limit in order to get elected."[54]

Newspaper editorial writers around the state chimed in agreement with that sentiment, adding one thing more. By declaring "I know the importance of judicial support for the police," Mattson was coming close to violating the canon forbidding judicial candidates from making promises about how they might rule in specific cases. "Does Mattson mean that Supreme Court justices should favor the police in cases challenging arrests or searches? Is he promising to do so?" the *Tribune* asked. The *St. Paul Dispatch* added, "Any reader of the Mattson ads can make the case that they violate the canons of ordinary decency as well."[55]

Rosalie was deemed the better-qualified candidate by 76 percent of respondents to the state Bar Association's judicial candidate survey. The four past and present presidents of the Minnesota Women Lawyers organization that Rosalie helped found issued an urgent appeal. "ALL OF US SHOULD BE GIVING 100% support to her campaign," it said, asking for money, endorsements, and volunteer time. In a gesture bound to be noticed, every major statewide candidate on both the DFL and Republican tickets, plus still-recovering primary loser Don Fraser and the mayors of Minneapolis and St. Paul, lent their names to a September 30 fundraiser for Rosalie's campaign. Connolly organized the impressive event, but the idea originated with Ramsey County district judge Joe Summers, Connolly revealed long after Summers's death. The tab was fifty dollars per person for cocktails and a buffet supper, ten dollars for the evening reception and music by the Westby Jazz Ensemble (Rahn's brother's group). Fittingly, the event was at the old federal courthouse in downtown St. Paul that had recently been renovated and reopened as the Landmark Center, a venue for civic events. Just as fittingly, since all of the luminaries at the top of the two parties' tickets were male, the fundraiser was also co-hosted by every female member of the legislature and featured remarks by Senator Muriel Humphrey. The gathering and its backers underscored Rosalie's standing within the state's political mainstream. It was meant to assure skeptics that there was nothing radical or partisan about her kind of feminism.[56]

Rosalie kept up a hectic pace of campaigning. "Nobody worked harder," recalled Joan Growe, who was seeking a second term as secretary of state that year and would occasionally encounter Rosalie at weeknight or weekend events far from St. Paul. Most afternoons that fall, Rosalie would leave the capitol and climb into a waiting car for a drive to a destination outside the Twin Cities. "It was a long time afterward when I'd come out of the court out back of the Capitol and expect to be picked up by someone who would take me somewhere," she would recall.[57]

Her best chance to defend herself against Mattson's charges came just four days before the election, at a debate between the two supreme court candidates sponsored by the Ramsey County Bar Association. When he reiterated his by-then familiar litany of accusations against Wahl, she was ready. She explained that she had upheld convictions in the vast majority of the approximately 130 criminal cases that the high court had seen in the previous year and added that the cases Mattson faulted were dissents based on U.S. Supreme Court decisions. "I was defending not only the rights of criminals, but your rights and my rights," she said. Noting that misrepresentation of facts is a violation of the code of judicial ethics, she continued, "If people want to judge between the candidates for this office, they might want to look no further than the kind of campaign that is being waged."[58]

Voters unaccustomed to such intense fire in a judicial campaign evidently were watching. Many Minnesota women identified with Rosalie. Many had themselves struggled against gender-based barriers to establish careers. Many had started or restarted careers after raising families, or looked forward to doing so one day, and valued Rosalie's example. Many knew the pain of divorce and admired a woman who achieved self-sufficiency in its aftermath. Many who heard Rosalie speak to female audiences were touched as she called on women to support each other's ambitions. "Most of us, imprinted by our culture with a sense of our own limits, need to know that the horizons are wider than we ever thought they were," she said to an AAUW chapter in May—one of only a few of her 1978 campaign speeches preserved with a full text. "We need to nourish in ourselves and each other a newfound sense of self-esteem." Even Rosalie's appearance helped connect her with voters. She looked like somebody's friendly grandmother—which she was. (Her eldest grandchild, Sean Christopher Wahl, was eight years old in 1978. Five more grandchildren would be born in the ensuing fourteen years.)[59]

The court appointee who represented a breakthrough for the state's feminist movement seventeen months earlier had become an emblem of the aspirations of half the population. Rosalie won a bigger victory on November 6 than her most ardent supporters six months earlier had dared to predict. She took 57 percent of the vote, 719,234 to 551,521. That solid victory assured that, though she would stand for election again in 1984 and 1990, she would not again face serious electoral opposition to remain on the court. But its import was much larger. Wahl's success gave future governors a green light to appoint women to the state's judicial benches. The political establishment was now on notice that women in judicial robes were acceptable to Minnesotans.[60]

All over the state on election night, Rosalie's backers exulted as the votes were counted. Rosalie herself celebrated in characteristic low-key fashion, with family, friends, and song. Her party at the University Club

Rosalie joins friends in a song on election night, 1978. *Courtesy Minneapolis Star Tribune.*

in St. Paul "bore no resemblance to an Election Night party," the *Minneapolis Tribune's* Jim Parsons reported. Instead of clustering around a television set and hanging on every tally update, Rosalie and a number of fellow Friends Meeting regulars gathered around a piano for a spirited round of "Solidarity Forever" and a sweet rendition of "Amazing Grace." They fitted the seventeenth-century Puritan hymn "He Who Would Valiant Be" to the occasion by changing "he" to "she" on verses such as

> There's no discouragement
> shall make her once relent
> her first avowed intent
> to be a pilgrim.

On that hymn, Rosalie's voice was said to be particularly strong.[61]

Years later, her fellow Nightingales would report, Rosalie gave them her own copy of that hymn's lyrics. In her version, "he" was changed to "we."[62]

Chapter Seven

Seeking Systemic Change

M innesota feminists were euphoric about Rosalie's landslide victory, but the rest of the 1978 election results were deflating, particularly to DFLers. Governor Rudy Perpich was unseated by Independent-Republican (IR) Al Quie, who had represented southeastern Minnesota in the U.S. House for nearly eleven terms. The DFL governor of whom feminists had been wary two years earlier had become a hero in many eyes, despite his opposition to legal abortion.[1]

Ironically, abortion opponents also found Perpich's stance objectionable. Minnesota Citizens Concerned for Life (MCCL), the state's leading anti-abortion lobby, faulted him for not outspokenly seeking the reversal of *Roe v. Wade*. They considered him a "weak pro-lifer"—an assessment not without foundation. As he campaigned, Perpich never raised the subject of his own volition, and as governor he had initiated no policy at MCCL's behest. Many of his appointments had gone to supporters of abortion rights—including Rosalie Wahl.

On the Sunday before the election, a political committee allied with MCCL and headed by a tactically gifted GOP activist from Roseville, Marsie Leier, had arranged for anti-Perpich fliers to be placed under the windshield wipers of 250,000 cars parked near Roman Catholic and conservative Protestant churches. Perpich had declined to respond to an MCCL questionnaire, the flier said, while Quie had not only responded, but also had been a congressional sponsor of the proposed Human Life Amendment to constitutionally ban abortion.[2]

The fliers may not have affected the election's outcome. All three major statewide offices went to Independent-Republicans, and the state house—the only legislative chamber on the ballot that year—would end up tied, 67–67. Most analysts believed Minnesota voters in 1978 turned against the entire DFL ticket out of disapproval of Wendell Anderson's "self-appointment" to the U.S. Senate and dislike of DFL Senate primary winner Robert Short. But Lola Perpich maintained that Quie and abortion foes, with "a Bible in one hand and a bucket of mud in the other," had spoiled her husband's chances with an unfair smear. In a letter to the editors of state newspapers on November 24, Minnesota's first lady accused Quie of injecting religion into the campaign in violation of the state's tradition of separation of church and state. Perpich would be back—and he would remember MCCL's role in the 1978 campaign.

Independent-Republican feminists viewed Quie with misgivings similar to those with which DFL feminists greeted Perpich in late 1976. His abortion position troubled them. So did the 1978 Independent-Republican convention's selection of Bemidji school superintendent Lou Wangberg as its endorsee for lieutenant governor. Wangberg's rival for endorsement was Rochester's Nancy Brataas, who sought to make Independent-Republicans the first major party to nominate a woman for lieutenant governor.

Brataas, a state senator since 1975, had, through years of service to its organization and candidates, more than earned her party's backing. But she supported abortion rights, she was from the same part of the state as Quie, and she was a woman seeking an office no woman had held before. Before the convention, Quie had personally asked her to seek the lieutenant governor spot, but he did not push the convention to endorse her. With her senate seat not on the ballot in 1978, Brataas had ample reason to walk away from that year's campaign after the convention's rejection. Instead, she refused to fault Quie for the convention's decision and worked hard to elect the Quie-Wangberg ticket. Her selflessness won her praise from an unexpected source. DFL activist David Lebedoff observed in the *Minneapolis Star*, "What Nancy Brataas did between the IR convention and the November election has more to do with her party's landslide victory than the work of any other Republican in the state." She was hoping to keep her star shining for another day.[3]

Brataas's visible support for Quie made it easier for other GOP women to suspend harsh judgments as he took office. So did Quie's reputation as an honest, openhearted man who, during a long public career, had also demonstrated an open mind. Raised on a southeastern Minnesota dairy farm founded by his grandfather, a Norwegian immigrant and Civil War veteran, Quie had a natural conservative bent, but he was an independent thinker. A devout Christian, he viewed many public policy issues through a faith-inspired ideal of justice and human dignity.

While in Congress, Quie visited urban ghettos to school himself on race relations and poverty, building genuine relationships with the people he met. He surprised some constituents when he voted in favor of civil rights legislation in the mid-1960s. Those who were surprised likely did not know that his grandfather, Halvor Quie, had been an ardent abolitionist who nearly lost his leg at Antietam during the Civil War. As a state senator, Quie voted in 1955 for the Fair Employment Practices Act despite representing an all-white district because, as he said in a floor speech, "It's the right thing to do." Yet when, as Dakota County Republican chairwoman, Kathleen Ridder asked the First Congressional District GOP to pass a resolution commending Quie for his 1964 Civil Rights Act vote, her motion was scuttled. "They didn't want to believe he'd made that vote," she would say years later.[4]

In 1972, Quie stood with Democratic representatives Patsy Mink and Edith Green in support of the Equal Opportunity in Education Act. Better known as Title IX, that federal measure banned gender discrimination in schools that receive federal funds—which was virtually all of them. It triggered a revolution in school-based athletics in 1974 when the federal agency tasked with implementing the law decreed that it required equal opportunity for girls and women to participate. Almost overnight, women's teams formed and received the uniforms, equipment, transportation, and access to facilities that until then had been denied them at many schools. In addition, higher education institutions throughout the country began to examine their hiring and admissions policies to find gender bias and root it out, lest a lawsuit invite a judge to do it for them.[5]

GOP Feminist Caucus members including Kathleen Ridder and Marilyn Bryant aimed to put justice for women on Quie's gubernatorial agenda. On a cold day in December 1978, Ridder convened a meeting of fifty GOP feminists to listen to several women in the Perpich administration describe the effort that had been made to win their appointments. They gave much credit to Gloria Griffin as their advocate inside the governor's office. Plans were laid that day to duplicate her effort to the extent possible. They enlisted an ally in Quie's chief of staff, Jean

LeVander King, the daughter of former governor Harold LeVander and his spirited, politically active wife Iantha Powrie LeVander. Their strategy helped win women four cabinet or subcabinet spots—employee relations, human rights, securities and real estate, and consumer affairs. Kathleen Ridder snagged a seat on the sixteen-member Metropolitan Council, representing south-suburban Dakota County. While those were all second-tier spots in executive branch hierarchy, the record was strong enough that the Minnesota Women's Political Caucus convened their annual meeting at the governor's residence six months later, with Quie happy to be in attendance.[6]

Quie had vindicated their hopes in 1979 by signing into law a bill that included $3 million for battered women's shelters. It was an expansion of a first-in-the-nation pilot project that Perpich and the 1977 legislature established to bolster a pioneering effort in St. Paul to help victims of domestic abuse. In the early 1970s while working as a volunteer for Women's Advocates, a group affiliated with Legal Assistance of Ramsey County, Sharon Rice Vaughn became aware of the plight of physically vulnerable women. Many women had nowhere to go when the men in their lives turned violent, she learned. Vaughn repeatedly opened her large Victorian home in St. Paul to women in desperate circumstances. She eventually obtained foundation funding and established the nation's first battered women's shelter in October 1974. Three years later, state representative Phyllis Kahn and senator B. Robert Lewis, a DFLer from Golden Valley and the senate's first African American member, sponsored legislation for a $500,000 pilot program to establish four shelters. Their bill also established grants for the training of law enforcement officers and other professionals about battered women's trauma and needs. And, aptly, it applied a term that had been previously reserved for laid-off industrial employees to homemakers fleeing abuse: "displaced workers."[7]

The 1979 bill Quie signed not only established more places of refuge, but also made it easier for domestic abuse victims to obtain court orders for protection that required abusers to leave "the residence of the petitioner." Previously, such restraining orders were only available to women who had initiated divorce proceedings—and then judges often issued twin orders, one for the woman as well as the man, even though the woman had never been violent. The 1979 law began a process of change that would take several years, as judges slowly adjusted their patterns.

Nevertheless, its enactment was a major breakthrough and a model for other states.[8]

Quie also agreed to direct the state human services commissioner to create a childcare subsidy plan for low-income families and to spend an initial $1.5 million over two years on the project. Perpich had signed a 1978 bill authorizing that work but not directing that it be done. The 1979 bill changed "may" to "shall" and thus launched a program that by 2012 was helping about ten thousand low-income single parents afford child care and join the workforce.[9]

Nonetheless, in other ways Quie and the 1979 legislature disappointed feminists. "We had a very poor year in 1979," Gloria Griffin would recall decades later. She was at the capitol that year as a volunteer lobbyist carrying the agenda of the Minnesota Women's Political Caucus, a public policy wish list that was similar to that of the League of Women Voters, the Children's Lobby, the Council on the Economic Status of Women, the two parties' feminist caucuses, and other like-minded groups. On that list: defining sexual harassment on the job as discrimination, getting aid to longtime homemakers after divorce, reforming insurance and banking to allow wives economic independence from their husbands, and guaranteeing equity for girls in education, including curriculum reform. The list also included the most sought-after prize: requiring equal pay for equal work, if not in all employment, then at least in government, where so many women toiled in low-wage clerical positions.[10]

Several dozen women regularly lobbied for those causes at the capitol. Almost all were volunteers. Some were unprepared for the reception they received from male legislators. In March, the capitol's feminist grapevine overloaded when young family planning lobbyist Rochelle Davis reported that IR representative Gil Esau of Mountain Lake in southwestern Minnesota had turned a private lobbying session into an uncomfortable, personal conversation about sex. A few days later, testifying against a bill to deny family planning money to agencies that perform abortions (a punitive measure directed at Planned Parenthood) before Esau's health and welfare subcommittee, Koryne Horbal could not contain her anger: "We resent that we cannot lobby some of you as professionals on this subject but must contend with immature sexual overtures because you think we are talking dirty when we discuss human reproduction," Horbal said. The story was out. Headlines around the state followed as other women at the capitol told about their experiences with male legislators' inappropriate comments and unwelcome advances. Those stories were a marker of progress, assured representative Phyllis Kahn, then in her fourth term in the house. When she first came to the capitol as a lobbyist in 1971, the way she had been treated by male legislators "was a real gross-out," she said. With only one woman in the house in 1971, she felt isolated and unable to speak out without inviting retribution. With twenty women serving in the 1979 legislature, that fear was abating.[11]

Still, feminists went home frustrated. They weren't alone. The 1979 session was the only one in state history without a majority in the Minnesota house. The sixty-seven Independent-Republican/sixty-seven DFL division produced gridlock that was finally broken in the session's final days with the expulsion of IR representative Robert Pavlak Sr. He was charged with unfair campaign practices. The charge was a partisan stretch: Pavlak's sin was reproducing a *St. Paul Pioneer Press* endorsement editorial that unintentionally misstated his opponent's legislative attendance record. The error originated with the newspaper, not Pavlak's campaign, but that defense did not spare him. The DFL's power play put that party back in charge of both chambers in the 1980 session, but with a Republican in the governor's office and the nation's economy perceptibly weakening, DFL initiatives stalled.[12]

Quie's judicial appointments became another sore spot with women, even as he won praise from other judicial watchdogs for the new approach he was using to fill vacancies on the bench. Quie had long sided with critics who faulted Minnesota governors for appointing under-qualified political cronies, as they were free to do under Minnesota's constitution. Quie set out to do something different. He launched a semi-independent, merit-based screening process that he hoped would become a new norm. He established nominating commissions of eight members in each judicial district—four permanent members chosen by the judges and lawyers of each of the state's ten districts; two permanent members named by the governor; and two more chosen by the governor as "special temporary" members to consider each vacancy as it arose. Supreme court vacancies would be filled with the participation of a separate nominating commission of ten members. "Presumably the committee members will be in a position to cast the net more widely than has been done in the past and to recommend qualified people who would otherwise escape notice," one academic observer said.[13]

That sounded like a process in which female judicial applicants could fare well. But when two vacancies arose on the state supreme court in mid-1980 as associate justices Walter Rogosheske and Fallon Kelly retired, Quie's nominating commission presented him with the names of two white men: Douglas Amdahl, a district court judge in Hennepin County, and John Simonett, an attorney in Little Falls. Amdahl would go on to succeed Robert Sheran as chief justice and rank among the top jurists in state history. He and Simonett were both well qualified and highly regarded. But the July 3 appointments disappointed feminists, especially when they read in the next day's *Minneapolis Tribune* that "only one woman and no minority group members were among the twenty-five applicants considered for the Supreme Court appointments." Quie staffer Carl "Buzz" Cummins, assigned to the nominating commission, told reporters that it made no special effort to seek women or minority applicants. "The burden is on them to apply," Cummins said.[14]

"The burden is on them." Those were irritating but motivating words for the state's most active feminists in the summer of 1980. Ten years of protesting, preaching, and politicking had scored them gains that would have seemed unimaginable a quarter century earlier. Women held twenty of 201 legislative seats, and Rosalie Wahl was one of nine justices on the supreme court. But by 1980, ten-percent tokenism was not good enough. Women's labor force participation rose faster in Minnesota in the 1970s than in the rest of the nation—a pattern that would continue for the rest of the twentieth century—and stood at 54 percent in 1980. Expectations rose as fast. Women—and a growing share of the state's men—wanted Minnesota power structures to reflect the fact that half of the population is female. They were seeking systemic change.[15]

During legislative sessions, Nina Rothchild, director of the Council on the Economic Status of Women, often informally convened feminist lobbyists to share information, "cry on each other's shoulders and grow stronger." By phone and in person that summer, members of that group talked about how to quicken the pace of change. They asked each other whether a new organizational infrastructure was needed to achieve greater leverage on the economic, political, and judicial systems. They engaged their female legislative allies—Brataas, Kahn, Berglin, and others—for advice. "We all said we ought to do something about this," Gloria Griffin said.[16]

It was time for a big meeting. Griffin, Rothchild, Minnesota Women's Political Caucus chair Elin Skinner, and irrepressible Sue Rockne of Zumbrota, the DFL's most dedicated abortion rights defender, called to a meeting on September 24, 1980, every lobbyist and equity-seeking organization they could think of. They gathered at the Roseville home of Kay Taylor, a Goldwater-backing conservative Republican in the early 1960s who, by the late 1960s, was defending women's right to choose abortion well before the U.S. Supreme Court did. Fifty-three organizations sent representatives. Rothchild brought cold cuts. Griffin took charge and divided the attendees into several small discussion groups to afford everyone a chance to speak. A consensus soon formed. A network of organizations, the Minnesota Women's Consortium, would be established. It would be a clearinghouse of information and a promoter of the overall agenda embodied in the Plan of Action developed at the 1977 International Women's Year conference in Houston. The consortium would not take positions on individual issues and it would leave direct lobbying to its member organizations. It would not require its member organizations to back every element of the Houston Plan, but it asked that they not actively oppose any part of it. That much flexibility, plus inexpensive dues, made joining the consortium an easy decision for organizations. By June 1981, fifty-five organizations—two more than "everybody we could think of" nine months earlier—had their names on the consortium roster. Minnesota feminists had given birth to a potent feminist network unlike any other in the country.[17]

Gloria Griffin was unanimously chosen as consortium coordinator and assigned to recruit a staff. That task was difficult because, like Griffin herself, the staffers would be unpaid until sufficient funds could be raised—in other words, indefinitely. Nevertheless, Gloria could count on volunteer help from a personal friend, Leone Carstens, a recently divorced mother of several grown children who lived in Minneapolis. Gloria also had the youthful enthusiasm of Bonnie Peace Watkins, who had been Griffin's twenty-six-year-old assistant when she went to work for Perpich in 1977. Soon thereafter, Watkins became Nina Rothchild's one and only staffer at the Council for the Economic Status of Women. (Rothchild cut her own salary to afford the hiring of an assistant.) But Watkins remained in Griffin's orbit and looked to her as a mentor. Watkins's "day job" overlapped with her feminist avocation, which included involvement in Women in State Employment, or WISE, a network of like-minded women in state agency jobs that Watkins had helped form as an idealistic young clerical worker in governor Wendell Anderson's administration in 1974–75.[18]

At the organizing meeting at Kay Taylor's house, someone suggested that the consortium ought to produce a weekly newsletter. The idea appealed to Griffin. Watkins typed the first edition of the consortium's *Capitol Bulletin* in February 1981. It was newsy, brash, and a must-read for women seeking equality and journalists seeking tips for stories about the women's movement.

Weeks later, Griffin recruited a permanent editor—Grace Harkness, a Presbyterian missionary couple's daughter, Minneapolis physician's wife, Peace Corps alumna, antiwar and civil rights activist, chair of Perpich's Governor's Task Force on Families, and unsuccessful 1980 DFL legislative candidate from southwest Minneapolis. Out of frustration, Harkness challenged representative Bill Dean that year. The task force she chaired had recommended legislation to encourage or require Minnesota employers to adopt employment policies that would aid working families, such as flexible work schedules and parental leave after the birth or adoption of a child. "What I met with was almost total indifference, or rather sort of a patronizing pat on the head, as if to say, 'There, there, little woman, we big men are doing work on important things like sports stadiums, roads and bridges, so don't bother us,'" Harkness would write in her autobiography. Harkness lost to Dean by 1,100 votes in 1980, but she wasn't through fighting. Though the consortium could not pay her a salary, Harkness threw herself into the new organization. Years later Griffin would often say that the original "office" for the consortium was Grace Harkness's station wagon, where the organization's only typewriter resided between *Capitol Bulletin* production sessions.[19]

The consortium amplified the voices of dozens of small organizations that sought better lives for women and children. It provided the connective tissue that disparate advocates needed to become a coherent, strategic force for change. It taught rookies how to lobby and gave veterans new allies. Over time, the consortium's value would be proven time and again.

But feminist disappointment continued in 1981, both with the legislature, which struggled against stiff economic headwinds to keep the state budget balanced, and with the Quie administration over judicial appointments. That June, Quie called the first of six special sessions that would be needed in an eighteen-month span to keep the state budget in the black. About that same time, Quie learned that Chief Justice Robert Sheran intended to retire from the supreme court in December at age sixty-five, five years earlier than the court's age seventy retirement rule required. Quie wanted Douglas Amdahl, the associate justice he had appointed the year before, to succeed Sheran as chief. Like Quie, Amdahl hailed from Norwegian stock in southeastern Minnesota. Unassuming, friendly, and humbly wise, Amdahl was a popular choice. He was a seasoned court administrator, having been chief judge in Hennepin County for six years, and he was already at work on what would be his signal achievement, the creation of an intermediate Minnesota Court of Appeals. Amdahl's promotion created an associate justice opening for Quie to fill. It was another chance for him to put the second woman on the high court.

Again, Quie did not seize the opportunity. He adhered strictly to the recommendation of the merit screening process he created. Though he added two women to the screening panel for this vacancy—Reatha Clark King, president of Metropolitan State University, and Sharon Litynski, a nurse from St. Peter, Minnesota—no woman's name rose to the top. Instead, the appointment in December 1981 went to Glenn Kelley, a Third District Court chief judge who again hailed from southeastern Minnesota. "He came up the highest quality candidate," Quie would say years later in defense of his choice. "His sense of fairness and justice in everything he did made him a highly respected member of the community."[20]

Feminists did not fault Kelley's suitability for the high court, but they objected to the male dominance his appointment preserved. In a broadside in the *Minneapolis Tribune*, freelance journalist Dulcie Lawrence reported that of twenty applications screened by Quie's panel, six were submitted by women: assistant Hennepin County attorney Ann Alton, Edina attorney M. Jeanne Coyne, Hennepin Municipal Court judge Doris Huspeni, state supreme court commission member Cynthia Johnson,

St. Paul attorney Mary Louise Klas, and Ramsey Municipal Court judge Harriet Lansing. "These evidently are not the good old names the good old boys are comfortable with," Lawrence wrote. "By turning its back on these women, the Supreme Court advisory committee is telling the governor that more than 50 percent of the state's population and 11 percent of the state's legal profession needn't be taken too seriously. When the next selection panel is set up, can it be taken seriously either?"[21]

Two weeks after Lawrence's biting essay was published, Kathleen Ridder found herself on a train to Duluth in a snowstorm, on her way to visit relatives for Thanksgiving. In the same Amtrak car was Marlene Johnson, the St. Paul DFLer with whom Ridder was allied in the bipartisan Minnesota Women's Political Caucus (MWPC).

Johnson and Ridder were involved in a project of the MWPC called the Minnesota Women's Educational Council, a tax-exempt entity created in 1979 to school candidates and other interested women about the feminist public policy agenda. It had in turn schooled its founders about fundraising. To launch the council, the MWPC executive committee planned a fundraising luncheon chaired by Laura Miles. After much debate and anxiety, they agreed to charge one hundred dollars per attendee. To their surprise, the core group easily found thirty-two supporters willing to pay what was then a considerable sum.

As Ridder and Johnson reflected on that experience, Johnson shared a bigger idea. She had seen women candidates for elective office struggle to raise the "upfront" money required to be taken seriously by the male political establishment. What if a special campaign fund existed for the express purpose of providing promising women early campaign money? As snow swirled outside their train window, Johnson outlined her vision of a fund that would make significant donations to female, pro-choice candidates deemed viable by a bipartisan steering committee. It could begin with as little as $10,000, which Johnson recommended raising by asking ten women—five IR, five DFL—each to contribute $1,000. It was an audacious sum compared with the $5, $10, and $25 dues that were typical of women's organizations—but not out of line with the major donations routinely solicited by male candidates for statewide office. That was the league in which Johnson wanted women to play.

Ridder's initial reaction: "I thought it was as wild as the blizzard raging outside." But a seed had been planted. The next week, Quie made Kelley's appointment official. Days thereafter, the Minnesota Women's Education Council raised a surprising $13,000 at one luncheon—and Ridder contacted Johnson. She wanted to give the campaign fund idea a try. Ridder pledged $1,000 and set out to find four other Republican women who would make the same two-year pledge. She was surprised at how quickly the likes of Marilyn Bryant, Sally Pillsbury, Perrin Lilly, and Martha Atwater agreed, and began asking others. Marlene was making the same request of affluent DFL women, and quickly exceeded her quota. They soon had twenty-six founding donors of $1,000 each. The Minnesota Women's Campaign Fund, then and still in 2013 the only state-based organization of its kind, was on its way to a June 30, 1982, launch at the Landmark Center in St. Paul. The date was consciously chosen to give a tone of determined resolve to what otherwise would be a dark day in the annals of the women's movement. On that date, the federal Equal Rights Amendment so confidently launched in 1972 would expire three states short of ratification. Featured speakers at the inaugural luncheon were Elizabeth Griffith, co-chair of the National Women's Campaign Fund, and Madeline Kunin, lieutenant governor of Vermont and a gubernatorial candidate. Kunin's presence added to the fledgling organization's excitement about the newly chosen candidate for lieutenant governor running with former governor Rudy Perpich as he pursued a comeback. Perpich had tapped the group's DFL co-founder, Marlene Johnson. Minnesota's feminists resolved that 1982 was going to be a banner year.[22]

Two months after Ridder and Johnson's train ride to Duluth, Minnesotans were surprised to learn that their governor would not seek a second term. After a prayerful weekend, Quie had decided that he could better lift the state he loved from its fiscal distress if he were able to fly above the partisan fray as a lame duck. His assessment proved accurate. Over IR objections, Quie and the DFL-controlled legislature opted to right the state's listing fiscal ship by raising taxes rather than by ravaging education and other public services. They not only ended the crisis but also positioned the state for a prosperous finish to the twentieth century.[23]

Quie's last year also redeemed him in Minnesota feminist annals. He signed into law the most significant anti-discrimination legislation to date—a requirement that state government employees receive equal pay for work of equal or comparable value. And in August, he finally appointed a woman to the Minnesota Supreme Court.

The 1981 supreme court still included only one woman, despite two fresh appointments by Governor Al Quie. The justices: Chief Justice Robert Sheran, seated; associates from left: George Scott, John Simonett, Lawrence Yetka, James C. Otis, Rosalie Wahl, John Todd, C. Donald Peterson, and Doug Amdahl. *Wahl Papers, Minnesota Historical Society.*

The pay equity bill was the culmination of six years of painstaking data collection and coalition building. The Council on the Economic Status of Women took the lead, under the guidance of executive director Rothchild and chair Linda Berglin, the Minneapolis legislator who advanced from the house to the senate in 1980. Since its 1976 founding, the council made pay equity in state government a priority in the hope that the state, with its 34,000 workers, could set a standard that would influence private sector employment practices. The council's first report detailed that women comprised only four percent of state managers and that, on average, female state employees were paid sixty-nine cents for every dollar paid to men. However, that report made barely a ripple. The council was determined to try again. In 1981 it created a task force to establish in more detail that gender-based discrimination existed in state employment and to press the 1982 legislature for change. The task force found consistent disparities, even among positions that were identically scored under the Hay system for evaluating jobs, adopted by state government in 1979. For example, the jobs of a delivery van driver and a second-tier clerk typist earned the same Hay system score. But drivers—all men in 1981—were paid a maximum monthly salary of $1,382, while the mostly female typists took home maximum monthly pay of $1,115. It was hard for critics to refute such findings.[24]

Meanwhile, starting in 1979, women leaders in organized labor campaigned to convince male-dominated state employees' unions that pay equity would not harm them—and in increasingly prevalent two-income households, would likely do them good. "It was a big educational process," said Bev Hall, the first woman elected to an AFSCME leadership council in Minnesota. "The strategy was, keep talking it. They heard it and saw it every time they turned around . . . We talked about some of the clerical workers who were strapped, sitting out there, 22 years old with a kid or two, trying to make ends meet on six bucks an hour. The men would see we're not joking. This is real stuff."[25]

Their groundwork was so successful that to observers new to the issue, the 1982 pay equity bill seemed non-controversial. Berglin, the issue's legislative general, made it so by crafting a bill that would not require an immediate infusion of scarce state money. Rather, inequities would be identified and wage adjustments would be phased in over time—a model approach for other issues, Berglin said years later. "Lurking in the shadows was the possibility of lawsuits" if the legislature had not acted, she said. That threat helped bring skeptical legislators around, and may have eased any qualms Quie had about signing the bill.[26]

While the pay equity bill chugged toward passage on the capitol's second floor that winter and spring, feminists—many of them Independent-Republicans—were registering their opinion of Quie's judicial selection performance on the first floor, in the governor's office. He had disappointed them again when he filled a vacancy on the Second District court bench in February. Two women were among the four who won the approval of Quie's merit selection panel, but the governor's nod went to a man. In March, Nancy Dreher, the Minneapolis attorney who had been Rosalie's campaign treasurer, fired off a memo to her fellow members of the Minnesota Women Lawyers appointments committee: "Marilyn Bryant, Kathy [Kathleen] Ridder, Susanne Sedgwick, Irene Scott [the first president of Minnesota Women Lawyers] and I met with Gov. Quie to encourage him to place more women on the nominating commissions. Also we urged him to appoint a woman to the Second Judicial District, which he failed to do the next week . . . This has been one of the most frustrating experiences of my professional career."[27]

Quie had one last chance to put a justice on the supreme court. In March 1982, Associate Justice James C. Otis—whom Rosalie considered "the other feminist on the court"—reached the mandatory retirement age of seventy. He would officially step down on September 1. The Yale-educated, community-minded son of a prominent St. Paul attorney, Otis was considered one of the court's leaders. He was leaving big shoes to fill. Minnesota Women Lawyers and their allies were determined that a woman would fill them.[28]

Rosalie's ability to participate in that effort was constrained by her position on the court. But undated notes filed amid her 1982 papers disclose that when she spoke to a group of women who came to the capitol that spring, likely to lobby the legislature, she had an assignment for them. She spoke about two "crying needs" for the judiciary: the creation of an intermediate appellate court and the appointment of more women to the bench. "Nothing is more important to women in this state than getting more women into the judiciary," she said, noting that out of seventy-two district court judges, just two were women. "Gov. Quie has appointed three members to [the Supreme] Court—all men—all good men—he will have one more appointment. That appointment should be a woman. Let him know," Rosalie's notes say in bold scrawl. She urged women to seek elective office and "not to vote for men who won't support women . . . These are hard times, hard days for us—but we will give not one inch of ground to despair."

Kathleen Ridder took particular interest in this high court appointment, knowing it would be Quie's last. Ridder had served six years on the state's first Board of Continuing Legal Education, appointed by Chief Justice Robert Sheran in 1975. The board's composition illustrated the court system's hesitance to grant women decision-making roles. A dozen male attorneys dominated the fifteen-member board; Ridder was one of only two female members, neither a lawyer. (The other was Wenda Moore, then chair of the University of Minnesota Board of Regents.) Ridder was not easily marginalized, however. She learned how to join constructively in the deliberations of loquacious attorneys, winning public praise from the board's chair. She perfected that skill as one of sixteen members of the Metropolitan Council, a body charged with planning, operation, and coordination of transit, sewer, and other region-wide infrastructure-based government services. There, she learned that indirect lobbying is often more effective than the in-your-face kind.[29]

Ridder applied that lesson when Otis's retirement neared. Instead of pleading with Quie directly, she contacted Joseph O'Neill of St. Paul, who headed Quie's screening panel for the Otis position. An outgoing Irish American canny enough to win election to the legislature four times as a Republican in a DFL town, O'Neill counted nearly everyone he had ever met in politics as his friend. That included Ridder, who had been his ally on civil rights matters in the 1960s. She knew that attorney Mary Jeanne Coyne—Jeanne to her friends—had been O'Neill's contemporary at the University of Minnesota Law School in the 1950s, graduating second in her class. Knowing O'Neill—and knowing how few women would have been in his cohort—Ridder guessed that he would be favorably disposed toward her candidacy. She called him to make the case for Coyne. She'd guessed right.[30]

Unbeknownst to Ridder and other feminists, another important private phone call already had been made about the appointment. Al Quie had never met Coyne. Though nominally a Republican, she had not participated in Republican Party activities. Nevertheless, Quie had heard Coyne's name often enough in connection with judicial appointments that he wanted to learn more. He called an acquaintance in the law firm at which she had worked for twenty-five years, Meagher, Geer, Markham, Anderson, Adamson, Flaskamp and Brennan of Minneapolis. He heard fulsome praise for her integrity, intelligence, and capacity to ask rigorous, independent-minded questions. The more significant call came next: "I called her and asked her to apply" for the supreme court vacancy, the former governor related three decades later. He did not promise her that she would win his nod. "I said, 'I want you to go through the process.' I didn't think it would look right for me to just appoint her out of the blue. I wanted to make sure that when I appointed a woman, it wasn't just because she was a woman. I wanted a woman who was better than any man who applied—and she was."[31]

Justice M. Jeanne Coyne. *Courtesy Minnesota Supreme Court.*

Coyne agreed to submit to screening by Quie's panel. As he had hoped, she rose to the top, besting four male applicants, one of whom was Rosalie's 1978 primary rival, J. Jerome Plunkett. Quie announced Coyne's appointment on August 17, 1982, noting that she would make Minnesota the first state supreme court in the nation that included two female justices. Rosalie got the word while she was vacationing in northern British Columbia. She telegraphed the governor to convey her appreciation.[32]

Unlike Wahl, Coyne had been a lawyer for most of her adult life. She never married, had no children, lived in Edina, and rooted for the NFL Vikings and NHL North Stars, Minnesota's home teams. Appellate business law was her specialty. In that role, she was said to have appeared before the state supreme court at least one hundred times, which undoubtedly eased her transition to the court. Most of the male justices she joined on September 1, 1982, were personally acquainted with her. Rosalie, whose legal specialty had been criminal appellate law, was not, though she had watched Coyne in action on several occasions. But no collegial welcome was more sincere than the one Justice Coyne received from Justice Wahl.[33]

"The day she was sworn in in the morning, we heard cases in the afternoon," Rosalie related years later. "At about 5 or 5:30, as we were going out of the conference room, I said something inconsequential as I went by her. It was something I probably wouldn't have said to one of the men . . . I realized at that point that I had been lonely in a way I hadn't even realized" for five years. "I realized there had been this burden, this tremendous pressure that I was, in a sense, the representative of women there. If I made mistakes, anything I did would be held against all my gender." That burden began to lift when there was another woman in the justices' suite, someone with whom she could share a laugh, a cup of tea, and a wry observation about male foibles. Rosalie was no longer an anomaly. With a second woman present, "you can be just who you are," Rosalie said, switching from first to second person as she thought of the many other feminist pioneers who had been similarly alone and under scrutiny. "You don't have to be *all* women."[34]

Chapter Eight

Gender Justice

W omen in the judiciary "have the exhilarating sense of making history," Rosalie told an audience in the mid-1980s. That sense was
alive not only in the Minnesota judiciary, but also the legislative and the
executive branches. Rudy Perpich returned to the governor's office in
January 1983 and brought with him Marlene Johnson as the state's first
female lieutenant governor. Perpich tapped Rosalie to administer the
oath of office to him on January 3 at Hibbing High School. The return of
the governor who had been their champion lifted feminist spirits.[1]

Just thirty-six years old when elected, Johnson had ranked among
the leaders of the state's women's movement since graduating from
Macalester College in 1968. As chair, she energized a flagging Minnesota Women's Political Caucus in the mid-1970s, then became founder
and president of the Minnesota chapter of the National Association of
Women Business Owners, and later that organization's national president. Choosing her as his running mate was Perpich's signal to feminist
voters that, unlike others in the running in 1982, he could be trusted to
advance women in state government. That signal undoubtedly helped
him defeat attorney general Warren Spannaus in the 1982 DFL primary.
Spannaus had made a conventional choice for lieutenant governor, state
representative Carl Johnson of St. Peter. In doing so, he bypassed the
woman whom many DFLers considered an obvious choice, secretary of
state Joan Growe. Feminist irritation with Spannaus gave Perpich a primary election advantage and Growe a leg up as she sought her party's
nod for the U.S. Senate in 1984.

But Perpich may not have intended Johnson to be a feminist agitator
within his own office. He likely didn't think he needed one. Even before

he won his comeback bid, he was at work recruiting and appointing more women to head state agencies than Minnesota had seen to date. His cabinet included Sandra Hale at administration, Barbara Beerhalter at economic security, Ruth Randall at education, Mary Madonna Ashton at health, Irene Gomez Bethke at human rights, and Sandra Gardebring, back again at pollution control after four years as director of the U.S. Environmental Protection Agency's regional enforcement division.[2]

For the Department of Employee Relations, charged with implementing the new pay equity requirements for state employees, he tapped pay equity's leading Minnesota advocate, Nina Rothchild of the Council on the Economic Status of Women. He interviewed her twice because of the personal rule he used when he appointed Rosalie in 1977: he wanted to feel that he could comfortably hug a potential candidate before deciding that he or she was acceptable. Rothchild, a Smith College math major, was supremely professional in her first meeting with Perpich, so much so that he couldn't bring himself to offer her the employee relations post. But he valued her work at the council enough to call her back for a second try. That did the trick. Perpich told Rothchild to push the legislature to extend pay equity requirements to the state's local governments. She dove into that assignment, and he signed a ground-breaking local government pay equity bill into law in 1984.

Nevertheless, as Perpich contemplated the rare opportunity to appoint the first twelve members of a new court of appeals that the 1982 voters had given him, Johnson detected that the governor needed a feminist push. Unlike Quie, Perpich did not assign the initial screening of judicial candidates to an appointed selection panel. He and a tight-knit team of in-house advisers did their own screening. Via the office grapevine, Johnson learned that Ramsey County Municipal Court judge Harriet Lansing was at risk of being removed from the list of candidates. Two of Perpich's allies, former legislators Peter Popovich and Donald Wozniak, were at the top of his list for the first six appointments. Popovich and Wozniak were cool to Lansing, and Johnson was convinced that her gender, age (thirty-eight), and perceived pro-choice position on abortion were the reasons. Lansing had been St. Paul's city attorney—the first woman to hold that position at any large American city—through divisive litigation over expansion of the Highland Park Planned Parenthood Clinic. Although she successfully navigated those battles and went on in 1978 to be the first woman judge appointed to the Ramsey County bench, she was an object of suspicion among abortion opponents. Lansing had been Johnson's contemporary at Macalester College. Johnson went to bat for her.[3]

"I said, 'Governor, you told me you'd give me [the chance to name] a judge. If I only get one, this is the one,'" Johnson related years later. When Perpich told her Wozniak and Popovich had reservations about Lansing, Johnson countered that those two men had begun their public careers as politicians. Lansing had not. The new court needed the balance that her apolitical background would bring, she argued. "Harriet's not political. When you get Harriet, you're getting a judge for life," Johnson said. She recited the names of numerous prominent Minnesotans who backed Lansing, including Rosalie Wahl, who weighed in with a strong letter of support.

Perpich called Johnson a few days later to tell her that Lansing was on the first list of six court of appeals judges. It was not the last time the governor and lieutenant governor would tangle over judicial appointments. Their personal relationship likely suffered as a result, but Johnson was convinced that Perpich had put her on his ticket because "he wanted me there to talk him into doing the right thing" for women when he was tempted to do otherwise. "He didn't have to bring me into his office. He let me hound him on this. I was there to balance the people who were pushing him in other directions."

During the weeks prior to his July 1983 appellate court announcement, Perpich also met with Gloria Griffin, his 1977 appointments director and executive director of the new Minnesota Women's Consortium, and Ember Reichgott, the state senate sponsor of the court's enabling legislation. The first-term DFLer from New Hope was then the only female member of the Senate Judiciary Committee. Carrying the enabling bill for the new court had been a legislative plum whose taste would be soured by anything less than three women appointees to the twelve-member court, she told the governor. While in college, she had been an intern for U.S. Senator Walter Mondale, doing research for the future vice president on domestic violence prevention. The issue stayed with her. She believed the law needed to do more to shield women from violence in their homes, and she was convinced that it would take more women on the state's high courts to make that happen. Her first bill as a state senator was one to make an arrest mandatory when police found probable cause that an assault had occurred between two adults sharing a home. Too often prior to enactment of that 1983 bill, police would break up domestic disturbances but fail to arrest the perpetrator. Unbeknownst to Reichgott, she was touching on an issue that resonated with Perpich. He remembered being a grocery delivery boy on the Iron Range and encountering bruised women cowering in their own homes.[4]

In characteristic Perpich fashion, he got ahead of his own official announcement and leaked to the *Star Tribune* the names of the first six appeals court appointees. On the list were both Harriet Lansing and Susanne Sedgwick, the pioneering Hennepin County district judge who won her seat in the 1970 election. So was district judge Daniel Foley of Rochester. Rosalie's 1978 primary election rival's ambition to climb the judicial ranks was finally requited. (After 1978, he sufficiently patched his personal relationship with Wahl for her to say late in life, "I liked Dan Foley. He didn't hold grudges.") The next six names were announced in early 1984. That roster included Doris Ohlsen Huspeni, Rosalie's former colleague at the state public defender's office whom Governor Al Quie had appointed to the Hennepin County District Court bench. (In the mid-1990s, someone referred to Huspeni as "the mother" of the appeals court. Appeals court chief judge Paul Anderson privately advised her not to "sell herself short by accepting this title too readily." She tartly replied, "Paul, it is obvious that you have never been a mother.")[5]

With Wahl and Coyne on the state supreme court and Sedgwick, Lansing, and Huspeni on the court of appeals, Minnesota's leading courts changed in both subtle and distinct ways. Anderson, who would serve on both courts, attested that "the very presence of women—or for that matter, any person who is part of a minority—makes or permits the majority to think of issues and problem-solve differently." Sexist jokes aren't told. Hiring decisions are fairer to both genders. Childcare concerns among court personnel are taken seriously. Cases involving family law and crimes in which women and children are victims take on greater significance.[6]

These things did not happen automatically. Rosalie and her fellow female judges had to work for those changes. They were active agents of what Rosalie described as "the slow erosion of individual and institutional sexism."[7]

Advancing that erosion was a day-by-day, case-by-case effort for Rosa-

Rosalie on the bench, about 1985. *Courtesy Minneapolis Star Tribune.*

lie on the collegial court, which shrank from nine to seven members in 1986 as directed by the law that created the court of appeals. She employed considerable powers of persuasion, both in person and in written arguments. She had a mother's warmth, a professor's gravitas, and a poet's ability to marshal language for maximum effect. Her "sense of humor and fairness often dominated the conference room" where justices deliberated and decided cases, Chief Justice A. M. "Sandy" Keith would say. "There is no one on earth who could so effectively tell me I was wrong or misled." One of her law clerks wrote that Rosalie brought to the court "not just her fine mind and elegant words, but the best of her spirit, her feeling and her human experience . . . I saw the gift given to every case."[8]

Rosalie viewed her role as helping her colleagues see justice "from the bottom up"—that is, from the vantage not only of women, but also of disadvantaged people of all kinds, including those accused of serious crimes. She understood the Minnesota Constitution to be a document with a distinct history and relationship with the state's citizens, and one which afforded stronger protection for individual rights than does the U.S. Constitution. She respected the policymaking role of the legislature and did not try to usurp it—though she would insist from time to time that the laws pursue legitimate policy ends. But she held that Minnesota's judicial branch had a special responsibility to guard and respect the rights of every citizen, and to make sure that state government was both just and humane. She practiced what appeals court judge Lansing would call "the jurisprudence of inclusivity."[9]

While Rosalie advocated from that perspective in judicial conferences on every case, her contributions are most visible in the 529 opinions she wrote for the majority or as a minority dissenter between 1977 and 1994. One topical summary list of those opinions runs to 113 categories. The single biggest category: criminal law, one hundred cases. For most of her seventeen years on the court she remained the only justice with criminal defense experience. That may explain why she often wrote the majority opinion on criminal cases. But particularly in her early years on the court, she was known for her eloquent dissents. In 1981, the *Star Tribune* reported that Rosalie had become the court's most frequent dissenter, adding that "one expects dissent from a woman who describes herself as a 'libertarian.'"[10]

Among those cases, one stands out for the national attention it received. Though it was issued in 1991, late in her career, it merits getting ahead of our story to describe it here. In *State v. Russell*, the court invalidated a statute that imposed a sentence for possession of crack cocaine that was much stiffer than the sentence for possession of powder cocaine. That disparity in sentencing for similar illegal drugs amounted to racial discrimination, Rosalie wrote for the court, since crack was being used then in Minnesota almost exclusively by African Americans. "The predominantly black possessors of three grams of crack cocaine face a long term of imprisonment with presumptive execution of sentence, while the predominantly white possessors of three grams of powder cocaine face a lesser term of imprisonment with presumptive probation and stay of sentence," the opinion said. It did not matter to the Minnesota court whether the legislature's intention was to discriminate against one racial group—even though in 1976 the U.S. Supreme Court had ruled that evidence of discriminatory intent was necessary to warrant striking down a statute for racial bias. The Minnesota justices grounded their decision on the state constitution, not the federal one, and on an overriding sense of justice that was pure Rosalie Wahl.[11]

"There comes a time when we cannot and must not close our eyes when presented with evidence that certain laws, regardless of the purpose for which they were enacted, discriminate unfairly on the basis of race," Rosalie wrote. Legal scholars around the country took note. The opinion was praised for ending overt racial injustice and criticized as judicial overreach in law journals for years.[12]

By the reckoning of Jane Larson, a Wahl law clerk in 1985–86 who went on to a career as a professor of law at the University of Wisconsin, Rosalie's "longest-running struggle with other members of the Supreme Court" came in cases involving middle-aged women displaced by divorce from long careers as stay-at-home mothers. The divorce settlements afforded these "displaced homemakers" were adversely affected by the legislature's 1974 enactment of no-fault divorce and 1978 replacement of traditional post-divorce alimony with "spousal maintenance." With those changes came an interpretation by many family-law judges that an able-bodied woman under the age of sixty-five should not be awarded a permanent or long-enduring income supplement from her ex-husband. Courts paid less heed than they had previously to how long a midlife divorcing woman had been married, how much she had contributed to her husband's success, or how long she had been away from paid employment.[13]

Rosalie's objection to this trend appeared first in a 1980 divorce case, *Otis v. Otis*. Georgia Contos Otis was forty-five at the time of her divorce from Emmanuel Otis, age forty-six and executive vice president of Control Data, a Minneapolis-based computer company that enjoyed much success in the 1980s. His income was $120,000 per year plus bonuses; her earning potential was deemed by the trial court to be between $12,000 and $18,000 per year. That was speculation on the district judge's part. Georgia Otis had not been a paid employee since leaving an executive secretary's position shortly after her 1974 marriage. She sought to return to work at one point, but her husband forbade it. She was a regular hostess for his business gatherings, a role considered so important by Control Data that when he was interviewed for a promotion, so was she.[14]

Yet the supreme court's majority upheld the trial judge's modest maintenance award—$2,000 per month for two years, $1,000 per month for the next two years, and nothing thereafter. Rosalie joined Justice James C. Otis (no relation to the litigants) in a minority dissenting opinion. "There is no evidentiary support for the trial court's finding that her earning capacity is substantial," Otis wrote.

The *Otis* decision made waves among feminists and was noticed at the legislature. State senator Linda Berglin was busy in 1982 with landmark pay equity legislation, but she made time to sponsor an amendment to the state's spousal maintenance statute specifically to permit permanent as well as temporary awards, and to direct judges to consider the extent to which a homemaker's employable skills had diminished during years spent out of the paid workforce.[15]

Yet two more women divorcing at midlife fared no better at the hands of the high court's majority in cases that arose not long after the legislature's clarification. Beverly Abuzzahab and Helen McClelland were both married for twenty years to men who rose in their professional ranks to high-income status. Both women had pursued careers in medicine, Beverly as a psychiatric nurse, Helen as a chemistry major heading for medical school. Both had dropped their career plans when they married in the early 1960s and stayed at home, each to raise four children. In these cases, the husbands successfully appealed trial court awards of permanent maintenance to their ex-wives.[16]

Rosalie had herself experienced divorce at midlife. Though her career was well established when her marriage dissolved in 1972, she could easily identify with women in their late forties and fifties who "entered marriage under a very different set of rules" than did women "growing up in the 1960s and 1970s with careers and job skills and every expectation of sharing equally in the parenting, household work and finances of marriage." Her fury at the court majority's decision to deny Abuzzahab and McClelland permanent awards is unmistakable in strongly worded dissents, in which she was joined by the court's new female justice, M. Jeanne Coyne. "There is no indication . . . that the Minnesota legislature intended the court to turn this group of women out to lives of poverty in their later years," Rosalie wrote, quoting Berglin's 1982 senate subcommittee presentation of the revised spousal maintenance language to back up her point. "The legislature intended permanent maintenance to be, not a 'lifetime pension' in every case, but an option in those cases where the earning capacity of a long-term homemaker has become permanently diminished during the course of the marriage."[17]

"You got it right," a dismayed Berglin assured Rosalie when they had a chance meeting at the capitol in December 1984, a few days after the Abuzzahab and McClelland decisions were handed down. Berglin "was wringing her hands, saying, 'What can we say to make the court understand?'" Wahl told a sympathetic audience not long afterward.[18]

It had been a tough season for Minnesota feminists. The state's first major-party female candidate for the U.S. Senate, DFLer Joan Growe, had suffered a drubbing at the hands of Republican senator Rudy Boschwitz as he won his second term. Her defeat was disappointing but not unexpected in a year and political climate that swept Republican Ronald Reagan back into the White House for a second term. The Democratic presidential challenger, Minnesota's Walter Mondale, carried but one state—his own—and that by a spare 3,761-vote margin. Nevertheless, the patronizing tone the campaign against Growe acquired shortly before the election disheartened her supporters. Growe had made an issue of Boschwitz's failure to release his income tax returns to the public. A retail entrepreneur and the son of a successful physician and refugee from Hitler's Germany, Boschwitz was a wealthy man who refused to let voters inspect the sources of his income or the nature of his investments beyond the minimal disclosure required of U.S. senators. Boschwitz's fellow Minnesota Republican, U.S. Senator Dave Durenberger, took to the airwaves with an ad chiding Growe for her calls on Boschwitz to release his tax returns. The ad worked so well for Boschwitz that it was aired for twelve days. Durenberger's scolding tone rankled feminists, and its effectiveness with the electorate discouraged them. The ad took the tax return issue "from a question of [Boschwitz's] integrity, and shifted it to whether the campaign was a nice campaign and whose fault that was," Growe campaign consultant Bob Meek told the *Star Tribune*. Growe won just 41.3 percent of the vote. She was back in the secretary of state's office the next day, on her way to becoming one of the nation's foremost authorities on election administration. She stayed in the office for fourteen more years but did not seek higher office again. "We've paved the way, and hopefully made it easier for the women who come behind us," a prescient Growe said the day after her defeat.[19]

Rosalie's keen mind was at work on Berglin's question—"What can we say, or do, to make the courts understand?" She, too, was discouraged, judging by her remarks at a Women's Law Caucus conference in April 1986. "The struggle never ends," she said. "If women falter in their efforts, if they pause to regain strength, if the many dimensions of their lives distract them for the moment, the pervasive sexism of our social institutions sweeps like an incoming tide over the field of their endeavors, erasing all evidence of progress . . . The truth is, despite proclamations of equality, the lives of many women today are impoverished, sometimes violent and most often marginal in terms of participation, power and self-determination." Particularly galling was the status of women in her own profession, purportedly dedicated to justice. A 1984 study commissioned by Minnesota Women Lawyers Inc. found that women who graduated from Minnesota law schools between 1975 and 1981 had a median 1982 employment income of $26,810, while the comparable sum for men from the same law schools was $33,400. "For change to occur in this basic inequity of power, we must challenge the belief that the imbalance is somehow right, natural or unavoidable," Wahl said.

Six months later, Rosalie was sounding more hopeful. At an October 1986 conference jointly sponsored by Minnesota Women Lawyers and the Minnesota Women's Consortium she revealed that she had thought deeply about the stereotypes that interfered with justice for women, and that she was developing a plan of action to eradicate them. As she attended national judicial conferences, she had made connections with like-minded counterparts in other states. Citing Lynn Hecht Schafran, director of the National Judicial Education Program to Promote Equality for Women and Men in the Courts, Rosalie said she detected three prevalent stereotypes about women among judges and lawyers. She called them Mary, Eve, and Superwoman.[20]

"Mary is a woman for whom motherhood is the only appropriate goal, who remains at home participating in a limited range of activities in the domestic sphere, who does not assume positions of authority, whose chastity is unassailable," Rosalie said. Men who hold this stereotype respond harshly to women who abandon family life or put careers first, she said. Their preconceived notion gets in the way of fair consideration of questions about workplace discrimination and children's custody after divorce. Other men categorize women as the Eve of Genesis, an eternal temptress. Judges who think of women in those terms tend to be sympathetic to male defendants in cases of criminal sexual assault. The Superwoman stereotype came into play in her colleagues' thinking about Georgia Otis, Helen McClelland, and Beverly Abuzzahab, Rosalie said. Judges assumed that these women could find work at acceptable middle-class wages despite being away from the workforce for twenty years. That's what Superwoman could do, she said.

Her analysis of the male mindset about women in mid-1980s America might have been amusing had the analogy not been so apt and the consequences so damaging. Women suffered because of the biases of the men who dominated the legal system. Women were left in poverty after divorce or unprotected after abuse. They were denied fair compensation both in the workplace and in child support after divorce, diminishing their comfort and security throughout their lifetimes and pinching the lives of their children as well. When women in the courtroom—lawyers as well as their clients—were patronized with labels like "little lady" and "sweetheart" or comments about their appearance, their credibility was diminished and their ability to obtain justice compromised.

This problem was not exclusive to Minnesota, or to the courts. But Rosalie was convinced that Minnesota's supreme court had a responsibility to do something about it within its domain. By 1986, state high courts in three states—New Jersey, Rhode Island, and New York—had task forces at work studying gender bias in their courts. Assistance with those efforts was provided by Schafran's National Judicial Education Program. Rosalie had been acquainted for several years with Schafran's predecessor at the program, founding director Norma Wikler.

A sociologist at the University of California–Santa Cruz whose interest in the courts could be traced from her upbringing as the daughter of a prison psychiatrist, Wikler took a two-year leave of absence from academe in 1979 to launch the program with funds provided by the brand-new National Association of Women Judges and the National Organization of Women's Legal and Education Fund. The latter had been around for ten years, but its work had been slow to develop because, as Rosalie described the situation, "no one could figure out how to educate the judges in state and federal courts about [their own] stereotypes and biases." Wikler could. She designed a two-hour seminar on gender bias and first presented it at the National Judicial College in Reno, Nevada, in 1980. The mostly male audience "booed her and threw spit balls," Rosalie would recall years later. But female judges in the audience deemed the program a great success. It sought not to impose a "feminist agenda," as Rosalie put it, but to impart facts and instill new sensitivity about women in the courts.[21]

Wahl and Wikler first met when the latter came to Minnesota in 1981 to speak to the Minnesota Women Lawyers, whose program committee included Rosalie's daughter Sara. The hospitality shown Wikler included a tour of the state capitol, led by Rosalie. The two women clicked as friends and fellow sociologists and stayed in touch. Their correspondence in the summer of 1986 reported the positive response of a number of state chief justices at a national meeting in Omaha when Wikler reported on the New York Task Force on Women and the Courts, which she was advising as a consultant. Ten chief justices expressed interest in establishing task forces of their own. Wikler wrote that while "I do not recall hearing from [Minnesota] Chief Justice Amdahl, perhaps he could be persuaded to follow suit." In fact, Amdahl had been present and was intrigued by what he heard.[22]

Wikler's August letter ended with an enticing offer: "Now that my duties with the New York Task Force are over, and those with the New Jersey Task Force quite diminished, I would have time to serve" as a technical adviser "for a few state task forces, and Minnesota would be at the top of my list." She added that she and Schafran had just completed a how-to handbook for state gender fairness task forces, and offered to discuss how Minnesota might proceed when they gathered at a National Association of Women Judges meeting in a few weeks. Excitedly, Wahl took Wikler's letter to Chief Justice Amdahl and asked how she should respond. "He said, 'Well, when this manual is out and we get it, well, then we'll proceed,'" Rosalie recounted a few years later, adding, "Judge Amdahl is a wonderful person." At the women judges' meeting, Wikler's commitment to help Minnesota conduct its own gender fairness study was sealed.[23]

With that assurance, Rosalie got busy. She started selling the idea as she spoke to audiences. She invited court of appeals judges Harriet Lansing and Susanne Sedgwick and Hennepin district judge Cara Lee Neville, an activist in the National Association of Women Judges, to a brainstorming session about who might populate a task force. With Amdahl's blessing, their core group grew into an official planning committee that included a key figure in all state court activities, Sue Dosal, who served for thirty years as chief administrator of the state courts. By early 1987, the planning group included the president and secretary of the Minnesota State Bar Association, Richard Pemberton and Thomas Tinkham, respectively; the president of the state district judges' association, Robert Schiefelbein; Minnesota Women Lawyers president Ann Huntrods; and executive director Aviva Breen of the Legislative Commission on the

Economic Status of Women. (The council by that name had been reconstituted as a legislative commission in 1983.) Tinkham, Huntrods, and Breen would go on to serve on the task force itself.[24]

To audiences and her colleagues, Rosalie pitched the idea that the courts ought to be the first major societal institution to root out sexism by conducting a systematic self-examination. "No other institution has such profound power over our lives," Rosalie would say. She understood that the independence that judges need in order to uphold constitutional principles against popular will often breeds an undesirable insularity. It can leave judges blind to their own limitations and spare them from the challenges to their perceptions and preconceived notions that arise routinely in the other two branches of government. Rosalie envisioned a gender bias evaluation that would shine a light bright enough to show even judges where change was needed.[25]

The pitch worked. In May 1987, the seven members of the supreme court voted unanimously to proceed with the "Minnesota Supreme Court Task Force for Gender Fairness in the Courts." The official suggestion that Rosalie should be its lead came from the then-longest serving justice, Lawrence Yetka, a former Liberal Caucus legislator from Cloquet who had been a member of the court since 1973. Rosalie recalled in 1989 that Yetka said, "This task force should be headed by a member of this court to show we mean business, and that member should be Justice Wahl."

Yetka may have been the formal nominator, but the choice was obvious. By her tenth year on the court, Rosalie had become its most visible and popular member. Through written opinions and frequent speeches to female-dominated audiences, she had taught the Minnesota women's movement the importance of the judiciary and the value of the law as a force for positive change. She was a heroine among those working to improve the lot of women at midlife. "We know of no other person who speaks so eloquently on and personifies the lives of women who have made the move from 'homemaker to breadwinner' and beyond as yourself," two such admirers wrote. Rosalie's reputation as a champion for the wronged and disadvantaged had grown to match the slogan on the 1978 campaign button she had rejected: "Wahl for justice, justice for all." After one of her many speaking engagements, an African American single mother approached her to let her know that she and her thirteen-year-old daughter had clipped Rosalie's photo from the newspaper and taped it to the wall of the stair landing in their home to serve as daily inspiration. It's doubtful that any other state supreme court justice had that kind of following.[26]

Yet while the gender fairness project had strong backing from her six supreme court colleagues, some quarters of the state's judiciary were less supportive. Judges were supposed to epitomize fairness. A report pointing out their shortcomings could dent public respect for the judiciary, some argued. Rosalie said in 1988 that she was being approached with some frequency by male judges who said "in confidence that[,] of course, there is gender bias out here. But that's the way it is and the study will make us look bad." Rosalie heard the complaints but pressed on, putting her own reputation on the line as she did. "She wanted the reality of fairness, not the appearance of fairness," Lansing said.[27]

Sedgwick signed on as the task force's vice chair. In 1987, Sedgwick was fifty-five years old—eight years Rosalie's junior—and had been a judge for more than sixteen years, longer than any other woman in Minnesota. She was among the founders of the National Association of Women Judges. She also had been battling breast cancer for seven years. Her spirits were high. "She was an unremitting blast of positive sunshine even in the worst of times," Lansing said of her colleague. No doubt Wahl and Sedgwick discussed "what if" questions as the project began. Sedgwick maintained that if this was the work that consumed the last of her strength, it was a worthy choice. The trio quietly agreed that Lansing would function as "co-vice chair" and increase her involvement if Sedgwick's health deteriorated.

Twenty-seven others joined Wahl, Sedgwick, and Lansing. They included ten male and three female judges representing each of the three tiers of the state court

Minnesota Court of Appeals judge Susanne Sedgwick, about 1986. *Courtesy Harriet Lansing.*

Harriet Lansing, Rosalie Wahl, and Norma Wikler, likely at the National
Association of Women Judges conference in 1986. Of this photo, Lansing would
say, "I am not sure whether the 'danger' and 'hard hat area' warnings were intended
to be part of the picture or not—but I think they accurately capture its spirit."
Courtesy Harriet Lansing.

system; three public members; and eleven attorneys, one of them a legislator, senator Ember Reichgott, well positioned to take the task force
recommendations for statutory change to the legislature. Every part of
the state was represented. The roster included a well-known Rochester
attorney, A. M. "Sandy" Keith. A brilliant, gregarious charmer, Keith
had served as lieutenant governor from 1963 through 1966. His 1966 bid
to replace Governor Karl Rolvaag, his fellow DFLer, faltered in the DFL
primary, and the party's split contributed to the election of Republican
governor Harold LeVander that year. Twenty years later, Keith was a respected attorney and Governor Rudy Perpich's friend and political ally.
His presence on the task force enhanced its credibility with the male judicial establishment. It was a fortuitous choice for another reason: in 1990,

Keith would become the supreme court's chief justice, and the changes the task force recommended for the courts would be his to oversee.[28]

The group came together quickly, aided with funding for staffing and research provided by the 1987 legislature, the State Bar Association and Foundation, the State Justice Institute, the Women Judges Fund for Justice, and the supreme court itself. But the task force's biggest re-cruiting and organizing advantage was Rosalie. "No one could say no to her," Kathleen Ridder said. Lansing added, "Everybody knew she wasn't asking for herself, but for a greater good." Besides, Lansing said, those who knew Rosalie were aware that if they rejected her request for help, whatever needed doing would be done by Rosalie herself—and she was already overbooked. "If she were scheduled to give a speech, the light above her bed would be on until the early morning hours," Lansing said. As the task force ramped up in the summer of 1987, Rosalie marked her sixty-third birthday.[29]

Norma Wikler was good as her word. As the task force's consultant and adviser-in-chief, "she was our guru," said Aviva Breen. Wikler spent many hours in conversation with Rosalie as they decided how to proceed. The task force's budget was tight. To reduce costs, Norma often stayed with Rosalie at the Lake Elmo farmhouse when she came to Minnesota for meetings. She told the task force that a survey of judges and attorneys should be part of their research, but that a survey alone was not suffi-cient. Low response rates to gender fairness surveys in other states had undercut their credibility. The Minnesotans should also invite public comment in writing and at a series of well-publicized hearings.[30]

Six such evening meetings, three hours in length, occurred between March 29 and June 7, 1988, one each in Moorhead, Marshall, Duluth, and Rochester and two in St. Paul. In addition, four open-microphone meet-ings, exclusively for attorneys, unfolded in Minneapolis, Duluth, Roch-ester, and St. Cloud. Each task force member committed to attending at least three of the meetings; Rosalie attended them all. Given the driving distance involved for some members and the fact that most of them had to be at work early the next morning, this was a major commitment.

The hearings were emotionally as well as physically taxing for task force members. The public turned out in unexpectedly large numbers, and, in Quaker meeting style, Rosalie wanted to hear from all who desired to speak. More than sixty people testified. The stories were "instructive and sobering," Rosalie said. Anger and frustration poured out as testifiers related episodes of disrespect and injustice for which no remedy seemed available. "Ordinary, indeed extraordinary, citizens— men and women—came forward with great difficulty and obvious effort to share their agonizing experiences of how the court system had dealt with them," Rosalie would say later. One of the reasons they came was Rosalie's understanding of the underdog, Ember Reichgott Junge said years later. "She was the leader we absolutely had to have. I did not realize how difficult it was going to be to roll this rock up the hill. You needed a strong voice that people respected, and she was that, and also firm, really firm—someone who would not take the excuses that had been given by the courts for years."[31]

Accounts involving family law and domestic violence predominated. For example, an attorney in greater Minnesota described a case in which a man and woman were both charged with assault. The woman had broken the man's glasses, and there was a long history of more serious assaults by the man on the woman. Instead of focusing on that history, the judge joked with the man, "I'll bet you $20 that you'll be back together within a week." The woman asked that the situation not be treated as a joke. The judge responded dismissively, "You know what the joke is, it's this relationship."[32]

Many of the stories that would be told and retold originated outside the Twin Cities metro area. At a hearing in Rochester, a woman said that a judge in a family law case stated that he believed her husband's testimony "because he was under oath." She pointed out to the task force, "I was under oath too." A women's advocate told of a woman who had managed a dairy and grain farm with the assistance of her sons while her husband was employed elsewhere. When the couple divorced, the judge awarded the farm to the husband. "It was his livelihood and source of income," the judge explained. In another divorce case, a judge accepted a husband's argument that the wife was an unfit mother because "she kept a messy house," even though both parents were living in the home at the time that a custody evaluator investigated the situation.

Reichgott Junge easily recalled one witness's testimony twenty-five years later. It was the story of a trial at which, after evidence was presented about a husband who had assaulted his wife, the judge turned to the victim. "You know, if you had had dinner on the table, this wouldn't have happened," he said. Task force members audibly gasped at that account, Reichgott Junge said. "It forever changed my thinking about the psychology that can justify abuse."

The task force heard about a judge who made light of the complaints of a woman alleging domestic abuse: "So he slapped you around a little, didn't he?" They heard about another who told a woman seeking help in getting her ex-husband to make court-ordered monthly payments: "I'm tired of seeing you here." They heard frequently about court orders for protection that were not enforced, leading to more injury and occasionally to murder at the hands of ex-boyfriends and husbands. "We were told in many different ways that we judges forget how enormously powerful we are," Rosalie said.[33]

To an extent that surprised task force members, the testimony was also replete with anecdotes about demeaning treatment of women in every courtroom role—lawyers, reporters, and administrators, as well as litigants and defendants. At hearings in the Twin Cities, the task force heard about an "old boys' network" involving judges and male attorneys from which female attorneys were excluded, to the disadvantage of their clients. When judges and male attorneys banter about sports and hunting, it "leads clients to think the judge likes the male attorney and doesn't like the female attorney . . . It creates client management difficulties and casts a shadow on the judicial system," a female attorney said.

A common complaint concerned questions about women lawyers' status as attorneys. Seventy percent of women lawyers surveyed said that at least sometimes a judge, other attorneys, or court personnel questioned whether they were attorneys or surmised that they were assistants or secretaries to male attorneys. Some women told of being forced to show the judge their licenses to practice law, which diminished their standing in the eyes of clients and jurors. A woman attorney in the Twin Cities described this incident: "There were four attorneys sitting at the counsel table—three men and myself. The judge said, 'Would the three attorneys please approach the bench?' The other attorneys, somewhat embarrassed, said, 'Which three?' The judge then turned to me and said, 'Oh, I'm sorry [first name], you can come too.'"[34]

Some women reported judges commenting about their sexuality, either directly to them or to male attorneys who related the remarks to them. A male attorney in greater Minnesota reported that a judge said in chambers that it was really hard to listen to female attorneys when "really all you can do is think of screwing them." A female attorney in the metropolitan area reported hearing judges and male lawyers agree in chambers that certain female attorneys "needed a good lay." One male judge stated that he was glad a particular female attorney was wearing a pantsuit so that he wouldn't be tempted to look up her dress. A female public defender in Ramsey County said she had been a waitress in restaurants and bars "so it's not like I haven't experienced this stuff before. But when you are up there [at the bench] trying to do something on behalf of your client and the judge can't peel his eyes off your chest, well, it pisses me off."[35]

"Going into this, we thought these things happened rarely," said task force member Aviva Breen. After all, by the late 1980s, the share of female graduates in the state's law schools had surpassed 40 percent. One out of every five practicing attorneys in Minnesota was a woman. The task force had reason to expect that the courts had adjusted to the presence of women. "But we were wrong. It was everywhere—every corner of the state. We began to see that the way women were treated in our courts was a broad problem that we had to take more seriously."

As significant as the hearings were the results of a survey of the state's attorneys, scientifically structured so that it represented the same proportion of male and female, metro and outstate attorneys as existed in the state as a whole. The large sample—4,288—and high 83.5 percent response rate to the mail-in survey allowed for a margin of error of less than two percent. The fact that the survey results corroborated the hearing testimony gave a high degree of credibility to both. In addition, all 281 of the state's trial court judges were surveyed by mail. Likely because of strong encouragement by Chief Justice Amdahl, 93 percent of them responded.[36]

The surveys painted a picture of routine disparate treatment. A third of female attorneys reported that judges did not address them in a professional manner in courtrooms. Their names were replaced by "Dearie" or "Little Lady," or their first names were used while male lawyers were addressed as "Counselor" or "Mr. Jones." Their fellow attorneys were worse. "In a deposition, a male attorney called me a 'whore' and told my client to hire a 'real attorney,'" one woman wrote on her survey questionnaire. Women judges were not immune from being addressed in a substandard manner. They reported being called "Ma'am" or even "sir" by attorneys, rather than "Judge Jones" or "Your Honor."[37]

Two out of five women attorneys said judges made public comments about their appearance; three out of five said that male attorneys did the same. "After the verdict I stopped in chambers to discuss the trial," one woman wrote on the survey. "I asked the judge if he had any feedback to offer me. The judge told me that I should wear high heels in front of a jury and not shoes with a flat heel."

Big differences emerged in the survey responses of male and female attorneys. Episodes of unequal treatment were not only widespread; they were invisible to many of the men who were witness or party to them. Half of male attorneys, but only nine percent of female attorneys, surveyed said they had never seen gender bias exhibited in courtrooms. Nearly a third of women reported that judges used disparate forms of address for women litigants, while only seven percent of male attorneys said that happened. While 40 percent of women reported that judges often made comments about women's appearance, only 15 percent of male survey respondents reported hearing such remarks. Jokes in the courtroom or in judicial chambers that poked fun at women were heard "sometimes" or "often" by 47 percent of the female attorneys but only 13 percent of the males. Such jokes were deemed objectionable by 83 percent of women judges but only 37 percent of their male counterparts.[38]

Just as the task force's fact-gathering was at its peak, a sad blow came. Vice chair Susanne Sedgwick died on April 8, 1988, at the age of fifty-six. Her office at the state court of appeals had been vacant for some weeks as her cancer progressed. But Judge Dan Foley—Rosalie's 1978 primary rival—made a point to turn on her office's lights each workday. "I will not let that room be dark," he told the *Star Tribune*'s Jim Parsons on the day she died. "Sue was a giant sequoia. I miss her terribly." Rosalie added, "She was No. 1 to all the women lawyers in the state . . . By all rights, she should have been the first woman on the [state] Supreme Court." Rosalie said the "last work [Sedgwick] put down" before her death pertained to the task force.[39]

The task force decided to dedicate its report to her. "Some leaders have a way of casting a shadow, and those who follow walk in that shadow. But with Sue, we always walked in her sunshine," Lansing wrote for the dedication page. Task force member Laura Miles and feminist allies Barbara

Adams and Marilyn Bryant organized a fundraiser for the task force as a tribute to Sedgwick. The June 29, 1988, event, with Rosalie as its featured speaker, raised more than $25,000 to fill a funding gap that had emerged in what would eventually be a $200,000 project. About half of that total came in the form of in-kind staffing contributions by the Commission on the Economic Status of Women, which Breen headed, and the supreme court's administrative office, headed by task force member Sue Dosal.

By the end of 1988, an interim report—largely the handiwork of Harriet Lansing—had been delivered to Chief Justice Amdahl, and the drafting of what would be the final 203-page report had started. It was divided into four sections: domestic violence, family law, criminal and civil law, and courtroom environment. The project's staff director, Mary Grau, and its reporter, Marsha Freeman of the Humphrey Institute of Public Affairs, asked the drafters to draw liberally from survey results and hearing testimony, so that their findings and recommendations would be well grounded in evidence. Recommendations would be of two kinds: changes that would require legislation and remedies that the judicial branch could engineer on its own. Wikler instructed the writers to keep their focus on judges. While "gender bias in the courts is a systemic problem, and . . . many other court players are involved, the unique mission of this task force is to promote judicial self-scrutiny," Wikler counseled.[40]

Meanwhile, change was coming at the top of the state's court hierarchy. Chief Justice Amdahl, a champion of the task force and its mission, had reached the mandatory retirement age of seventy and would step down on January 31, 1989. Governor Perpich chose Associate Justice Peter Popovich to succeed Amdahl, and appointed A. M. "Sandy" Keith—the member of the Gender Fairness Task Force whom Rosalie would call "our stalwart"—to the high court. Though Popovich was sixty-eight years old and would be required to retire less than two years later, Perpich rewarded his old friend with a promotion in recognition of his groundbreaking service as the state court of appeals' founding chief justice from 1983 to 1987. Popovich was highly regarded, but not known for feminist sympathies, which may have been the reason that, almost nine months before its final report was ready for release and a month before his retirement, Amdahl issued an order creating a nine-person standing committee of the court to implement the task force's recommendations. It was signed on December 22, 1988, and stipulated that the committee's chair, for a term of three years, would be Associate Justice Rosalie Wahl.[41]

Giving that much running room to the implementation committee before the report went public proved a smart strategy. Stepped-up judicial education and sensitivity training would figure prominently in the recommendations. As other task force members put the finishing touches on their drafts, Rosalie and her new committee developed preliminary plans for teaching judges how to eradicate gender bias in their courtrooms. They wanted that plan ready when the report went public, to assure Minnesotans that the courts were already at work correcting the problems the task force had found.[42]

They also wanted to frame their findings in a way that would ease their acceptance by their primary audience, the state's judges. To that end, Rosalie went to the Minnesota district judges' annual conference on June 15, 1989, with a carefully crafted message. Without disclosing details, she allowed that the report would show that "we need some work" in family law, domestic abuse, acquaintance rape, and access to the courts for low-income women. It would show that "judges could be more conscious of the impact their words and behaviors have." But her chief message was positive. "By your participation, you showed that you realize the significance of gender bias and its capacity to undermine the personal goals you have set for yourselves and for the system in terms of objectivity and fairness," she said. "It stands to reason that if we want to influence society to be fair and just and free of limiting beliefs, that we, in the judiciary, are in a prime position to lead the way." Rosalie assured the district judges that, when it was time to go public, she would praise the judiciary as "the first major societal institution to conduct a far-reaching self analysis on this issue."[43]

That was the theme she pounded when the report was released on September 6 and in the days thereafter. Its public debut came at a rare 6:30 PM news conference at the capitol, "the heart of the state's judicial system." It was tactically scheduled to follow the day's judicial conference in Brainerd, at which the task force's report was presented and a three-hour training session about domestic abuse was conducted for the first time. That timing allowed Rosalie to announce to reporters: "We have gone beyond naming the problem, gone beyond identifying it, to coming up with an action plan to address it. Our intention is to eradicate any remnants of gender bias that may exist in the Minnesota court system." Chief Justice Popovich and former Chief Justice Amdahl both stood at her side. Popovich said he was "shocked as to the extent of the problem." Henceforth, "attitudes that result in undermining women and their credibility are not acceptable and will not be tolerated," he said.[44]

Media interest in the report was considerable. The next day, Rosalie did twenty five-minute radio interviews before 9 AM and eight more with newspapers and television stations before 11 AM. While Rosalie accentuated the positives—the Minnesota judiciary's commitment to fairness, its precedent-setting self-scrutiny, and its already-begun effort to correct lapses—journalists ferreted out the bad news. "Gender Bias Found in Courts," a *St. Paul Pioneer Press* headline announced on September 7. The *Star Tribune* of the same day reported that Minnesota judges often display insensitivity when dealing with domestic abuse victims. State statutes outlawing such abuse and requiring abusers to leave the home were strong, the task force concluded, but police often failed to make arrests in such cases, believing prosecutors would not pursue them. Prosecutors in turn believed judges would not hold offenders accountable. The upshot was an unrealistic burden on abuse victims themselves to follow through in enforcement. "Often the very women seeking orders for protection understandably lack the courage to follow through," commented Ramsey County district judge Mary Louise Klas. "I'm gravely concerned over the extent to which domestic violence exists and the extent to which our protection laws are not being enforced."[45]

Reporters found plenty of grist for stories in the report's family law section. It told that financial settlements in marriage dissolution cases are stacked against women, especially when they are the custodial parent of minor children. Child support awards in Minnesota were deemed inadequate. Property divisions in divorce typically left men, not women, with income-generating assets. Judges consistently overestimated the earning capacity of divorcing women who had been out of the workforce for long periods. The custodial mother and children's standard of living decreased 45 percent after divorce, while the non-custodial father's increased by 50 percent, the task force found. Further, gender-based stereotypes too often governed child custody decisions, to the disadvantage of both fathers and working and/or impoverished mothers. As task force member A. M. "Sandy" Keith put it, child-support guidelines "function as a ceiling," reducing the standard of living of the custodial parent and children while leaving the non-custodial parent far better off. "We've got to educate the courts and all involved and see to it that custodial spouses have enough money to raise the children," Keith told an audience of St. Paul attorneys in one of many meetings aimed at acquainting the state's entire legal community with the report's findings.[46]

Cases involving rape by an acquaintance also revealed systemic bias. The courts too often treated such victims as though they had implicitly consented to the violent act, the report concluded. Disparate treatment of the genders extended to juvenile cases. Teenage girls were being punished more often and more severely than juvenile males committing the same misdeeds. Female runaways in particular received harsher sentences.[47]

While those were compelling findings, journalists were drawn to descriptions of the sexist gauntlet women had been running in Minnesota courtrooms. "If a person ignored the title page on the report of the Minnesota Supreme Court Task Force for Gender Fairness and began paging through the abundant anecdotes sprinkled throughout, she or he might conclude the environment being described was not a courtroom, but a locker room," reported a feature story in *Minnesota Lawyer* magazine. Another account likened the experience of women attorneys in court to "what they might expect when passing a construction site." Those embarrassing words were keenly felt in some judicial quarters, despite the fact that the report did not name names or lay blame. Judge Roberta Levy (Rosalie's 1977 rival for Perpich's supreme court appointment was by then chief judge of Hennepin County District Court) felt obliged to comment that "the anecdotes are shocking, and they were obviously meant to be shocking, in order to affect even more change. But that doesn't mean that enormous changes haven't already taken place."[48]

The legislature's leadership, senate majority leader Roger Moe and house speaker Robert Vanasek, took great interest in the report and sent a copy to every legislator with a cover letter asking that it be read and studied. The legislature's two judiciary committees invited Rosalie to a rare joint meeting on October 31, 1989, while the legislature was not in session, to present the report's findings. She also testified at hearings during the 1990 session. "This is your report too," she told legislators in thanks for the $50,000 state appropriation that gave the project its financial foundation. Her prepared remarks for the 1990 hearings focused on domestic abuse, noting that 1,500 American women were murdered by their husbands or boyfriends in 1986. "You have given us excellent domestic abuse statutes—some of the nation's most progressive—and knowledgeable advocates of enforcement. But our task force found compelling evidence that domestic abuse victims do not receive the relief, either civil or criminal, which you intended."[49]

Spurred by senator Ember Reichgott, the task force's sole legislative member, the 1990 legislature set out to change that. Rosalie was her partner in explaining and selling the report's long list of recommendations. Lawmakers embraced most items on that list, and Governor Perpich eagerly signed them into law. As a result, police no longer needed to witness a violation of an order for protection by a domestic abuser in order to make an arrest. Courts were authorized to require violators of orders for protection to post bonds "sufficient to deter the respondent from further violations." Violations were deemed criminal misdemeanors, not just matters for contempt citations. Causing a death while committing domestic abuse after a pattern of such misconduct became a qualification for a charge of first-degree murder.[50]

The task force recommended that all of the state's prosecuting county attorneys be required to have a plan for the effective prosecution of domestic violence cases. On that point, the legislature decided to proceed gradually, with five pilot projects aimed at reducing the share of domestic abuse charges that are dismissed before prosecution. It also ordered a feasibility study of a statewide computer database on domestic assaults, accelerating the development of a new crime-fighting tool. A few years later, both the database and an every-county requirement for a domestic violence prosecution plan were reality.[51]

The family law statutory changes that the task force sought also came quickly. Child custody language was amended to include a presumption that joint legal custody is not in the best interests of the child if domestic abuse has occurred. The factors that judges are required to consider in determining custody were changed to focus on the child's relationship with the parents and his or her need for stability, not on the parents' wishes. Judges were required to make detailed findings on each of the factors outlined in the statute and to explain how the factors led to its conclusion. Judges were also directed to be more generous in awarding temporary attorneys' fees to low-income parties to divorce, so that each spouse could press effectively for justice in family court.

Meanwhile, Popovich was true to his word. Effective January 1, 1990, he issued amendments to the rules of conduct for judges and attorneys that made gender discrimination or harassment explicit grounds for discipline. Later that year, the mandatory retirement rule that Popovich resented caught up with him, and he retired. Fortunately for the gender fairness cause, Perpich's selection to succeed him as chief justice was task force member A. M. "Sandy" Keith.[52]

More good news for the state's feminists was coming at the Minnesota Supreme Court. Two vacancies arose in 1990. The first was created when one of Governor Quie's appointees, Glenn Kelley, reached the age of seventy. That seat went to Esther Tomljanovich—Rosalie's Lake Elmo neighbor and friend—who had served to much acclaim as a Washington County district judge for thirteen years. Her appointment took the gender balance on the high court to four men and three women—Wahl, Coyne, and Tomljanovich.

The second arose when Popovich retired and Keith was elevated to chief justice. That move was announced in midsummer, and observers expected Perpich to fill the seat before Popovich hung up his robe in November. But Perpich was embroiled in one of the most tumultuous election campaigns in state history that fall, and he tarried with judicial appointments as he fought to hang on to the governorship. After ten years in office, Perpich had slipped considerably from his peak approval levels in public opinion polls, but he thought he had a shot against Republican primary winner Jon Grunseth, a businessman who had run unsuccessfully for Congress in 1974. Grunseth's personal life had included a messy divorce, which Perpich pointed out to voters against the better judgment of his advisers.[53]

No one in the Perpich camp knew that more salacious news about Grunseth was on the way. In a series of revelations by *Star Tribune* investigative reporters in October, Grunseth was accused of nude swimming with teenagers at a party and repeated marital infidelity. Less than two weeks before the election, Grunseth resigned from the race. His decision set up several days of high legal drama as first DFL secretary of state Joan Growe, then the supreme court itself, determined that the name of the Republican who had finished second in the September primary, state auditor Arne Carlson, should replace Grunseth's on the ballot for governor. Perpich was furious with that outcome, and particularly stung that three of his appointees—Wahl, Tomljanovich, and Keith—sided with the 5–2 majority. Among Perpich's appointees, only Popovich—who was literally on his way out of his office when the November 1 ruling was handed down—rejected the argument that Carlson deserved to be on the ballot.[54]

Five days later, Perpich lost to Carlson. It wounded Perpich deeply that he would go down in state annals not only as Minnesota's longest-serving governor but also as the first incumbent to be rejected twice by voters. His dark mood permeated the capitol as 1990 came to a close. For weeks it seemed that the last thing on his mind was how to fill one more supreme court vacancy. But as his term neared its end, Perpich set out to make judicial history once more. On January 4, 1991—his last full day in office—Perpich appointed appeals court judge Sandra Gardebring to

The four women of the Minnesota Supreme Court in 1991. From left, Esther Tomljanovich, Rosalie Wahl, M. Jeanne Coyne, Sandra Gardebring. *Wahl Papers, Minnesota Historical Society.*

be the fourth woman on the seven-member supreme court. That made Minnesota the first state in the nation to have a female majority on its high court. Gardebring was a talented Perpich loyalist who had served his administration as head of three state agencies before taking a seat on the court of appeals. She also supported abortion rights. Her appointment was a hat trick for Perpich: it made history, it rewarded a friend, and it was a parting shot at the state's increasingly Republican-allied anti-abortion forces.[55]

Political payback was Perpich's last-day theme in a flurry of district-level judicial appointments. He elevated his campaign manager, John Stanoch, and a number of other friends to the bench. He knew that awarding judgeships to cronies on his way out the door would trigger a howl of criticism. Nonetheless, he knew that those complaints would soon die down, but his transformation of the supreme court would be remembered. His legacy would be as the governor who did more than any other, in Minnesota and arguably in the nation, to bring women into full participation in the third branch of government. In so doing, he helped bring a fuller measure of justice to half the population. That achievement was prominently cited in the outpouring of tributes to Perpich that came in September 1995, when he died of cancer at age sixty-seven.[56]

Chapter Nine

Never Discouraged, Never Done

S ix months after the Gender Fairness Task Force's report was released, Rosalie sat down with Norma Wikler, her law clerk Laura Kadwell, and a tape recorder. They were conducting what Norma called "fireside chats," with the intended audiences of gender fairness analysts in other states and future historians. Rosalie could have launched into a litany of her accomplishments through three years on the task force and thirteen years on the supreme court. Instead, what poured from her that day was concern for the plight of homeless children, made recently fresh by the release of U.S. census data showing that 50 percent of Minnesota's homeless people were the very young. She had also learned that federal/state welfare payments to a single parent of one child were less than four hundred dollars per month, not enough to pay for rent in most of Minnesota, let alone life's other necessities. As she described society's weak response to the basic needs of impoverished children, her indignation showed.

"We are willing to spend money to bail out the savings and loan [industry] and we're willing to spend money for new prisons. We're building the new prison down in Faribault and as the projections go, we'll need more and more space to put people away when they break the law and frighten people—as these will when they get older and don't have anything," she said.[1]

Though Rosalie was sixty-five years old in early 1990, she wasn't about to retire from seeking justice for the homeless, disadvantaged, and victims of discrimination. To her, that quest was the purpose of both the law and the women's movement. She held that, as women advanced into previously all-male regions of power, they had a special responsibility to "transform our specific knowledge of shifting social rules and limiting assumptions about the individual capabilities" into "a broad ethic of fairness to all persons whose existences are controlled by such cultural limits."[2]

She was about to take on a new assignment. Admirers of the Gender Fairness Task Force in the state legislature began asking Chief Justice Peter Popovich in 1989 whether a similar study could spot and help root out racial bias in Minnesota's judicial system. Rosalie admired the impulse but voiced concern about whether the gender task force's approach was the right one for the more complex and emotionally charged phenomenon of racial disparities. Court records made the experiences of men and women fairly easy to distinguish. That wasn't so about race. Race-based data existed statewide on sentencing outcomes, but on not much else outside of Hennepin County. Rosalie also wondered about the timing of a study that would come hard on the heels of the gender report. Would a new report's conclusions and recommendations get the attention they deserved? She urged that a feasibility study be undertaken. But Senate Judiciary Committee chair Allan Spear, who represented an inner-city Minneapolis district, and representative Andy Dawkins, who served a similar population in St. Paul, saw the good that the Gender Fairness Task Force had done. They were convinced that the same approach would benefit Minnesota's minority populations. They put their conviction into a legislative directive in 1990 that appropriated $50,000 from state coffers for that purpose. Popovich responded by assembling a fourteen-member planning committee, headed by Associate Justice Rosalie Wahl.[3]

There would be no Norma Wikler this time to guide the work, and no Sue Sedgwick and Harriet Lansing as helpmates, but there were models in other states to follow. New Jersey, New York, Michigan, and Washington had completed analyses of their state judicial systems' disparate treatment of racial minorities, and five other states had such work in progress. And there was Hennepin County district judge Michael J. Davis, a brilliant jurist with a background in criminal defense for the disadvantaged. An African American and a native of Ohio, Davis had been a contemporary of Lansing and Marlene Johnson at Macalester College, an attorney at the Neighborhood Justice Center in St. Paul and the Legal Rights Center in Minneapolis, an assistant public defender in Hennepin County, and an adjunct professor at William Mitchell and the

University of Minnesota, all before becoming a judge in 1983. He was also Rosalie's son-in-law, married since 1980 to her elder daughter, Sara, and the father of two of Rosalie's grandchildren. Davis joined Rosalie on the planning committee, and when the task force was officially assembled, he took charge of its criminal process committee (a shared assignment with Hennepin district judge Pamela Alexander) and its editorial committee, which would draft the report.[4]

In Michael Davis, Rosalie had the able and committed partner that another major extracurricular project would require. She also had the assistance of Hennepin district judge LaJune Lange and Ramsey district judge Salvador Rosas as task force co-chairs. In December 1990, the Minnesota Supreme Court Task Force on Racial Bias in the Judicial System was launched with thirty-two members that included state government's top lawyer, attorney general Hubert Humphrey III, and state senator Linda Berglin. The scope of the report was set. It would focus on judicial practices, not police practices—a decision that disappointed some constituencies but was true to the task force's mission of judicial reform. Data collection had begun and an ambitious schedule of ten public hearings was set for the fall and winter of 1991–92—two in Minneapolis, three in St. Paul, and one each in Albert Lea, Bemidji, Duluth, Marshall, and Moorhead. In addition, fifteen focus groups representing elements of the judicial system were assembled.[5]

With Davis at her side for all but one public hearing, Rosalie led each one. Her forecast that this task force's work would be complicated and emotionally charged proved prescient as the hearings brought out angry stories of perceived and real discrimination. Task force members heard about police who refused to respond to violence in minority neighborhoods, minority victims of assault blamed for their own injuries, a black student sent to juvenile detention after a school altercation while the white students involved were simply sent home. They learned that black parents believed the purpose of juvenile court was to break up minority families. Minority children who might temporarily be placed with grandparents or other relatives were often sent to live with majority-race strangers instead.[6]

Just as with the gender study, the Racial Bias Task Force elicited many complaints about judges' treatment of not only minority defendants but also minority attorneys. Some judges routinely belittled minority mothers at hearings to determine whether their children should be placed in foster homes, the task force was told. One nineteen-year-old mother was badgered to accept a "deal" to give up custody permanently of one of her two children in order to be allowed to keep the other. One Minnesota judge reportedly asked a defendant with a black attorney if he would like a white attorney instead. Another judge continually mistook a black attorney for the defendant during a court proceeding.[7]

The hearings were exhausting, "but she never got exhausted," Davis said of Rosalie twenty years later. "She was able to bring everyone together. When you're talking about the minority community, you are talking about many different communities with a lot of different positions. Every group was jockeying for position to make sure its stories were told. She was able to bring everyone together because everybody respected her. They knew she was pure of heart and had fought long and hard for equal justice for all. She rallied the troops. No one else could have calmed the waters."

In Minnesota, the face of equal justice under the law was Rosalie Wahl's. She was an essential component of the trust on both sides of the racial divide that would be essential to the report's credibility. When the *Minneapolis Spokesman* newspaper, the state's oldest African American–owned business, published an appeal to its readers to participate in the task force's hearings, it quoted Rosalie at length to make the case: "Incidents of racially motivated crimes, as well as criticism of the treatment of minorities in contact with the legal system, have risen dramatically over the past few years. The people must know that even one instance of racism within the judicial system is one too many." Rosalie emphasized that this task force had staying power. "This task force is patterned after the Gender Fairness Task Force that spent two years gathering information about sexism and is now in its second year of implementing recommendations. The Gender Fairness Implementation Committee continues to meet on a monthly basis. It has put into action recommendations that have brought about changes in legislation and judicial education to aggressively work toward the elimination of gender bias in the court system."[8]

She was willing to stake her reputation on the promise that this task force would do the same. Her introduction to the final 138-page report pleaded for persistence:

People of color came forward at public hearings, angry
and anguished, saying, "This is just another study!" This
cannot be "just another study." People trusted us enough
to come and make their feelings known. We who are the
stewards of this justice system cannot fail the people it
belongs to . . . This we vow: That we will not cease our efforts until this court system, of which we are so proudly a
part, treats every person equally before the law—and with
dignity and respect—regardless of such irrelevancies as
race or gender or class.[9]

Her reassurance was needed to ease judges' qualms too. Racism was
more socially unacceptable than sexism in 1990s Minnesota. Few judges
could survive their next election if a credible task force pointed at them
as racists. Judicial fears about what the task force would find were not
trivial, but trust in Rosalie outweighed the jitters—or at least muted
them. Judges were loath to cast aspersions publicly on her efforts.

The report's findings, issued on June 10, 1993, were predictable, yet
dramatic. Although people of color comprised six percent of the state's
population in the 1990 U.S. census, they comprised 45 percent of its
prison population. People of color were imprisoned at a rate that was
at least 12 percent greater than the white imprisonment rate for iden-
tical convictions of aggravated robbery, criminal sexual conduct, and
weapons offenses. In Hennepin County, which kept the most comprehensive statistics about race in court proceedings, people of color ac-
counted for 11 percent of the population and 36 percent of arrests. The
fact that people of color also experienced higher dismissal rates following arrests for misdemeanor assault, theft, and prostitution suggested
that too many of their arrests lacked sufficient grounds for prosecution.
A Hennepin County study found that arrested African Americans were
significantly less likely than whites to be released with no bail required—
and African Americans were also less likely to be able to post bail once
set. As a result, African Americans comprised 65 percent of the county's
detained population.

The pattern continued in matters of family law. Minority children
were greatly over-represented in the foster care system. They comprised
more than one-third of out-of-home placements in Minnesota. Rosalie's

cheat-sheet from the report's rollout has the following notation scrawled in her own hand: "Native American children are removed from their homes and placed in foster care at 12 times the rate of white children, this despite the fact that we have the Indian Child Welfare Act and the Minnesota Minority Preservation Act."

The report inspired a raft of recommendations. Many of them involved better data collection. It called for the legislature to require counties to keep track of arrests and case dispositions by race, age, and gender as well as by type of offense. Sunlight was essential to change, the task force maintained. The hiring of more non-white court personnel, including as prosecutors, and stepped-up racial sensitivity training were also key recommendations.

Following the gender task force's example, an implementation committee was formed—but this time the assignment did not go to Rosalie. The newest member of the high court in 1993 got the nod, foreshadowing the role he would play on the court in her wake. Associate Justice Alan Page arrived at the court in an unconventional way with an unconventional résumé. An NFL Hall of Fame defensive tackle for the Minnesota Vikings, 1967–78, and the Chicago Bears, 1979–81, Page in 1971 was the first and one of only two defensive players ever to win the Associated Press sportswriters' Most Valuable Player Award. He was a fan favorite, even as his focus turned to a different dream at the University of Minnesota Law School from 1975 to 1978. Page practiced law in Minneapolis in the off-season beginning in 1979 and year-round beginning in 1982. In 1984, he moved to the attorney general's office, rising to assistant attorney general. Almost from the start, he had his eye on an appellate judgeship. A quiet, thoughtful scholar and excellent writer, Page knew himself well enough to realize that he was well suited to the dispassionate intellectual exertion required of an appellate judge.[10]

But he also accurately judged that waiting for a Republican governor to appoint him was not likely to bear fruit. Page instead went to the voters in 1992. He had to do so by way of court action. In 1992, Justice Lawrence Yetka's six-year term was expiring, and he was eighteen months away from his seventieth birthday and mandatory retirement. Page planned to file for Yetka's seat and run against him if he chose to seek another term. Yetka instead tried to take his seat off the 1992 ballot via an appeal to Governor Arne Carlson to extend his term until his retirement. It was an unconventional ploy, but Carlson played along. Page filed a lawsuit in response. The supreme court appointed a special panel of judges to hear the case, headed by Rosalie's old rival Daniel Foley, by then retired from the court of appeals. The panel voided Carlson's move; Yetka announced his retirement; and Page faced little-known Hennepin County prosecutor Kevin Johnson on the 1992 ballot. Page was a heavy favorite, yet he overcame his innate reserve to stump the state as if he were the underdog. He arrived on the supreme court as its first African American associate justice on January 4, 1993, with the tailwind of a 62-percent share of the 1992 vote.[11]

Rosalie immediately liked the tall, shy newcomer to the Minnesota Judicial Center, the remodeled and enlarged former Minnesota Historical Society building that became the high court's home in 1992. Her confidence in him bolstered these words from the Racial Bias Task Force report's executive summary: "After more than two years of research and study, one might assume that many of us have grown disillusioned. We have not. We have come to the end of this part of the process full of faith and great hope that the recommendations found here will soon be implemented, as was the case with the Gender Bias Task Force Report that preceded our work in 1989."

Another wellspring of the faith and hope that passage invoked came from within Rosalie herself. As she exhorted audiences through the years not to "give one inch to despair," she was sharing watchwords she had chosen for her own life. "Her strength comes from the waters of Birch Creek," Michael Davis said with a proud smile as he spoke about his mother-in-law's leadership. "In all the years I've known her, I've never heard her say a bad word about anybody. She is always so positive—but not naively. There is also an understanding that there's a battle to be won. I've never seen her lose hope."[12]

Rosalie's unique mixture of compassion and toughness undoubtedly sprang from the experiences of a farm girl raised by sturdy women in hardscrabble 1930s Kansas, as Davis suggested. But it was also tested by loss and disappointment, and renewed and sustained by the faith she shared at Friends Meetings. Participation in Quaker congregations was a constant in Rosalie's adult life. There, she gained and shared spiritual sustenance among people who shared her sense that a divine presence is real and abides in every member of the human family.[13]

Each summer, Rosalie invited her past and present law clerks to a picnic at her Lake Elmo farm. The occasion often included singing, led by Rosalie. *Courtesy Wahl family.*

Faith was an animating force in her professional life, those who know her best attest. "It informed her decision to go to law school," said Mary Alice Harvey, who outlived all the other members of the original Circle Pines intentional community that brought Rosalie to Minnesota. "She chose the law very intentionally to be of service to the entire community." Another good friend and Friend Gail Lewellan said that the belief that God is present in all and with all of humanity was central to Rosalie's thinking about the law and undergirded her work to improve the judicial system. The small-group worship practices of Friends Meetings encouraged Rosalie to apply her ideal of justice to here-and-now questions. After the meetings' trademark periods of silence, Rosalie was a frequent speaker. She adopted as her own the Quaker preference for plain, direct speech, as well as a Quaker's appreciation for the power of silence. "Over time, she became well able to articulate spiritual growth and development, and the social testimonies," Harvey said. "She became a leader."[14]

The Race Bias Task Force report was the third of Rosalie's lasting transformations of the Minnesota justice system. First, she opened the political door for the appointment of more women judges. Next, she led the fight to root out sexism in the way the courts treated women. The Racial Bias Task Force report raised judicial consciousness of the ways in which Minnesota courts were treating white and non-white people differently. It helped reduce that disparity as its recommendations to the legislature became law and those to the courts were implemented. But even as the judiciary became more alert and resistant to racial bias, Minnesota's white and non-white populations were growing apart in income, education, health, life expectancy, and opportunity. Regrettably, a racial imbalance in arrests, incarceration, criminal sentencing, and children's out-of-home placement has proven discouragingly enduring.[15]

One more major professional transformation bears Rosalie's strong imprint. All the while she served on the high court, she never stopped pushing for the inclusion of hands-on, practical experience in law school curricula in Minnesota and the nation. As a result, the American Bar Association Section of Legal Education and Admission to the Bar gave her its prestigious Robert J. Kutak Award in 1994 for exceptional contribution to the increase of understanding between legal education and the active practice of the law. No woman had achieved that honor before.

Rosalie's connection to the national clinical education movement started before she was appointed to the high court. When an American Bar Association accreditation team visited her new Mitchell clinical

Rosalie in 1994. *Courtesy Minneapolis Star Tribune.*

education program in the mid-1970s, she struck up a friendship with William Pincus, then the director of the ABA legal education section's governing council and later hailed as "the grandfather of the clinical movement" in law schools. He recruited her to join an accreditation team that visited the law school at her undergraduate alma mater, the University of Kansas.[16]

That positive experience sparked her willingness to become the state supreme court's liaison to the Board of Bar Examiners when that opportunity arose in 1980. In Minnesota, as in most states, the supreme court requires that those admitted to the legal bar must be graduates of ABA-accredited law schools. The liaison assignment and her accreditation team service positioned Rosalie for appointment to the ABA's Accreditation Committee, which she chaired in 1983–84. She was its first female leader and could choose who would fill the committee seat traditionally reserved for a non-lawyer. That's how Kathleen Ridder became an ABA committee member not long after completing a four-year term on Minnesota's Metropolitan Council.[17]

This was no small responsibility. Overseeing the ABA's inspection and review of the nation's law schools involved four meetings per year, each of three days' duration, and plenty of homework in between. Despite an intense workload in Minnesota, Rosalie performed at such a high level that she was invited to move up to the ABA legal education section's governing council, and then to take its chair in 1987—again as the first woman to hold its gavel. That put her into the orbit of Robert MacCrate, American Bar Association president during that same year. A New York attorney and son of a congressman, MacCrate had been chief counsel to Governor Nelson Rockefeller in the early 1960s and special counsel to the U.S. Department of the Army when, in 1969–70, it investigated what became known as the My Lai massacre by U.S. troops in Vietnam in 1968. Like Rosalie, he grew up in an active Methodist family and had a passion for extending the rule of law to women and minorities. He became Rosalie's collaborator in her effort to bring practical, experiential learning out of the shadows and into respected prominence in America's law schools.[18]

When, as the section council's chair in 1987, Rosalie arranged for a conference in Albuquerque, New Mexico, to discuss the state of clinical education, MacCrate agreed to be a featured speaker. Half of the

American Bar Association Accreditation Committee, Indianapolis, 1983. Rosalie sits in the chair's seat; Kathleen Ridder is standing, second from right. *Wahl Papers, Minnesota Historical Society.*

law schools in the country sent representatives to what she called the National Conference on Professional Skills and Legal Education. The meeting's goal was to assess the progress and acceptance of clinical legal education in the nation's law schools. One-third of the attendees were women—a fact that would have pleased Rosalie save her awareness that it signified the second-class status that clinical education still had. Rosalie's keynote address at the four-day confab set its agenda. She pointedly asked why the ABA's accreditation standards required law schools to offer "adequate training in professional skills," but neither defined what that meant nor required law school graduates to take part in such training. It was time to unify clinical teaching with traditional curricula, she argued.[19]

The Albuquerque meeting shifted the legal education reform movement into high gear. In its wake, just when Rosalie was ending one major judicial reform task force in Minnesota and launching another, she conceived the idea of a commission that would probe deeply into the heart of legal education. It would identify and define the skills required of an attorney and how best to impart them to law students. She sought the help of the ABA's consultant on legal education, Professor James White of Indiana University, and the chair of the ABA section's skills training committee, Professor Roy Stuckey of the University of South Carolina, in defining the commission's charge. Then she recruited MacCrate to head the effort and twenty-five other ABA leaders from around the country to join them, hand-picking each participant. The stellar cast she attracted, including law school deans at New York University and the University of California–Los Angeles, was a tribute to Rosalie's leadership.

She served as an active member of the commission and nothing more, leaving the spotlight to others. Together they produced a legal education landmark. Entitled *Legal Education and Professional Development: An Educational Continuum,* the 1992 report was known shortly and ever after as the MacCrate report. It identified ten fundamental skills that a lawyer should possess: problem solving, legal analysis and reasoning, legal research, factual investigation, communication, counseling, negotiation, litigation and alternative dispute resolution procedures, organization and management of legal work, and recognizing and resolving ethical dilemmas. It also identified four fundamental values the profession requires: providing competent representation, striving to improve the profession, offering professional self-development, and striving to promote justice, fairness, and morality. The emphasis on fairness and morality was pure Rosalie.[20]

The MacCrate report included sixty-four recommendations, many directed at law schools. Among them were calls to clarify the interaction between traditional core subjects and practical instruction and to require that schools prepare students not only to pass bar exams but also "to participate effectively in the legal profession." That language was added to the ABA's accreditation standards the following year.[21]

That change in wording was all that the ABA's Section on Legal Education and Admission to the Bar was willing to do to push law schools to change. Faculty members at some of the nation's most prestigious law schools had little experience actually practicing law, and they were loath to move outside their comfort zones. "They say, 'We are so good, why should you care whether we meet the standards or not? Do not bother us,'" Rosalie said in 1994 of the major schools' resistance to accreditation changes.[22]

The minimal acceptable change wasn't enough for Robert MacCrate or several other ABA leaders who admired the MacCrate task force's work. And it wasn't enough for Rosalie. In 1994, as she was closing in on her professionally significant seventieth birthday, she agreed to chair one more ABA panel, officially called the Commission to Review the Substance and Process of the ABA's Accreditation of American Law Schools. Informally, it was the Wahl Commission. Its report in 1995 recommended that, in order to achieve ABA accreditation, a law school must offer all its students instruction in professional skills, including one rigorous legal writing experience. Further, each school's pre-accreditation self-study needed to document how it prepared its students to do the actual work of lawyering. While that was still short of requiring that all graduates complete a practicum experience, it moved the needle in the direction of more clinical experiences for more students. Within a year, the ABA's House of Delegates adopted the Wahl Commission's recommendations.

Like the rest of American higher education, law schools change slowly. Fifteen years after the Wahl Commission issued its recommendations, the *New York Times* was still reporting about career-preparation deficiencies at American law schools. But Rosalie's goal of legal education that combines the scholarly with the practical advanced significantly because of the panels she crafted and the work they did.[23]

Within a week of turning seventy—and without the foot-dragging some of her male colleagues had exhibited—Rosalie retired from the supreme court on August 31, 1994. Her long nights at the farmhouse kitchen table, pouring over cases and drafting opinions in longhand until past midnight, were coming to an end. In line to replace her: Edward Stringer, Governor Arne Carlson's chief of staff and a former general counsel and chief administrative officer for the Pillsbury Company. He had also served as general counsel to the U.S. Department of Education under President George H. W. Bush. Stringer was highly qualified and able, but feminists sighed as his appointment took away the Minnesota Supreme Court's 4–3 female majority. Nineteen years later, that 1991–94 distinction still stands alone among high courts in U.S. states.[24]

Rosalie counseled against ruing the diminution of female representation on the court. "The important thing is that it happened at all," she told *Star Tribune* courts reporter Donna Halvorsen as she prepared to leave office. She left knowing that she had won over her critics. Former state senator Fritz Knaak, a Republican attorney who had led his party's criticism of Perpich's judicial appointments as too liberal and inexperienced, had only good to say. "She entered the court with a lot of raised eyebrows, and she leaves it with the respect of almost everyone," said the Roseville lawyer. "It's a reluctant concession, but I have to make it."

A *Star Tribune* editorial on the day she retired said, "In 17 years of wise and selfless service, the court's first female justice has opened countless doors: for women, for the poor, for people of color, for the unlucky. Even people who have never heard Wahl's voice should lament its absence from the high court's halls."[25]

Wahl went home to the Lake Elmo farmhouse, but she was not through speaking out. She was still in demand as a public speaker. With the judiciary's strictures against partisan political activity removed, she was again free to be an active DFLer. She had missed that kind of activism while a justice, she confessed during her 1990 "fireside chat" with Norma Wikler and Laura Kadwell. "I think that what I'm doing on the court is important. But I am no longer able to be active in the political process, and I guess I think that the political process is the way by which we've got to solve some of these problems," she said, referring to the widening income inequality in America that was leaving too many children homeless. "I just plain and simple don't believe that individuals . . . can solve these problems. I think we have to do it on a broader scale."

Retirement also meant more time for family, which by 2007 included six grandchildren and two great-grandchildren; the St. Croix Valley Friends Meeting, which looked to her for wise words each week; and her garden, books, poetry, and music. It provided a chance for more community service, including involvement with the young women's leadership training program of the American Association of University Women. Rosalie cheered in 2000 as Minnesota sent a woman, DFLer Betty McCollum, to the U.S. House of Representatives for the first time since voters sent representative Coya Knutson home in 1958. Six years later, she rejoiced when DFLer Amy Klobuchar became the state's first woman elected to the U.S. Senate. And she was elated when more women joined the Minnesota Supreme Court: Kathleen Blatz, appointed to the court in 1996, elevated to chief justice in 1998, and retired in 2006; Joan Ericksen Lancaster, 1998–2002; Helen Meyer, 2002–12; Lorie Skjerven Gildea, appointed to the court in 2006, elevated to chief justice in 2010; and Wilhelmina Wright, the court's first African American woman, appointed to Meyer's seat in 2012. Each of them acknowledged a debt of gratitude to Rosalie Wahl.[26]

Awards kept coming, too. The one that may have meant the most was the Joan Dempsey Klein Honoree of the Year Award, the top honor of the National Association of Women Judges. It had been given first, in 1982, to

Rosalie Wahl, 2008. *Photo by Ann Marsden.*

U.S. Supreme Court Justice Sandra Day O'Connor, and two years later, to Minnesota's Susanne Sedgwick. Rosalie was the winner in 2004, the year she turned eighty years old.

As she reached her mid-eighties, Rosalie's public voice fell silent. Age took its toll. She left her beloved farmhouse and joined the St. Paul household of her daughter and son-in-law, Jenny and Patrick Blaine. She enjoyed family gatherings, including one for son-in-law Michael Davis's birthday on Sunday, July 21, 2013. That evening, several brief blackouts led to her hospitalization at Region's Hospital in St. Paul. Early the next morning, Rosalie died.

Tributes flowed for weeks afterward. At a September 21 memorial service at Central Lutheran Church, former Minnesota chief justice Eric Magnuson, once Rosalie's student, called her "a beacon of compassion on the court . . . One of her deepest-held beliefs [was that] we are all human. We are all in this together. The law isn't a contest of strength. It's a collaborative effort to find justice."

Harriet Lansing, retired in 2011 after twenty-eight years on the Minnesota Court of Appeals, invoked the words of poet Emily Dickinson. Lansing and Wahl's last visits in 2012 and 2013 had included readings and recitations of Dickinson's work. "As our connections to Rosalie move, as Emily Dickinson would say, from syllable to sound, her clear, unwavering voice will remain with us," Lansing said.

> In the dreams and aspirations of young women all across
> Minnesota, we will continue to hear the sound of her
> voice. In the lives of young women and men who reach out
> to make this a fairer and more just world, we will continue
> to hear the sound of her voice. In the vibrant yellow of a
> Kansas sunflower on a beautiful blue morning, we will
> glimpse the sound of her spirit. In the concept of what it
> means to be a fully human judge with a jurisprudence of
> inclusivity, we will hear the sound of her voice. And in our
> hearts and souls, wherever the spirit prevails, we will be
> able to hear the notes of Rosalie's voice, maybe even lifted
> in song.

In 2012, Rosalie's voice was heard by new audiences through the release of a fine feature-length documentary, *The Girl from Birch Creek*. The work of Lightshed Productions filmmakers Emily Haddad and John Kaul, it came to fruition with a grant made possible by the voters of Minnesota in 2008. By a 56 percent majority—bigger than President Barack Obama's Minnesota margin that year—voters approved a 0.375 percent sales tax increase dedicated to the preservation and enhancement of natural resources and the arts. It was a demonstration of the power of the people's collective action. Rosalie undoubtedly approved.[27]

At William Mitchell College of Law—where Rosalie's portrait hangs in a well-trafficked corridor—she was strong enough to attend a January 29, 2013, screening of the film and acknowledge the audience's applause at the end. After the screening, a panel discussed women's past, present, and future contributions to the legal profession. It included Professor Ann Juergens, co-director of William Mitchell's clinical program, now housed in an office suite named the Rosalie Wahl Legal Practice Center; Jessie Nicholson, CEO of Southern Minnesota Regional Legal Services;

and three judges—Associate Justice Wilhelmina Wright of the Minnesota Supreme Court, Judge Susan Richard Nelson of the U.S. District Court, and retired judge Mary Louise Klas of Ramsey County District Court. They agreed that a key element of Rosalie's legacy is the law's greater embrace of the entire human experience.[28]

"I had been taught in law school that emotion had no place in law—that to be legally analytical, I needed to set my feelings and even my values aside," said Juergens, who graduated from the University of Minnesota Law School a year before Wahl was appointed to the supreme court. The male-dominated legal culture of that era reinforced the sense that participants in the judicial system, from defendants to judges, "had to set their feelings aside and stick to the facts." With Rosalie's arrival, that changed.

> Having strong women in my life and another like Rosalie on the bench helped me realize that there is a lot of important information in people's emotions and feelings. To give the best arguments, I needed not only intellectual analysis, but also I needed good in-touch emotional information and I needed my personal values . . . I wanted to know my clients' feelings. Why do you think this happened? When the boss did that, what was your reaction? Not just what did you do, but what did you feel? Rosalie Wahl, in her jurisprudence and in her teaching, always cared about how the law made people feel. Incorporating that into our advocacy and into justice is more possible because she was on the Supreme Court.[29]

Juergens made the same point in a 2003 article. Rosalie held that "the underlying unity that lawyers must seek is that of heart with intellect," she wrote. "Wahl prized goodness and kindness equally with intelligence, and found them everywhere in people. She listened to emotional information and valued it when solving problems. She was very good at reasoning, but never presumed that reason excludes perceptions gained from emotion." For generations, the iconic image of justice has been a blindfolded goddess holding a balanced scale, denying herself the impressions she would gain from her own eyes. Rosalie believed Lady

Justice should have her eyes open and all of her senses fully engaged. She pushed the legal system to value life's emotional and psychological components. As a result, today it responds with more alacrity than it once did to crimes such as acquaintance rape and child and spousal abuse. It better emphasizes the well-being of children in cases of marriage dissolution. It is more sensitive to discrimination in hiring, educational opportunity—and, recently, marriage.[30]

For Rosalie and for the feminists who strove to put women into all three branches of government, securing and safeguarding human wholeness was a primary purpose of the law. It was also the ultimate aim of the mid-twentieth-century women's movement. Participants in that movement sought equality for their own sakes, to be sure, but also for the good their elevated status and wider opportunity might bring to men and children. A more humane society for all would be the result, they maintained.

That goal is yet to be achieved, even within the legal profession. With female students comprising 42 percent of the University of Minnesota Law School student body and 49 percent at William Mitchell, the profession is now well populated with women. But like many other American professions, it has not adjusted its practice to accommodate society's need for each generation to raise the next one properly. As Judge Susan Richard Nelson said, it's still common at large law firms for promising women attorneys to lose ground when they become mothers, while male attorneys pay no such career penalty for becoming fathers.[31]

Justice Wilhelmina Wright said that the law has become "an equal-opportunity employer for a single-career family." Women can succeed as both lawyers and mothers provided their husbands are willing to be the primary caregivers of their children, but the legal workplace has not been willing to define the requirements of success as anything less than a sixty-, seventy-, or eighty-hour-per-week commitment, regardless of one's parental status. And an attorney's decision to pull back from her career while her children are small still often results in a permanent loss of opportunity and earning power. "I don't think we as a society and as a profession can afford to lose all of that talent," Wright said. "We need to have that talent working toward justice, equality, representation of diverse clients, bringing the way women think to problem-solving. I want to see the law provide greater opportunity for both men and women to have rich family lives *and* rich professional lives."

Wright's concern reaches far beyond the legal profession. For many Americans today—both men and women—the work-life balance tips too far in work's favor. It's as if male-dominated professions said to women in the 1970s and 1980s, "Sure, little lady, you can come to work here. But don't expect us to change one bit what we demand of workers because you've arrived. You must work as long and hard as any man—or harder, since we'll be watching you. What happens at home is your business, not ours." If anything, employers' expectations for more—often much more—than forty hours per week from their employees grew with the arrival of the ubiquitous Internet.

At home, more American men today report sharing household maintenance and childrearing chores than their fathers did, but women still carry a heavier load. Though more than 70 percent of mothers of Minnesota grade school children have been employed outside the home for more than a generation, schools continue to dismiss children for the day at mid-afternoon and offer little or no programming during the long summer recess. Most employers offer no on-site childcare or other provision for employees' small children. The recent trend has been toward ending, not expanding, corporate experiments in flexible work hours and sites. Federal law requires employers of fifty or more employees to provide up to three months of unpaid parental leave in the year after the birth of a child, and Minnesota law says employers of twenty-one or more workers must allow six weeks of unpaid leave. But parents employed by small employers enjoy no such protection, and nothing requires the paid parental leaves that are standard in many other developed countries.[32]

Altering the American workplace to be friendlier to mothers, fathers, and the children they raise together is a major unfinished item on the agenda pursued during the American women's movement's so-called "second wave." Historians use that term about the period from 1960 to 1990, to distinguish it from the women's suffrage movement, which started at an 1848 meeting in Seneca Falls and concluded sixty-eight years later with ratification of the Nineteenth Amendment to the U.S. Constitution. The second wave can be said to have reached its zenith in Minnesota in 1991, with the 4–3 female majority on the Minnesota Supreme Court.

A year later, Rosalie observed that some women lawyers were "unwilling—not unable, but unwilling—to do some of the things that are required if you practice law in a certain way, to give up all the things you have to put aside to be [a] successful lawyer in certain fields . . . Money is not the first thing in their lives." She was not criticizing their choices. To the contrary: she was praising them for refusing to bow to professional demands set predominantly by men. And she voiced a hope that was prevalent then: "If you get more women there as senior partners, there will be more change." That hope has been tempered in the intervening years, as a number of women who climbed into executive suites conspicuously opted to reinforce existing norms rather than reforming them. It increasingly appears that if a greater measure of humane wholeness is to come to all who populate the American workplace, the impetus for change will need to come not only from women at the top but also from the grassroots—just as it did in the women's movement's first two waves.[33]

There's more on the feminist agenda of the 1970s that remains relevant in the 2010s. Pay equity is still elusive. The U.S. Census Bureau reported in September 2013 that, on average, the nation's working women earned seventy-seven cents for every dollar men earned, a ratio that had not budged in five years despite considerable dislocation for male workers during the Great Recession. Though domestic violence rates have dropped significantly in the last twenty years, one-third of the women murdered in the United States each year still die at the hands of a current or former husband or boyfriend. Though women have made great inroads in previously male-dominated professions, in 2012 women still held only 16.6 percent of board of directors' seats at U.S. Fortune 500 corporations. Minnesota has yet to elect a female governor.[34]

What Harriet Lansing said of Rosalie at her memorial service, quoting an inscription that Rosalie herself often quoted from a nineteenth-century New Hampshire woman's tombstone, is a fitting epitaph for the twentieth-century Minnesota women's movement as well: "She done all she could." But more change is needed. More change is coming. The Baby Boomers' daughters are on their way. Bring on the next wave.

Notes

Notes to Chapter One

1. Much material in this chapter derives from the author's interviews with Rosalie Wahl on October 31 and November 7, 2009, and Jenny Blaine's interview with her mother on April 1, 2009.

2. Sarah Almeda Patterson was born February 20, 1902. She dropped the "h" from her first name while in high school. Transcript, "Interview with Minnesota Supreme Court Associate Justice Rosalie Wahl," by Laura Cooper, professor, University of Minnesota Law School, August 17, 1994. Courtesy of Ann Juergens, professor, William Mitchell College of Law.

3. Mary, born January 3, 1918, married Frank Drake and lived much of her adult life in Colorado. Jeanette, born April 13, 1920, married a man named Conlee; she worked in banking, played championship badminton, and lived in Seabrook, Texas. Cooper interview with Wahl.

Rosalie lived briefly with her father and his second wife in Towanda, Kansas, when she was in first grade, because her grandmother thought that the distance from the Patterson farm to the Birch Creek School was too far for the first grader to walk. American Bar Association Commission on Women in the Profession, Women Trailblazers in the Law, "Oral History of Rosalie E. Wahl," interviewed by Hennepin County district judge Cara Lee T. Neville, March 18 and July 8, 2006.

4. Cooper interview with Wahl, 17.

5. Rosalie's first presidential vote, cast in 1948, was for socialist Norman Thomas, she said in an oral history interview with Professor Ann Juergens of William Mitchell College of Law. She added that Aunt Sara was also a Thomas voter that year. "She wouldn't have ever told the family and I don't know how I happened to know, but I did," Rosalie said.

6. Speech to Retired Educators Association of Minnesota, 1995, included in Marvin Roger Anderson, ed., and Susan K. Larson, assistant ed., *The Social Justice, Legal and Judicial Career of Rosalie Erwin Wahl*, Minnesota Justices Series 12 (St. Paul: Minnesota State Law Library, June 2000). Transcript, *Rosalie Wahl: A Vision for a Better World*, film by Jonathan Quijano, John Knauss, and Evan

Beaumont, Minnesota's Greatest Generation "Moving Pictures" film festival, 2008.

7. For an overview of the Dust Bowl's causes and impact, see Timothy Egan, *The Worst Hard Times* (New York: Houghton Mifflin Harcourt, 2006).

8. Ann Juergens interview with Rosalie Wahl, August 13, 2002. Transcript, *Rosalie Wahl: A Vision for a Better World.*

9. Juergens interview with Wahl. Billie Young and Nancy Ankeny, *Minnesota Women in Politics: Stories of the Journey* (St. Cloud, MN: North Star Press, 2000), 132.

10. Cooper interview with Wahl.

11. Young and Ankeny, *Minnesota Women in Politics*, 133.

12. Transcribed from "Small Songs, 1943–1973" by Rosalie Wahl, a compact disc recording supplied to the author by former *Star Tribune* reporter Betty Wilson.

13. Rosalie Wahl oral history interview, March 27, 1990. Transcript courtesy of Ann Juergens, William Mitchell College of Law. During World War II the University of Kansas operated on a three-semester calendar in response to the national labor shortage.

14. Juergens interview with Wahl.

15. An account of the YWCA's early efforts at racial inclusivity can be found in the history section of the organization's website, www.ywca.org.

16. Rusty L. Monhollon, *This is America? The Sixties in Lawrence, Kansas* (New York: Palgrave, 2002), 66. *The Graduate Magazine of the University of Kansas* 20 (April 1922): 30. Author's interview with Fronzena Sizer, April 5, 2011.

17. Deane Waldo Malott biography, http://en.wikipedia.org/wiki/Deane_Waldo_Malott. Wahl oral history interview.

18. A description of the Quaker testimony on equality can be found on the Guilford College website: http://www.guilford.edu/about-guilford/quaker-heritage/quaker-testimony/equality. The importance of that testimony to Rosalie was described by attorney, Friends colleague, and former tenant Gail Lewellan in an interview with the author, June 21, 2013. Cooper interview with Wahl.

19. Speech at career day for high school women, Southwest State University, 1978, included in Anderson and Larson, *The Social Justice, Legal and Judicial Career of Rosalie Erwin Wahl.* Poem transcribed from "Small Songs, 1943–1973" by Rosalie Wahl.

20. About the William J. Reals Gallery of Art, University of Kansas School of Medicine, Wichita, http://wichita.kumc.edu/gallery/about.html. Author's interviews with Rosalie Wahl, Sara Wahl, and Jenny Blaine, November 7, 2009.

21. Author's interview with Mary Alice Harvey, June 16, 2013. About Circle Pines: http://www.ci.circle-pines.mn.us.

Notes to Chapter Two

1. An excellent account of the women's suffrage movement in Minnesota can be found in Barbara Stuhler, *Gentle Warriors: Clara Ueland and the Minnesota Struggle for Woman Suffrage* (St. Paul: Minnesota Historical Society Press, 1995). Minnesota achieved statehood on May 11, 1858.

2. The Minneapolis Collection, "A History of Minneapolis: University of Minnesota," Hennepin County Library, http://www.hclib.org/pub/search/specialcollections/mplshistory/?id=7. The University of Minnesota also ceased to operate soon thereafter and did not reopen until 1868. When it did, it was coeducational, a decision credited to John S. Pillsbury by his grandson Philip in the booklet "The Pioneering Pillsburys" (Minneapolis: Newcomen Society, 1950).

3. Lori Sturdevant with George S. Pillsbury, *The Pillsburys of Minnesota* (Minneapolis: Nodin Press, 2011), 222.

4. The transformation of the National American Woman Suffrage Association into the League of Women Voters was first proposed at a national meeting in St. Louis on March 24, 1919, three days after the Minnesota house voted to allow women to vote for president in the state. Stuhler, *Gentle Warriors*, 181–82. Author's interview with Arvonne Fraser, January 25, 2011.

5. National Women's History Museum, "Women Wielding Power: Pioneer Female State Legislators, Minnesota," http://www.nwhm.org/online-exhibits/legislators/Minnesota.html.

6. Barbara Stuhler and Gretchen Kreuter, *Women of Minnesota: Selected Biographical Essays* (St. Paul: Minnesota Historical Society Press, 1977), chapter about women in the Minnesota legislature written by Arvonne S. Fraser and Sue E. Holbert, 262. Minnesota Legislative Reference Library, Legislators Past and Present, "Sue Metzger Hough," http://www.leg.state.mn.us/legdb/fulldetail.aspx?ID=13426. See link to 1923 article by C. J. Buell, http://www.leg.mn/archive/LegDB/Articles/13426Buell.pdf.

7. Edward T. James, ed., *Notable American Women: A Biographical Dictionary* (Cambridge, MA: Belknap Press, 1971) II:327. Section on Kempfer written by Jon Wefald, state agriculture commissioner in 1971, who went on to become president of Kansas State University. Young and Ankeny, *Minnesota Women in Politics*, 4.

8. "Mrs. Paige, Legislator, Dies at 91," *Minneapolis Star*, August 19, 1961, 1A. Young and Ankeny, *Minnesota Women in Politics*, 5.

9. James, *Notable American Women*, III:498–89. Section about Ueland written by University of Minnesota history professor Clarke A. Chambers.

10. Stuhler and Kreuter, *Women of Minnesota*, 248, 250. Legislative Coordinating Commission, Office on the Economic Status of Women, "Women in the

Minnesota Legislature, 1923–1969," http://www.commissions.leg.state.mn.us/oesw/wmnpuboff/1923.htm.

11. Minnesota Legislative Reference Library, Legislators Past and Present, "Sally Luther," http://www.leg.state.mn.us/legdb/fulldetail.aspx?ID=13723.

12. Stuhler and Kreuter, *Women of Minnesota*, 265. Gretchen Urnes Beito, *Coya Come Home: A Congresswoman's Journey* (Los Angeles: Pomegranate Press, 1990), 50–52.

13. Beito, *Coya Come Home*, 62.

14. Material about Coya Knutson can be found on the History, Art and Archives website of the U.S. House of Representatives, http://history.house.gov/People/Listing/K/KNUTSON,-Coya-Gjesdal-(K000300)/. Beito, *Coya Come Home*, 72–73.

15. Bob Weber, "Coya Knutson Still Works in Capital," *Minneapolis Star*, January 18, 1964. Beito, *Coya Come Home*, 87. Chuck Haga, "Coya Came Home," *Minneapolis Star Tribune*, March 19, 1990.

16. Knutson would tell *Minneapolis Star* reporter Bob Weber in 1964 that she decided she wanted to run for Congress in 1942, when she heard First Lady Eleanor Roosevelt give a speech about the value of something her husband aimed to create, the United Nations. Weber, "Coya Knutson Still Works in Capital."

17. Fraser interview. Photo of Knutson with her legislative successor, *Minneapolis Star*, November 15, 1954. *Minneapolis Tribune*, November 4, 1954. "*Minneapolis Tribune*, November 15, 1956.

18. Congressional Record, House, 84th Cong., 1st sess. (July 30, 1955): 12445. Cooley also inserted a very favorable report on Knutson into the Congressional Record. See Congressional Record, House, 84th Cong., 2nd sess. (July 24, 1956): 14313. Beito, *Coya Come Home*, 179–80. Mary C. Pruitt, "Knutson Obit Gave Her Career Short Shrift," *Minneapolis Star Tribune*, October 26, 1996.

19. Another was businessman Robert Short, who in 1978 would again alienate the DFL establishment by defeating representative Don Fraser in that year's U.S. Senate primary. Short lost that fall's election to GOP U.S. Senator Dave Durenberger. United Press photo and caption, March 19, 1956, from *Star Tribune* photo archives.

20. "Mate Urges Coya Not to Run Again," *Minneapolis Tribune*, May 8, 1958.

21. "Mate Says Coya Need Not Quit," *Minneapolis Tribune*, May 10, 1958. Beito, *Coya Come Home*, 233.

22. Beito, *Coya Come Home*, 218.

23. Beito, *Coya Come Home*, 232, 238, 239. "Woman's Dilemma: Home or Politics?" *U.S. News and World Report*, May 23, 1958, 68–70.

24. Chuck Haga, "'Come Home' Coya Dies," *Minneapolis Star Tribune*, October 11, 1996.

25. Beito, *Coya Come Home*, 270.

26. Charles Bailey, "Coya May Not Pursue Fight, She Indicates," *Minneapolis Tribune*, December 18, 1958.

27. *Minneapolis Tribune*, May 6, 1958.

28. Legislative Coordinating Commission, Office on the Economic Status of Women, "Women in the Minnesota Legislature by Year(s) Elected," http://www .commissions.leg.state.mn.us/lcesw/wmnpuboff/wmnpuboffname.htm.

Notes to Chapter Three

1. Donna Halvorsen, "Credit Where Her Credit Is Due: Rosalie Wahl Has a Passion for the Law and for Books, and She Has Nurtured Both. Now, the Name of Lake Elmo's New Library Will Honor Her Efforts as a Longtime Advocate for the Community Library," Minneapolis *Star Tribune*, November 25, 2005, 3B.

2. Celsius: A Library Architecture Resource, "Mobile Libraries in Wisconsin and Minnesota," http://libraryarchitecture.wikispaces.com/Mobile+Libraries +in+Wisconsin+and+Minnesota. Much material for this chapter came from the author's interviews with Rosalie Wahl on November 7 and 21, 2009.

3. Sally J. Kenney, "Thank You for Being Ready: Rosalie Wahl Holds Her Place on the Minnesota Supreme Court," Center on Women and Public Policy Case Study, Humphrey Institute of Public Affairs, University of Minnesota, 2001, 6.

4. Harvey interview. As of late 2013, Mary Alice was the sole surviving member of the Circle Pines intentional community.

5. Ryan Dawson, "A Cooperative Experiment Spawns City," 2010, http:// anokahistory.wordpress.com/category/circle-pines/.

6. Author's interview with Timothy Wahl, December 3, 2011.

7. Minnesota Historical Society, Collection Finding Aids, "Gibas Family: An Inventory of Their Papers," http://www.mnhs.org/library/findaids/00431 .xml. "First Woman on State Supreme Court Was First Editor of *Circulating Pines*," *Circulating Pines*, June 9, 1977.

8. Neville interview with Wahl.

9. Neville interview with Wahl.

10. The William Mitchell campus was then at 2100 Summit Avenue, near the University of St. Thomas. Today it is several miles east, at 875 Summit. A timeline of the school's history can be found under the history section of its website, www.wmitchell.edu.

See also Douglas R. Heidenreich, *With Satisfaction and Honor: William Mitchell College of Law, 1900–2000* (St. Paul, MN: William Mitchell College of Law, 1999), timeline, xv–xxiii.

11. Author's interview with Douglas Heidenreich, November 21, 2011. Heidenrech, *With Satisfaction and Honor*, 39, reports that of the 638 graduates of the St. Paul College of Law in its first eighteen years of existence, only eight were women. Governor's Commission on the Status of Women, Education Committee, Women in Professional Careers Subcommittee, "Women in Law: Summary of a Report Submitted by Mrs. Esther Wattenberg," November 1, 1964.

12. Author's interview with Ellen Dresselhuis, December 8, 2011. Kenney, "Thank You for Being Ready," 7.

13. Neville interview with Wahl.

14. Author's interview with Raquel Wood, December 31, 2011.

15. "Attorney in City Named State Public Defender," *Minneapolis Tribune*, November 20, 1965. Bernie Shellum, "Minnesota Counsel System Improves Aid to Indigents," *Minneapolis Tribune*, April 2, 1967.

16. Richard Kleeman, "Miss Lehmann Tops School Race," *Minneapolis Tribune*, April 28, 1965.

17. Author's interview with Esther Tomljanovich, October 15, 2011.

18. Bob Von Sternberg, "C. Paul Jones, State's First Public Defender, Dies at 84," *Minneapolis Star Tribune*, April 23, 2011, http://www.startribune.com/local/west/120545424.html. Also: William Mitchell College of Law, "Remembering C. Paul Jones LL.M., '55, Longtime Mitchell Professor," April 20, 2011, http://web.wmitchell.edu/news/2011/04/remembering-c-paul-jones-ll-m-55/, and University of Minnesota Law School, "Law School Bids Farewell to Legal Pioneer C. Paul Jones ('50)," April 22, 2011, www.law.umn.edu/news/law-school-bids-farewell-to-legal-pioneer-c-paul-jones-4-22-2011.html. Tuttle interview.

19. "State Public Defender, Assistants Sworn In," *Minneapolis Star,* January 1, 1966. Commencement address by Rosalie Wahl, William Mitchell College of Law, May 21, 1978, included in Anderson and Larson, *The Social Justice, Legal and Judicial Career of Rosalie Erwin Wahl*.

20. Gwenyth Jones, "She Hopes to Enrich Court View," *Minneapolis Star,* June 21, 1977, 1C.

21. The size of the Minnesota Supreme Court would shrink from nine to seven after the Minnesota Court of Appeals was formed in 1983.

22. Wahl interview, included in the documentary film *Girl from Birch Creek,* Lightshed Productions, November 2012. Rosalie Wahl, "Equal Justice Under Law: Dream or Reality?" Putnam Lecture in Social Ethics, *Hamline Law Review* 1979.1.

23. Neville interview with Wahl.

Notes to Chapter Four

1. Gail Collins, *When Everything Changed: The Amazing Journey of American Women from 1960 to the Present* (New York: Little, Brown & Co., 2009), 95–96.

2. U.S. Census Bureau, "Median Family Income by State," http://www.census.gov/hhes/www/income/data/historical/state/state2.html. The gap would widen to 6.4 percent in 1979.

3. Minnesota Legislative Commission on the Economic Status of Women (LCESW) fact sheet, "Educational Attainment of Women, Minnesota and U.S.," January/February 2002, and report, "Women in Minnesota, 100 years, 1900–2000," June 2003. "Women in the Labor Force," www.infoplease.com/ipa/A0104673.html.

4. For a description of the enactment of both the Fair Employment Practices Act and the Fair Housing Act in Minnesota, see Elmer L. Andersen, *A Man's Reach: The Autobiography of Elmer L. Andersen,* ed. Lori Sturdevant (Minneapolis: University of Minnesota Press, 2000).

5. Fraser's feminist history is recounted in Arvonne Fraser, *She's No Lady: Politics, Family and International Feminism,* ed. Lori Sturdevant (Minneapolis: Nodin Press, 2007). For a timeline, see also Minnesota Historical Society, Collection Finding Aids, "Arvonne S. Fraser: An Inventory of Her Papers," http://www.mnhs.org/library/findaids/00034.xml.

6. Bonnie Watkins and Nina Rothchild, *In the Company of Women: Voices from the Women's Movement* (St. Paul: Minnesota Historical Society Press, 1996), 77–78. Ann Baker, "Feminist Groups Take Varying Approaches to Problems," *St. Paul Dispatch,* August 28, 1973, 10.

7. Governor's Commission on the Status of Women, interim report, November 1, 1964. Thanks to the Honorable Esther Tomljanovich for supplying her personal copy. Watkins and Rothchild, *In the Company of Women,* 9–10.

8. Collins, *When Everything Changed,* 78–81.

9. Watkins and Rothchild, *In the Company of Women,* 12.

10. Kathleen Ridder, *Shaping My Feminist Life: A Memoir* (St. Paul: Minnesota Historical Society Press, 1998), 38, 42–43. Author's interview with Chuck Slocum, former Republican state chairman, February 13, 2012.

11. Esther Wattenberg, "Women in the DFL . . . A Preliminary Report: Present but Powerless?" Contributors to the report include Yvette Oldendorf, Susan Christopherson, Delores Orey, Caroline Rose, Anne Truax, and Koryne Horbal. See also Wendy Ross, "Minnesota Women Want to Remove 'Men-Only' Sign from U.S. Politics," *Minneapolis Tribune,* February 27, 1972, 1A. Peg Meier, "DFL Women Attend Seminar," *Minneapolis Tribune,* October 29, 1971.

12. Author's interview with Koryne Horbal, May 14, 2011. Peter Ackerberg, "Koryne Horbal, Champion of the Feminist Caucus," *Minneapolis Star,* February 3, 1975.

13. Her model may have been Orville Freeman's similar organizing trips for the newly merged DFL Party immediately after World War II. Those trips planted the seeds for Humphrey's U.S. Senate win in 1948, Freeman's gubernatorial victory in 1954, and the party's climb to majority status at the legislature in 1972. Wattenberg, "Present but Powerless," 18, 19. Geri Joseph would serve as ambassador to the Netherlands during President Jimmy Carter's administration.

14. Meier, "DFL Women Attend Seminar." Ross, "Minnesota Women Want to Remove 'Men-Only' Sign."

15. Fraser, *She's No Lady,* 157–58.

16. Author's interview with Emily Anne Tuttle, August 24, 2011. Emily Anne Staples was married to Loring M. Staples Jr., mayor of Plymouth. He died in 1988. She married Gedney Tuttle on January 14, 1995, and is known today as Emily Anne Tuttle.

17. Susanne Braun Levine and Mary Thom, *Bella Abzug: How One Tough Broad from the Bronx Fought Jim Crow and Joe McCarthy, Pissed Off Jimmy Carter, Battled for the Rights of Women and Workers, Rallied against War and for the Planet, and Shook Up Politics along the Way* (New York: Farrar, Straus and Giroux, 2007), 136, 138. National Women's Political Caucus, "History: About the Caucus," http://www.nwpc.org/history. "Background of the Minnesota Women's Political Caucus," complied by Ann Burns, temporary chairwoman, speakers' bureau MWPC, undated but clearly from late 1971, since it refers to a "January 1972 conference being planned." "Gloria Steinem Addresses the Women of America," video, www.history.com/audio/gloria-steinem-addresses-the-nwpc#gloria-steinem-addresses-the-nwpc.

18. Burns, "Background of the Minnesota Women's Political Caucus."

19. Burns, "Background of the Minnesota Women's Political Caucus," lists Kahn as "delegate at-large" of the new organization. Author's interview with Phyllis Kahn, April 9, 2011. Cheri Register, "When Women Went Public: Feminist Reforms in the 1970s," *Minnesota History* 61.2 (summer 2008): 75.

20. Watkins and Rothchild, *In the Company of Women,* 46. The Conservative label was the de facto Republican caucus between 1913, when party designation ended at the legislature, and its return in 1973. Sturdevant and Pillsbury *The Pillsburys of Minnesota,* 348.

21. Tom Brokaw, *Boom! Voices of the Sixties: Personal Reflections on the '60s and Today* (New York: Random House Publishing Group, 2007), 168. In

addition, the author drew from her *Minneapolis Star Tribune* coverage of Joan Anderson Growe's 1984 U.S. Senate campaign.

22. Kay Miller, "Joan Growe's Political Legacy: Her 1972 Housewives' Campaign Proved Women Could Take the Heat Outside the Kitchen," *Minneapolis Star Tribune* Sunday Magazine, January 3, 1993. Author's interviews with Gretchen Fogo and Judy Schuck, January 25, 2012.

23. Author's interview with Joan Growe, April 14, 2012.

24. Register, "When Women Went Public," 67. *Minnesota Legislative Manual, 1973–74* (St. Paul: State of Minnesota, 1973), 93.

25. Author's interview with Linda Berglin, April 16, 2011. "2 Contestants in 59A Split on Tax Views," *Minneapolis Star,* October 3, 1972. Author's interview with Marlene Johnson, November 11, 2011.

26. "Record 6 Women Win Seats in the Legislature," *Minneapolis Star,* November 8, 1972.

27. The closest of the six winning women's elections was in District 31B in Mower County, where Helen McMillan won her fifth and final term by 798 votes. See *Minnesota Legislative Manual, 1973-74,* 540–54.

28. Linda Napikoski, "Which States Ratified the ERA During 1973? Another Year of Equal Rights Amendment Victories," http://womenshistory.about.com/od/equalrightsamendment/a/States-Ratified-ERA-1973.htm.

29. "Women's Lobby Seeks to Educate," *St. Petersburg [FL] Times,* March 12, 1973, 16A. Linda Napikoski, "Stop ERA: A Campaign Against the Equal Rights Amendment," womenshistory.about.com/od/equalrightsamendment/a/Stop_ERA.htm.

30. Pattock would drop her husband's surname, Bremer, when their marriage ended. Stocker won a seat on the newly established Falcon Heights City Council in 1973, as Falcon Heights was reorganized from village to city status. See also Stocker's obituary, *Green Valley News and Sun,* December 22, 2011, available: www.legacy.com/obituaries/gvnews/obituary.aspx?n=luella-heine-stocker&pid=155147869.

31. "The Minnesota Coalition to Ratify the ERA," letter to 1972 candidates, Emily Anne Staples Tuttle papers, Minnesota Historical Society, St. Paul. "Organizations in Minnesota Coalition to Ratify the Equal Rights Amendment," as of January 19, 1973, Mary Pattock personal papers. News release from the Archdiocese of St. Paul and Minneapolis, January 16, 1972 (*sic*), Pattock personal papers.

32. Pattock personal papers; Pattock drafted the letter that Humphrey and Mondale signed.

33. *St. Cloud Daily Times,* January 8, 1973, found in the Minnesota Legislative Reference Library's 1973 session clippings scrapbook.

34. Bernie Shellum, "DFL Feminists May Quit Party," *Minneapolis Tribune,* March 22, 1973, 1B.

35. Handwritten notes taken by Mary Pattock Bremer as she watched the senate floor debate in the gallery, February 5, 1973. (Pattock dropped the name Bremer several years later.)

36. Pattock handwritten notes.

37. Vote totals from the 1973 *Journal of the House* and *Journal of the Senate,* Minnesota Legislative Reference Library, with thanks to deputy director/reference librarian Elizabeth Lincoln. And thanks to Mary Pattock for photos of Cain.

38. Bernie Shellum, "Feminist Group Gains DFL Party Regulars," *Minneapolis Tribune,* April 27, 1973, 1A.

39. Carol Lacey, "GOP Women's Caucus Formed," *St. Paul Pioneer Press,* July 1, 1973, Family Life section.

40. Wattenberg, "Present but Powerless," 14. Slocum interview.

41. Author's interview with Dottie Rietow, September 21, 2009.

42. Interview with Mary Pattock, February 18, 2012.

43. Shellum, "Feminist Group Gains DFL Party Regulars." The six other "founding mothers," according to Horbal, were Jeri Rasmussen, Yvette Oldendorf, Mary Bremer, Mary Peek, Cynthia Kitlinski, and Peggy Specktor. Other early members of the DFL Feminist Caucus include Sue Rockne of Zumbrota, Janet Sigford of Winona, Fran Naftalin of Minneapolis, and legislators Linda Berglin and Phyllis Kahn.

Notes to Chapter Five

1. Author's interview with Mary Pattock, March 10, 2012.

2. Minnesota Women Lawyers, "History," http://www.mwlawyers.org/displaycommon.cfm?an=1&subarticlenbr=2. Kenney, "Thank You for Being Ready," 5. Sedgwick was not Minnesota's first female judge. That distinction belongs to Betty Whitlock Washburn, who was appointed a Hennepin County municipal judge in 1950 by governor Luther Youngdahl and died twelve years later of cancer at age forty-five. From Minnesota Law and Politics, "Minnesota's Legal Hall of Fame," http://www.lawandpolitics.com/minnesota/Minnesotas-Legal-Hall-of-Fame/9fe5f62c-aded-102a-ab50-000e0c6dcf76.html.

3. Author's interview with Rosalie Wahl, November 21, 2009.

4. Roger S. Haydock, "Clinical Legal Education: The History and Development of a Law Clinic," *William Mitchell Law Review* 9.1 (1984): 106.

5. Author's interview with Roger Haydock, December 19, 2011.

6. Haydock, "Clinical Legal Education," 108. Four "clinics" were established in the program's first semester. In addition to criminal law and civil practice, clinics were established in welfare law and criminal appeals. In the spring semester, demand was so strong that three more clinics were added: in consumer law, civil rights, and prisoner assistance. However, only the criminal and civil practice clinics functioned like independent law firms. The other clinics offered experiences akin to internships supervised by Legal Assistance of Ramsey County, the state attorney general's office, the state public defender's office, and the Minnesota Human Rights Department. Heidenreich interview.

7. Juergens interview with Wahl.

8. Ann Juergens, "Rosalie Wahl's Vision for Legal Education: Clinics at the Heart," *William Mitchell Law Review* 30 (2003): 9.

9. Author's interview with Ross Kramer, March 9, 2012.

10. Haydock, "Clinical Legal Education," 107.

11. Juergens interview with Wahl. Cooper interview with Wahl.

12. Haydock, "Clinical Legal Education," 108. Memo to ten public defenders in the Ramsey County Municipal Court, and Roger S. Haydock, "A Tribute to Rosalie E. Wahl," both included in Anderson and Larson, *The Social Justice, Legal and Judicial Career of Rosalie Erwin Wahl*.

13. Author's e-mail exchange with Judge Harriet Lansing, retired member of the Minnesota Court of Appeals, February 23, 2013.

14. Student evaluations, 1975 criminal practice clinic, William Mitchell College of Law.

15. Kenney, "Thank You for Being Ready," 8, citing Nadine Strossen, "The Leadership Role of the Legal Community in Promoting Both Civil Liberties and National Security post 9/11," *Minnesota Women Lawyers*, Minneapolis, February 13, 2003.

16. Minnesota Legislative Reference Library, "Party Control of the Minnesota House of Representatives, 1951–present," http://www.leg.state.mn.us/lrl/histleg/caucus.aspx?body=h.

17. 1952.MN.168, 55 N.W.2d 302, 238 Minn. 25.

18. "Senate Perspective '75," March 21, 1975, http://www.leg.mn/archive/LegDB/Articles/10074SenatePerspective75.pdf. Ridder, *Shaping My Feminist Life*, 71–72.

19. Johnson interview.

20. Minnesota Legislative Reference Library, Legislators Past and Present, "Oscar Albert 'O. A.' Naplin," http://www.leg.state.mn.us/legdb/fulldetail.aspx?ID=13606.

21. "Senate Perspective '75."

22. Amy Caucutt, *A Woman's Place Is in the House . . . and the Senate*, ch. 4, "Taking the Lead: Rochester Women in Public Policy, 1970–1990" (St. Cloud, MN: Polaris Publishing, 2013), 31–42. Brataas, then Nancy Osborn, was a University of Minnesota classmate and friend of Emily Anne Mayer, who became Emily Anne Staples Tuttle.

23. Author's interview with Gloria Griffin, April 30, 2011.

24. Betty Wilson, "Ford Gets 8 State Delegates, Reagan 2," *Minneapolis Star,* April 26, 1976, 1A. See also Betty Wilson, "DFLers Will Weigh Woman's Bid to Challenge Hagedorn," *Minneapolis Star,* April 24, 1976. Also, "Obituary: Gloria Griffin, Leader in Women's Issues," *Minneapolis Star Tribune,* December 24, 2011. Associated Press, "Man Drops Idea of 2nd District DFL challenge," *Minneapolis Star,* May 14, 1976.

25. Watkins and Rothchild, *In the Company of Women*, 236. "United States House of Representatives Elections, 1976, Minnesota," http://en.wikipedia.org/wiki/United_States_House_of_Representatives_elections,_1976#Minnesota.

26. Gerry Nelson, "Anderson to Take U.S. Senate Seat," *Brainerd Daily Dispatch,* November 10, 1976, 1A. See also a fine biography by *Minneapolis Star* and *Star Tribune* journalist Betty Wilson: *Rudy! The People's Governor* (Minneapolis: Nodin Press, 2005). The Minnesota Poll results from October 1976 are described on pages 65-66.

27. Author covered Governor Rudy Perpich for the *Minneapolis Tribune* and *Star Tribune* from 1978 until 1990.

28. Wilson, *Rudy!* 68, 289. Perpich and Murray had both been opponents of the Vietnam War, which helped cement their friendship. In addition, Murray is cited as a judge who "allegedly heard a pay discrimination complaint by Perpich's mother," Mary Vukelich Perpich: see Kenney, "Thank You for Being Ready." Mary Perpich was employed in a hospital laundry in Hibbing after her sons were grown. Her daughter-in-law Lola Perpich and grandson Rudy Perpich Jr. told the author they have no knowledge of Mary Perpich's involvement in a pay equity suit.

29. Author's e-mail exchange with Rudy Perpich Jr., March 18, 2012. Ann Brown oral history 2007.0064, Iron Range Research Center, Chisholm, MN. Ann Brown was Mary Vukelich Perpich's youngest sister. She was interviewed in her home in Roseville, Minnesota, on September 10, 1997. She indicates that two Vukelich children, a son and a daughter, were born in Croatia. The baby boy died soon after birth; the fate of the daughter is not clear, but Brown indicates that by the 1920s, Mary is the "oldest daughter."

30. Wilson, *Rudy!* 4. Author's interview with Rudy Perpich Jr., March 17, 2012.

31. "In Memoriam: Gov. Rudy Perpich (1928–1995)," chronology, http://www.reocities.com/heartland/1302/perpich.html#1.

32. Carol Lacey, "Woman in Top Court Promised," *St. Paul Pioneer Press*, January 16, 1977, A1.

33. Author's interviews with Rudy Perpich Jr. and Hy Berman, Perpich kitchen cabinet member and personal friend, January 29, 2011.

34. Kenney, "Thank You for Being Ready," 7. When an older women's legal sorority, Phi Delta Delta, merged nationally with the male legal fraternity Phi Alpha Delta, Minnesota women attorneys opted in September 1972 to regroup and rename their chapter. Transcript, *Rosalie Wahl: A Vision for a Better World.*

35. Harry H. MacLaughlin obituary, *Minneapolis Star Tribune*, May 5, 2005, http://www.legacy.com/obituaries/startribune/obituary.aspx?n=harry-h-maclaughlin&pid=3505793.

36. Kenney, "Thank You for Being Ready," 4. Author's interview with Rahn Westby, August 18, 2012.

37. Michael Novak, *Washington Star*, "The End of the ERA," *Minneapolis Star*, May 10, 1977.

38. Minnesota Historical Society, Collection Finding Aids, "Minnesota Women's Meeting: An Inventory of Its Records," http://www.mnhs.org/library/findaids/00724.xml.

39. Young and Ankeny, *Minnesota Women in Politics*, 137. Wilson, *Rudy!* 78.

40. Gwenyth Jones, "Three Women Believed to Lead Race for Spot on State Supreme Court," *Minneapolis Star*, May 25, 1977. Federal Judicial Center, Biographical Directory of Federal Judges, "Diana E. Murphy," http://www.fjc.gov/servlet/nGetInfo?jid=1720&cid=999&ctype=na&instate=na. Hy Berman's list of six finalists omitted Sedgwick and added Doris Huspeni, who would go on to serve on the Hennepin County District Court and the Minnesota Court of Appeals. Kenney's list of three finalists ("Thank You for Being Ready," 10) substitutes Murphy for Orey.

41. Kenney, "Thank You for Being Ready," 10.

42. The *Minneapolis Tribune*, June 3, 1977, 1A, mentions two other gubernatorial screeners: University of Minnesota professor Forrest Harris, who was treasurer of Perpich's 1978 reelection campaign, and state energy agency director John Millhone. Kenney adds the name Ray Bohn, a communications staffer in Perpich's office.

43. Wilson, *Rudy!* 90.

44. Author's interview with Carol Connolly, July 16, 2011.

45. Horbal interview.

46. Author's interview with Ray Bohn, June 8, 2011.

47. Young and Ankeny, *Minnesota Women in Politics*, 138. Other sources estimate the crowd as between two and four thousand.

48. Text of Rosalie Wahl's acceptance speech, *Minneapolis Star*, June 7, 1977.

Notes to Chapter Six

1. Much material for this chapter derives from the author's interview with Rosalie Wahl, January 2, 2010. Rosalie Wahl, "Women and the Law," speech, April 21, 1985, First Unitarian Society, Minneapolis; also the Thursday Club, St. Paul, May 9, 1985, box 5, Rosalie Wahl Papers, Minnesota History Center Library, St. Paul.

2. Doug Stone, "Ms. Wahl Hopes to Please Her Rooters," *Minneapolis Tribune*, June 13, 1977, 1A. Brenda Ingersoll, "Ms. Wahl Is Named to State High Court," *Minneapolis Star*, June 4, 1977, 1A.

3. Gwenyth Jones, "She Hopes to Enrich Court View," *Minneapolis Star*, June 21, 1977, 1C.

4. "First Woman on State Supreme Court was First Editor of *Circulating Pines*," *Circulating Pines*, June 9, 1977.

5. Speech to the St. Croix Valley School District, July 7, 1977, box 2, Rosalie Wahl Papers.

6. Minnesota Judicial Branch, Minnesota Supreme Court Oral Histories— A Brief View, "Justice Rosalie Wahl," http://www.mncourts.gov/?siteID= 0&page=3687. "Remarks of Justice Rosalie E. Wahl, October 3, 1977," http:// www.mnhs.org/library/findaids/00430/00430_SwearingInRemarks.htm. She was referring to the Henry Wadsworth Longfellow poem "The Sicilian's Tale: The Bell of Atri," from his *Tales of a Wayside Inn*, first published in 1863.

7. "The Horizon 100," speech given July 15, 1986, at St. Paul College Club, Rosalie Wahl Papers.

8. Rosalie Wahl interview with Marvin R. Anderson, May 13, 2000, transcribed in Anderson and Larson, *The Social Justice, Legal and Judicial Career of Rosalie Erwin Wahl*.

9. "The Horizon 100" speech. The St. Croix Valley Friends Meeting began when Herb Crocker—one of the original Circle Pines "intentional community" members—became ill with cancer. Traveling to southwest Minneapolis for Sunday meetings became difficult for him, so Rosalie, Ed and Peg Stevens, and several other Friends in the Stillwater/Lake Elmo area began meeting with the Crockers on Wednesday nights. As Crocker's health improved, the group decided to continue weekly meetings but to shift to Sundays so families with children could more easily participate. Author's interview with Wayne Kassera,

St. Croix Valley Friends Meeting member and archivist, June 16, 2013. Speech to AAUW [chapter unstated], May 19, 1978, Rosalie Wahl Papers.

10. Supreme Court Study Commission on the Mentally Disabled and the Courts, "Civil Commitment in Minnesota," final report, 1979.

11. *The Professional, Public and Judicial Career of C. Donald Peterson*, Minnesota Justices Series 4 (St. Paul: Minnesota State Law Library, 1987).

12. Perpich repeated the same story to future supreme court justice Esther Tomljanovich.

13. 261 N.W.2d 88; 1977 Minn. LEXIS 1296.

14. Nick Coleman, "Judge Foley Will Run for High Court," *Minneapolis Tribune*, May 12, 1978. Lucy Y. Her, "J. Jerome Plunkett, Retired Judge, Dies: He Earned Respect as a Great Lawyer in 38 Years on Ramsey County Bench," *Minneapolis Star Tribune*, December 7, 2000.

15. "Jane Hodgson, 91, Supporter of Abortion Rights, Is Dead," *New York Times*, November 5, 2006, http://www.nytimes.com/2006/11/05/us/05hodgson.html?_r=0. Betty Jane Reed, Minnesota Association of Volunteer Directors, letter to editor, "Resolutions Should Go Forward," *Minneapolis Star*, June 25, 1977.

16. Coleman, "Judge Foley Will Run for High Court." Liz Fedor, "Obituary: Daniel Foley, Original Member of Minnesota Court of Appeals," *Minneapolis Star Tribune*, August 17, 2002. Tom Foley for U.S. Senate Committee (201 East Hennepin Avenue, Minneapolis, MN 55414), "Tom Foley: A Biography."

17. Gene Lahammer, "Stenvig, Former Atty. Gen. Mattson Offer Surprises as Filings Close for State Elections," *Minneapolis Star*, July 19, 1978.

18. *Minnesota Legislative Manual, 1965–66* (St. Paul: State of Minnesota, 1965), 144.

19. David Peterson, "Police Report Says Mattson Intoxicated during Incident," *Minneapolis Star*, July 7, 1978. Robert Mattson Jr. would lose the auditor's seat in 1978 but win election as state treasurer in 1982. His service in that office was laden with controversy over his prolonged absences in Florida. He did not seek reelection in 1986.

20. Gwenyth Jones, "State Judges Are Subjected to Stiff Election Challenges," *Minneapolis Star*, August 1, 1978.

21. Burton R. Hanson, "A Profile of Justice C. Donald Peterson on His Retirement," *The Hennepin Lawyer* (November-December 1985).

22. Peterson lost to lieutenant governor A. M. "Sandy" Keith, a future supreme court chief justice, by only 4,699 votes. It was the last election in which a governor and lieutenant governor ran separately rather than as a team. That same year, GOP governor Elmer L. Andersen lost to DFL governor Karl Rolvaag by 91 votes. That remains at this writing the closest gubernatorial election in U.S.

history. Joe Rigert, "Ballot to Have Gallagher's Middle Name," *Minneapolis Tribune*, n.d., included in *The Professional, Public and Judicial Career of C. Donald Peterson*.

23. Editorial, "Vote for Experience," *New Ulm Daily Journal*, November 3, 1966. Editorial, "Attorneys for Peterson," *Waseca Journal*, October 26, 1966. *The Professional, Public and Judicial Career of C. Donald Peterson*. Finlay Lewis, "Gallagher–Peterson Contest Lively by Judicial Standards," *Minneapolis Tribune*, October 23, 1966.

24. E-mail from Connolly to author, December 10, 2012.

25. Lindquist and Vennum, LLP, tribute, "Leonard E. Lindquist," http://www.lindquist.com/leonard_lindquist/xprGeneralContentLindquist.aspx?xpST=GeneralContent.

26. Minnesota Judicial Branch, "Judge Profile: Senior Judge John S. Connelly," http://www.mncourts.gov/?page=JudgeBio_v2&ID=30451.

27. "List of U.S. Ballot Initiatives to Repeal LGBT Anti-discrimination Laws," http://en.wikipedia.org/wiki/List_of_US_ballot_initiatives_to_repeal_LGBT_anti-discrimination_laws. Author's interview with Carol Connolly, July 16, 2011.

28. Author's interview with Kathleen Ridder, December 7, 2010. Dreher went on to appointment as a U.S. bankruptcy judge in 1988. She died in November 2012. See her obituary in the *Minneapolis Star Tribune*, November 29, 2012, http://www.legacy.com/obituaries/startribune/obituary.aspx?page=lifestory&pid=161310480#fbLoggedOut.

29. In a 2002 decision, *Republican Party of Minnesota v. White*, the U.S. Supreme Court ruled 5–4 that Minnesota's prohibition on judicial candidates commenting on pending cases was unconstitutional.

30. Obituary, "James Gillespie Miles," *Minneapolis Star Tribune*, April 24, 2012. Author's interview with Laura Miles, December 13, 2012. Doug Stone, "Challengers in High Court Race Question Wahl's Trial Experience," *Minneapolis Tribune*, September 9, 1978.

31. Minnesota Historical Society, Collection Finding Aids, "GOP Feminist Caucus of Minnesota: An Inventory of Its Records," http://www.mnhs.org/library/findaids/00828.xml.

32. "Deaths for the Week of January 5, 2005: Mary Peek, Inver Grove Heights," *Woodbury [MN] Bulletin*. Robert T. Smith column, *Minneapolis Tribune*, October 23, 1970.

33. "7 Minnesotans on Women's Panel," *Minneapolis Star*, March 22, 1978. E-mail to author from Nina Rothchild, December 19, 2012.

34. Minnesota Legislative Reference Library, Minnesota Women's Legislative Timeline, http://www.leg.state.mn.us/lrl/womenstimeline/details.aspx?recid=24.

35. Watkins and Rothchild, *In the Company of Women,* 353. Lori Sturdevant, "Women's Council Strives to Continue Record of Success," *Minneapolis Tribune,* February 5, 1979.

36. Author's interview with Nina Rothchild, November 27, 2012.

37. KQRS radio debate, August 27, 1978, audio tapes, box 5, and speech to AAUW [chapter unstated], May 19, 1978, box 2, both Rosalie Wahl Papers.

38. The Coalition for Impartial Justice is at work in Minnesota seeking to replace contested judicial elections with yes-or-no retention elections, which it deems less prone to special interest influence and negative campaigning. See http://www.impartialcourts.org/.

39. Radio debate, August 27, 1978, box 5, Rosalie Wahl Papers.

40. Stone, "Challengers in High Court Race Question Wahl's Trial Experience."

41. Larry Purdy, attorney at law, former Wahl student, letter to editor, *Minneapolis Star,* August 14, 1978. Stone, "Challengers in High Court Race Question Wahl's Trial Experience."

42. Author's interview with Marcia Fluer, December 14, 2012. Kenney, "Thank You for Being Ready."

43. Author's interview with Frank and Raquel Wood, June 16, 2013.

44. Ridder, *Shaping My Feminist Life,* 106. Seaberg would lose the 1978 election to DFLer Ray Kempe but go on to win the District 38B seat in 1983 and hold it for the next ten years. Author's interview with Kathleen Ridder, December 29, 2012.

45. Author's interviews with Ember Reichgott Junge, March 15, 2013, and with Carol Connolly, May 12, 2013. Lester Munson, "New Book Chronicles Alan Page's Story," http://sports.espn.go.com/espn/commentary/news/story?page=munson/101021.

46. Author's interview with Carol Connolly, December 29, 2012.

47. Mott would go on to appointment as a Ramsey County district judge by governor Rudy Perpich in 1988.

48. Doug Stone, "Challengers in High Court Race Question Wahl's Trial Experience." Anderson interview with Wahl, included in Anderson and Larson, *The Social Justice, Legal and Judicial Career of Rosalie Erwin Wahl.* Author's interview with Deborah Fisher, March 16, 2013.

49. Doug Stone and Jim Parsons, "Court," *Minneapolis Tribune,* September 13, 1978.

50. Gwenyth Jones "Ad Claiming Justice 'Soft on Rape' Gives State Race a California Tone," *Minneapolis Star,* October 12, 1978. Also Sally J. Kenney, *Gender and Justice: Why Women in the Judiciary Really Matter* (New York: Routledge, 2013), 149–59. Gwenyth Jones, "Group Charges Mattson Breaking Canons in Campaign Against Wahl," *Minneapolis Star,* October 19, 1978. Also, ad,

"Compare, Then Decide/Bob Mattson vs. Rosalie Wahl," *Minneapolis Tribune*, October 17, 1978.

51. *Chimel v. California*, 395 U.S. 752 (1969). Jones "Ad Claiming Justice 'Soft on Rape' Gives State Race a California Tone."

52. Jones, "Group Charges Mattson Breaking Canons in Campaign Against Wahl."

53. "Mattsons Blast Wahl, Endorsement Process," *Worthington Daily Globe*, October 1978 [full date omitted], photocopy in box 5, Rosalie Wahl Papers. "Mattson Files Complaint against Justice Wahl," *St. Cloud Times*, September 30, 1978. Doug Stone, "Robert Mattson Sr. Ads Bring Complaints," *Minneapolis Tribune*, October 14, 1978. Also, "Mattson Charges Violation," *St. Paul Dispatch*, September 30, 1978.

54. Attorney Si Weisman, letter to editor, *Minneapolis Tribune*, October 19, 1978. "Rosalie Wahl Favored over Mattson," *Fergus Falls Daily Journal*, October 20, 1978.

55. Editorial, "Mattson's Injudicious Campaign," *Minneapolis Tribune*, October 22, 1978. "Those Mudslinging Ads," *St. Paul Dispatch*, October 20, 1978.

56. Gwenyth Jones, "Race Against Mattson Brings Out Defense Lawyer in Justice Wahl," *Minneapolis Star*, November 3, 1978. Also, Doug Stone, "Mattson Brings Out Campaigner in Wahl," *Minneapolis Tribune*, November 3, 1978. Letter on Wahl-Peterson letterhead, September 15, 1978, signed by Judith Oakes, Phyllis Jones, Helen Kelly, and Margaret Johnson, and Invitation, both box 5, Rosalie Wahl Papers. Author's interview with Connolly, May 12, 2013. "Fundraiser to Honor Rosalie Wahl," *Stillwater Gazette*, September 29, 1978.

57. Growe interview.

58. Jones, "Race Against Mattson Brings Out Defense Lawyer in Justice Wahl."

59. A fulsome discussion of the emotional bond that was forged between Wahl and Minnesota women can be found in Kenney, *Gender and Justice*, ch. 3. See also Kenney's article "Mobilizing Emotions to Elect Women: The Symbolic Meaning of Minnesota's First Woman Supreme Court Justice," *Mobilization: An International Journal* 15.2 (2010): 135–58. AAUW [chapter unstated], May 19, 1978, box 5, Rosalie Wahl Papers. Rosalie's grandchildren and their birthdates: Sean Christopher Wahl, January 22, 1970; Abbie Wahl, December 23, 1980; Michael James Davis II, August 3, 1981; Turner Wahl, August 4, 1982; Alexander Nathan Davis, August 26, 1986; Henry Wahl, June 24, 1992. Abbie Wahl and her husband Gustavo Ramirez are the parents of Rosalie's two great-grandchildren, Alina Ramirez, May 29, 2004, and Rosalie Ramirez, August 21, 2007.

60. The 1978 election also saw the defeat of Robert Mattson Jr. and the launch

of the statewide career of Republican Arne Carlson, who would serve twelve years as state auditor before being elected governor in 1990. Mattson Jr. was elected state treasurer in 1982, the year Robert Mattson Sr. died.

61. Jim Parsons, "TV Set Escapes Attention at Rosalie's Party," *Minneapolis Tribune*, November 8, 1978.

62. Lewellan interview.

Notes to Chapter Seven

1. The Minnesota Republican Party was named the Independent-Republican Party from 1976 until 1995.

2. Wilson, *Rudy!* 105–8.

3. Author's interview with Nancy Brataas, January 20, 2013. "XXXtitle," *Minneapolis Star*, December 18, 1978. Caucutt, "Taking the Lead." Her hopes were dashed again in 1984, when she was rejected in a bid for IR endorsement for the First District congressional seat. The man who defeated her, Keith Spicer, went on to lose to Democratic U.S. representative Tim Penny.

4. Lori Sturdevant, "What the Civil War Wrought in Minnesota," *Minneapolis Star Tribune*, March 31, 2013. Author's interview with Kathleen Ridder, December 7, 2010.

5. Quie's career is described in the book by Mitch Pearlstein, *Riding into the Sunrise: Al Quie, a Life of Faith, Service and Civility* (Lakeville, MN: Pogo Press, 2008). Material for this chapter also derives from the author's interview with Quie on March 7, 2013, and coverage of his career since 1978. Collins, *When Everything Changed*, 248–49.

6. The women were employee relations commissioner Barbara Sundquist, human rights commissioner Marilyn McClure, securities and real estate commissioner Mary Alice Brophy, and consumer affairs director Kris Sanda. *Minnesota Legislative Manual, 1981–82* (St. Paul: State of Minnesota, 1981). Ridder, *Shaping My Feminist Life*, 119.

7. Council on the Economic Status of Women newsletter 29 (June 1979). Watkins and Rothchild, *In the Company of Women*, 67–75. Minnesota Legislative Reference Library, Minnesota Women's Legislative Timeline, http://www.leg.state.mn.us/lrl/womenstimeline/details.aspx?recid=26; also Laws of Minnesota for 1977, Chapter 428, https://www.revisor.mn.gov/data/revisor/law/1977/0/1977-428.pdf. Lewis's untimely death on April 25, 1979, was a much-felt loss for social justice advocates of all stripes.

8. Laws of Minnesota for 1979, Chapter 214, https://www.revisor.mn.gov/data/revisor/law/1979/0/1979-214.pdf. E-mail correspondence with Lansing, February 2013.

9. Danyell Punneli, "Child Care Assistance," Minnesota House Research, July 2013, http://www.house.leg.state.mn.us/hrd/pubs/ss/sscca.pdf.

10. Griffin interview.

11. Suzanne Perry, Patrick Marx, and Debra Stone, "Legislator, 59, Is Accused," *Minneapolis Star,* April 9, 1979, 1A.

12. The year's one advance was the inauguration of childcare subsidies for low-income working families, which were often headed by single mothers. What became known as Basic Sliding Fee Child Care was started with a modest $1.5 million appropriation that year. It's described on the Minnesota Women's Legislative Timeline, http://www.leg.state.mn.us/lrl/womenstimeline/details.aspx ?recid=all. David Chanen, "Robert Pavlak, 70, Dies; U.S. Marshal and St. Paul Officer," *Minneapolis Star Tribune,* October 11, 1994.

13. John E. Turner, regents professor of political science, University of Minnesota, "Quie's Step Toward Better Judges," *Minneapolis Star,* June 26, 1979.

14. Steve Brandt and Doug Stone, "Quie Selects Two for Supreme Court," *Minneapolis Tribune,* July 4, 1980.

15. Legislative Coordinating Commission, Office on the Economic Status of Women, Women in the Minnesota Legislature, 1971–1979, http://www .commissions.leg.state.mn.us/oesw/wmnpuboff/1971.htm. Legislative Commission on the Economic Status of Women, Status Report, June 21, 2004, http:// www.commissions.leg.state.mn.us/oesw/fs/lfpMN00.pdf.

16. Minnesota Women's Consortium, "History," http://mnwomen.org/ about-us/history/.

17. Rockne was a native of Connecticut whose marriage to David Rockne brought her to Minnesota as a young woman. David was the grandson of Minnesota legislative legend A. J. Rockne, whose forty-four years in the legislature (1903–46) tied him for longest service in state history. In 2013, the consortium consisted of 150 member organizations.

18. Author's interview with Bonnie Peace Watkins, August 9, 2011.

19. Grace Underwood Harkness, *Living Carelessly: My Life Story* (Minneapolis: self-published, December 2009), 115.

20. Dan Freeborn, "Glenn E. Kelley Dies; Retired Justice of the State Supreme Court," *Minneapolis Star Tribune,* April 13, 1992.

21. Dulcie Lawrence, Minneapolis, freelance writer, "Women Needed on Supreme Court," *Minneapolis Tribune,* November 11, 1981. Of that group, all but Johnson would eventually become a judge.

22. Ridder, *Shaping My Feminist Life,* 120–21. Womenwinning archives provided this list of the original thousand-dollar donors: Martha B. Alworth, Martha Atwater, Marilyn Bryant, Sage Fuller Cowles, Laura A. Crosby, Karen

Desnick. Arvonne Fraser, Kay Fredericks, Alene Grossman, Rosalie Heffelfinger Hall, Jean Heilman, Marlene Johnson, Geri Joseph, Perrin Lilly, Sally Martin, Katherine B. Murphy, Sally Pillsbury, Kathleen Ridder, Susan Sands, Kathleen Scott, Mary Stringer, Barbara Stuhler, Mary Vaughan, Katherine Watters, Ruth Ann Wefald, Jean West. Lilly, a Republican, and Joseph, a DFLer, were the original co-chairs. E-mail to author from Meagan Bachmeyer, womenwinning communication director, April 13, 2013. Also, Roberta W. Francis, "The History Behind the Equal Rights Movement," http://www.equalrightsamendment.org/history.htm. Wilson, *Rudy!* 121.

23. Wilson, *Rudy!* 115. See also Pearlstein, *Riding into the Sunrise*, 185–86.

24. Bonnie Watkins, "Pay Equity: The Minnesota Experience," a report to the Legislative Commission on the Economic Status of Women, April 1994, fifth edition, 11.

25. Watkins and Rothchild, *In the Company of Women*, interview with Bev Hall, 118.

26. Minnesota Legislative Reference Library, Minnesota Women's Legislative Timeline, http://www.leg.state.mn.us/lrl/womenstimeline/details.aspx?recid=37. Berglin interview.

27. Nancy Dreher, memo to MWL Appointments Committee members, March 8, 1982, box 7, Rosalie Wahl Papers.

28. At Jeanne Coyne's retirement dinner in St. Paul, November 21, 1996, Rosalie related that soon before Coyne joined the court, she and Justice Otis encountered *Minneapolis Star Tribune* reporter Betty Wilson in the capitol cafeteria. Wilson said to Wahl, "You're going to have company on the court." Otis "drew himself up with great dignity" and said, "She's HAD company on the court." "The Horizon 100" speech.

29. Ridder, *Shaping My Feminist Life*, 110, 114. The other woman on the board was Wenda Moore, who went on to serve as the first African American chair of the University of Minnesota Board of Regents.

30. Ridder, *Shaping My Feminist Life*, 124.

31. Quie interview.

32. Robert Whereatt, "Quie Names Second Woman to Supreme Court," *Minneapolis Star Tribune*, August 18, 1982. Rosalie Wahl's remarks at Jeanne Coyne's retirement dinner in St. Paul, November 21, 1996, contained in Anderson and Larson, *The Social Justice, Legal and Judicial Career of Rosalie Erwin Wahl.*

33. Wahl's remarks at Coyne's retirement dinner included, "From the other side of the bench, I had been the recipient of her sound arguments, the integrity of her presentation of the law."

34. Watkins and Rothchild, *In the Company of Women*, 179.

Notes to Chapter Eight

1. Rosalie Wahl keynote address, "Women in the House/Women in the Courts," April 10, 1986, meeting of the Women's Law Caucus of William Mitchell College of Law, St. Paul, MN, box 2, Rosalie Wahl Papers.

2. As a *Minneapolis Star Tribune* reporter, the author traveled with candidate Perpich on several occasions in October 1982 and was sworn to secrecy as he went about discussing potential cabinet appointees and recruiting several of them. *Minnesota Legislative Manual, 1983–84* (St. Paul: State of Minnesota, 1983). Also, Minnesota State Law Library, Biographies of the Justices of the Minnesota Supreme Court, http://mn.gov/lawlib/judgebio.html.

3. Johnson interview.

4. Reichgott married in 1993 and took the name Ember Reichgott Junge.

5. The leak was shared with the author, who was about to begin a six-month maternity leave. Perpich characterized the tip as an early baby gift. Paul H. Anderson, "Women in the Judiciary: Do They Make a Difference?" *Minnesota Women Lawyers* (February 11, 2004), available: http://www.mncourts.gov/default .aspx?siteID=0&page=NewsItemDisplay&item=20239&printFriendly=true.

6. Anderson, "Women in the Judiciary."

7. Wahl keynote address, "Women in the House/Women in the Courts."

8. Justices John Todd and C. Donald Peterson left the court in 1985 and 1986, respectively, and were not replaced. A. M. Keith tribute to Rosalie Wahl, June 9, 2000, on the occasion of the presentation of her papers to the state law library, included in Anderson and Larson, *The Social Justice, Legal and Judicial Career of Rosalie Erwin Wahl.* Jane E. Larson, "The Jurisprudence of Justice Rosalie E. Wahl." Larson clerked for Justice Wahl in 1985–86. Her essay was commissioned by Marvin Anderson and the Minnesota State Law Library and appears in Anderson and Larson, *The Social Justice, Legal and Judicial Career of Rosalie Erwin Wahl.*

9. Author's interview with Marvin Anderson, May 13, 2000. Larson, "The Jurisprudence of Justice Rosalie E. Wahl." Harriet Lansing, "Rosalie Wahl and the Jurisprudence of Inclusivity," *William Mitchell Law Review* 21 (1995–96): 11; also, Mary Divine, "Minnesota Judge Inspired Many Lawyers, and Now a Film," *St. Paul Pioneer Press,* November 10, 2012.

10. Anderson and Larson, *The Social Justice, Legal and Judicial Career of Rosalie Erwin Wahl.* David Peterson, "Otis: Unlikely Dissenter on State Supreme Court," *Minneapolis Star,* June 22, 1981.

11. 477.N.W. 2d 886 (Minn. 1993).

12. Criticism of Wahl's opinion can be found in Jeffery A. Kruse, "Substantive Equal Protection Analysis under *State v. Russell* and the Potential Impact

NOTES TO PAGES 167–72 ‖ 231

on the Criminal Justice System," *Washington and Lee Law Review* 50 (1993): 1791, available: http://scholarlycommons.law.wlu.edu/wlulr/vol50/iss4/19. A more positive review: Knoll D. Lowney, "Smoked Not Snorted: Is Racism Inherent in Our Crack Cocaine Laws?" *Washington University Journal of Urban and Contemporary Law* 45 (1994): 121.

13. Larson, "The Jurisprudence of Justice Rosalie E. Wahl."

14. 299 N.W. 144 (Minn. 1980).

15. Minn. Stat. 518.552 Subd. 2 (1982).

16. *Abuzzahab v Abuzzahab,* 359 N.W. 12 (Minn. 1984). *McClelland v. McClelland,* 359 N.W. 2d 7 (Minn. 1984).

17. Wahl dissent, *Abuzzahab.*

18. Wahl keynote address, "Women and the Law: Finding your Way through the System," October 25, 1986, at a conference jointly sponsored by Minnesota Women Lawyers, Chrysalis, and the Minnesota Women's Consortium, Rosalie Wahl Papers. Gloria Griffin introduced Rosalie's keynote address.

19. Lori Sturdevant, "Growe's Gamble Couldn't Tarnish Boschwitz Image," *Minneapolis Star Tribune,* November 7, 1984. Lori Sturdevant, "Boschwitz Winds Up; Growe Still Pitching," *Minneapolis Star Tribune,* November 4, 1984. Lori Sturdevant, "'Unbeatable' Boschwitz Still Working the Crowd," *Minneapolis Star Tribune,* November 8, 1984.

20. Rosalie refused an honorarium for speaking at this conference, suggesting that any sum that might have gone to her be used to compensate the visiting keynoter from Harvard or for "a few of those extra hours given by G. Harkness et al., which make possible the wonderful work of the consortium. Bless you." Letter to Grace Harkness, September 2, 1986. Evidently the Minnesota Women's Consortium's finances were still skimpy six years after its founding. Lynn Hecht Schafran, "Eve, Mary, Superwoman: How Stereotypes About Women Influence Judges," *Judges Journal* 24 (1985): 12.

21. Wahl's speech at a memorial service for Norma Wikler, June 30, 2002, in New York City, http://www.wikler.net/writings/rosaliewahl.html. Wikler died at her own hand in Costa Rica on May 27, 2002, after battling depression for many years.

22. Letter to Rosalie from Norma Wikler, August 28, 1986, University of California letterhead, Rosalie Wahl Papers. Minnesota Supreme Court Task Force for Gender Fairness in the Courts, report summary, 1989, S2.

23. At Norma Wikler's memorial service in New York on June 30, 2002, Rosalie reported that funds raised in Minnesota in 1985 in connection with the National Women Judges Association meeting in Minneapolis were instrumental in funding the manual's development. "That money allowed there to be a truly national movement," Norma reported in her final letter to Rosalie before

her death. Transcript, Rosalie Wahl oral history interview with Norma Wikler, March 25, 1990. Courtesy Professor Ann Juergens, William Mitchell College of Law.

24. "State Court Administrator Sue K. Dosal Receives Minnesota State Bar Association's Most Prestigious Award," July 2, 2012, http://www.mncourts.gov /?page=NewsItemDisplay&item=55575. Minnesota Supreme Court Task Force for Gender Fairness in the Courts, interim report, October 1988, 3.

25. Wahl speech, Minneapolis Business and Professional Women's Clubs, October 18, 1989, box 3, Rosalie Wahl Papers. E-mail to author from Harriet Lansing, February 23, 2013, analyzed Rosalie's thinking as the task force began.

26. Letter to Rosalie from Laura Turner, state coordinator, Displaced Home-maker Program, and Yvette Oldendorf, executive director, Working Opportu-nities for Women, August 8, 1988, and Wahl speech to Working Opportunities for Women, tenth anniversary of the enactment of displaced homemaker legis-lation, October 20, 1988, both Rosalie Wahl Papers.

27. Wahl's remarks at the Susanne Sedgwick memorial "to benefit the Min-nesota Task Force for Gender Fairness in the courts," June 29, 1988, Rosalie Wahl Papers.

28. The members of the Gender Fairness Task Force are listed on page v of the final report of the Minnesota Supreme Court Task Force for Gender Fairness in the Courts, 1989, http://www.mncourts.gov/Documents/0/Public/ Other/Gender1.pdf.

29. A $50,000 appropriation was secured via a bill sponsored by senator Allan Spear, DFL-Minneapolis, and representative Sandy Pappas, DFL–St. Paul. E-mail to the author from Harriet Lansing, March 24, 2013.

30. Author's interview with Aviva Breen, April 21, 2013.

31. Minnesota Supreme Court Task Force for Gender Fairness in the Courts, interim report, October 1988, 8. Wahl's notes for her presentation to the Minne-sota Judges Annual Conference in Brainerd, September 6, 1989, box 10, Rosalie Wahl Papers. Reichgott added Junge to her name in 1994, after her marriage to Michael Junge.

32. From the draft report of Gender Fairness Task Force's Committee on Courtroom Interaction, May 2, 1989, Rosalie Wahl Papers.

33. Wahl's remarks at Sedgwick memorial.

34. Wahl's remarks at Sedgwick memorial.

35. Gender Fairness Task Force's Committee on Courtroom Interaction, draft, May 2, 1989, Rosalie Wahl Papers. David Carr, "A Sexist System? A New Survey on Gender Bias in the Courts Has Just Been Released. Horror Stories Abound," *Minnesota Lawyer*, November 1989, 18–30.

36. Minnesota Supreme Court Task Force for Gender Fairness in the Courts,

appendix, survey methodology, 1989. Rollout of Gender Fairness Task Force, Box 10, Rosalie Wahl Papers.

37. Carr, "A Sexist System?" Gender Fairness Task Force's Committee on Courtroom Interaction, draft.

38. Carr, "A Sexist System?"

39. Jim Parsons, "Judge Susanne Sedgwick Dies at 56," *Minneapolis Star Tribune*, April 9, 1988.

40. Marsha Freeman, reporter, memo to Gender Fairness Task Force committee chairs and vice chairs regarding preparation of final report, December 13, 1988, and Norma Wikler letter to Mary Grau, Gender Fairness Task Force, April 10, 1989, both box 9, Rosalie Wahl Papers.

41. Wahl's prepared remarks for a legislative committee hearing, October 31, 1989, Rosalie Wahl Papers. Among Rosalie's papers at the Minnesota History Center is an undated memo addressed to Justice Keith, signed by "Ann Nonymous." It gently advises the new member of the high court to remember one of the lessons of the task force: "I was surprised to notice that in a recent case, *State v. Michael W. Fenney*, you referred to all of the men by their surnames, but you referred to the female victim by her first name. You did so even though there was no one else involved in the case who had the same surname as the victim. Calling women by their first names while calling men by their surnames is a sexist practice, and is offensive to some people. I know you're not a sexist man, and I hope you'll refrain from using this practice in the future, so people won't get the wrong impression of you. Best of luck in your new job on the court." In an interview with the author, May 10, 2013, Keith said he considered Wahl "my judicial mother."

42. The text was put in final form by an editorial committee headed by Harriet Lansing and including Martin Costello, Jan Symchych, Sue Dosal, Marsha Freeman, and Christina Baldwin. Rosalie wrote the preface, which she signed. E-mail exchange with Lansing, March 24, 2013.

43. Gender Fairness Task Force preliminary report to trial judges, Rosalie Wahl's remarks, Minnesota District Judges Association Conference, June 15, 1989, Rosalie Wahl Papers.

44. Rosalie's notes/script of news conference announcing release of the GFTF report, 6:30 PM September 6, 1989, Supreme Court chamber, box 3, Rosalie Wahl Papers. Virginia Rybin, "Gender Bias Found in Courts; Chief Justice Shocked by Extent of Problem," *St. Paul Pioneer Press-Dispatch*, September 7, 1989.

45. Rosalind Bentley, "Report Says Gender Bias Afflicts State Legal System," *Minneapolis Star Tribune*, September 9, 1989. "Face to Face/The Judiciary: Ramsey County District Judge Mary Lou Klas," *Minnesota Law Journal* (January

1990): 10. A quarter century earlier, Klas's comments at a chance conversation at a DFL fundraising event helped convince Rosalie to enroll in law school.

46. William Mitchell College of Law campus newsletter, October 17, 1989.

47. Minnesota Supreme Court Task Force for Gender Fairness in the Courts, report summary.

48. Carr, "A Sexist System?" Marsha Freeman, "A Fair Day in Court for Women; Can Women Receive a Fair Shake in Minnesota's Court System?" *Humphrey Institute News*, December 1989, 13–14.

49. Prepared remarks for 1990 legislative hearings, box 10a, Rosalie Wahl Papers.

50. Professor Ann Juergens, William Mitchell College of Law, at a forum about Rosalie's impact on women in the law, January 29, 2013. Letter from Rudy Perpich to Peter Popovich, December 5, 1989, thanking Popovich and Wahl for an "outstanding job," box 3, Rosalie Wahl Papers. "I'd like to see the timetable and any priorities you may have set for implementing change at various levels within the justice system . . . You can count on my support when you need it," in Kathleen E. Pontius, senate counsel, memo to Senator Ember D. Reichgott, "Re: Summary of Laws 1990, Chapter 583: Domestic Abuse and Crime Victim Amendments," May 22, 1990, private papers of Ember Reichgott Junge.

51. Bill summaries, GFTF Legislation file, 1989–90, box 10, Rosalie Wahl Papers.

52. *Implementation Committee Newsletter* 1.1 (June 1990), box 10, Rosalie Wahl Papers. Dan Oberdorfer, "Judge Fights Mandatory Retirement Laws," *Minneapolis Star Tribune*, August 6, 1990.

53. Minnesota General Election Results, 1974, compiled by Secretary of State Joan Growe, November 5, 1974: Richard Nolan, 96,465 votes; Jon Grunseth, 77,797.

54. The author was the assignment editor at the *Star Tribune* who supervised news coverage of the 1990 gubernatorial campaign. Robert Whereatt, "IR Team Is Carlson-Dyrstad; Justices Reject Clark's Challenge," *Minneapolis Star Tribune*, November 2, 1990. Popovich was joined in dissent by Associate Justice Lawrence Yetka, a former state legislator who had been appointed to the court by DFL governor Wendell Anderson.

55. Dane Smith, "Gardebring Named to Supreme Court; State Becomes First in U.S. with Female Majority," *Minneapolis Star Tribune*, January 5, 1991.

56. " 'I don't know of any governor anywhere in the country who appointed so many women—in the judiciary, in his Cabinet,' said Jan Smaby, who served in Perpich's administration in 1989 and 1990." Robert Whereatt and Patricia Lopez Baden, "Minnesota Loses a Leader Both Brilliant and Baffling; Perpich:

A Man of Vision; Former Governor Dies of Cancer at Age 67," *Minneapolis Star Tribune*, September 22, 1995.

Notes to Chapter Nine

1. Wahl oral history interview.

2. Wahl keynote address, "Women in the House, Women in the Courts."

3. Senator Allan Spear letter to Chief Justice Peter Popovich, March 23, 1989, box 11, Rosalie Wahl Papers.

4. U.S. District Court, District of Minnesota, Chief Judge Michael J. Davis biography, http://www.mnd.uscourts.gov/MDL-Baycol/judge-michael-davis.shtml.

5. Author's interview with U.S. District Court Chief Judge Michael Davis, June 4, 2013.

6. MSBA in Brief, Minnesota State Bar Association newsletter, December 1991, box 12, Rosalie Wahl Papers. Jim Parsons, "Task Force Is Told That Racism Pervades State's Court System," *Minneapolis Star Tribune*, November 14, 1991.

7. Kurt Errickson, "Task Force Studies Bias in State Courts," *Twin Cities Reader*, November 6–12, 1991.

8. "State Supreme Court Wants Testimony on Race Bias in the Court System," *Minneapolis Spokesman*, October 3, 1991.

9. Minnesota Supreme Court Task Force on Racial Bias in the Judicial System, final report, Wahl introduction, dated April 30, 1993.

10. Bill McGrane, *All Rise: The Remarkable Journey of Alan Page* (Chicago: Triumph Books, 2010).

11. Page defeated Johnson 1,240,633 to 750,228. He was overwhelmingly reelected in 1998, 2004, and 2010.

12. Wahl's handwritten notes, undated but clearly prior to the August 1982 appointment of M. Jeanne Coyne to the state supreme court, Rosalie Wahl Papers.

13. E-mail from fellow Friends member and former Wahl law clerk Paul Landskroener, June 22, 2013.

14. Lewellan interview.

15. Documentation of Minnesota's persistent socioeconomic racial divide can be found online at Minnesota Compass: www.mncompass.org/disparities.

16. Cooper interview with Wahl. Juergens, "Rosalie Wahl's Vision for Legal Education: Clinics at the Heart." Juergens interview with Wahl.

17. Ridder served on the ABA Accreditation Committee for four years and was awarded an honorary degree by William Mitchell College of Law in 1985 in

appreciation for her service. Author's interview with Ridder, June 22, 2013; and Ridder, *Shaping My Feminist Life,* 144.

18. "ABA Confers Medal of Honor on Robert MacCrate," from *Syllabus,* the newsletter of the American Bar Association Section of Legal Education and Admission to the Bar, 32.3 (Summer 2001).

19. Juergens interview with Wahl.

20. Helen Pratt Mickens, "Professional Responsibility: Bridging the Gap Between Law School and the Practice of Law," *Michigan Bar Journal* 11.

21. Juergens, "Rosalie Wahl's Vision for Legal Education: Clinics at the Heart."

22. James Hogg, "Rosalie Wahl: Her Extraordinary Contributions to Legal Education," *William Mitchell Law Review* 21.1. Hogg was a professor, dean, and president of William Mitchell College of Law. Cooper interview with Wahl.

23. David Segal, "What They Don't Teach Law Students: Lawyering," *New York Times,* November 19, 2011.

24. Lewellan interview. Margaret Zack, "The Law's in His Blood; Minnesota's Next Supreme Court Justice Brings a Wide Range of Legal Experience," *Minneapolis Star Tribune,* August 28, 1994.

25. Donna Halvorsen, "Judge Wahl Leaves Historic and Personal Mark on Court," *Minneapolis Star Tribune,* August 28, 1994. Editorial, "Rosalie Wahl: A Trailblazing Justice Opens a New Book," *Minneapolis Star Tribune,* August 31, 1994.

26. Minnesota State Law Library, Biographies of the Justices of the Minnesota Supreme Court, http://mn.gov/lawlib/judgebio.html.

27. A trailer is available for viewing at http://girlfrombirchcreek.com/.

28. Klas had been a member of the Gender Fairness Task Force. The January 29 panel was moderated by the author. It was presented jointly by William Mitchell College of Law and Minnesota Women Lawyers.

29. Author's transcript of January 29, 2013, forum at William Mitchell College of Law.

30. Juergens, "Rosalie Wahl's Vision for Legal Education: Clinics at the Heart."

31. *U.S. News and World Report* Grad Compass, University of Minnesota—Twin Cities, http://grad-schools.usnews.rankingsandreviews.com/best-graduate-schools/top-law-schools/university-of-minnesota-twin-cities-03085?int=c6b9e3. William Mitchell College of Law, Student Profile, Fall 2013 Entering Class, http://web.wmitchell.edu/admissions/student-profile/.

32. Yahoo! CEO Marissa Mayer dismayed many American workers when in February 2013 she ended her firm's longstanding policy of allowing work to be accomplished at a location of the employee's choosing rather than exclusively in the office. Minnesota's Best Buy Corporation made a similar move one week

later, ending its "Results Only Work Environment" system of flexible hours that had been established to much acclaim in 2006. See Bureau of Labor Statistics, "Married Parents' Use of Time Summary," 2008, http://www.bls.gov/news .release/atus2.nro.htm.

33. Rosalie Wahl interview with Nina Rothchild, February 26, 1992, Watkins and Rothchild, *In the Company of Women.* Facebook chief operating officer Sheryl Sandberg triggered a national debate about what success requires of women with her book *Lean In: Women, Work, and the Will To Lead* (New York: Knopf, 2013). She argued that women's careers often faltered because of insecurity, lack of ambition, and failure to set aside conflicting priorities, and urged women to overcome those inner deficiencies. She did not argue for a change in the corporate environment.

34. U.S. Census Bureau, "Income, Poverty and Health Insurance Coverage in the United States, 2012," 11, http://www.census.gov/prod/2013pubs/p60-245. pdf. U.S. Bureau of Justice Statistics, "Intimate Partner Violence, 1993–2010," http://www.bjs.gov/index.cfm?ty=pbdetail&iid=4536. National Organization for Women, "Violence Against Women in the United States: Statistics," http:// www.now.org/issues/violence/stats.html.

Index

Note: page numbers in *italics* refer to photographs and captions.